C
HAROL

D0422771

R000072

PR
4754
.T5

Thurley, Geoffrey

The psychology of
Hardy's novels

DATE DUE

REF.

FORM 125 M

LITERATURE & PHILOSOPHY DIVISION

The Chicago Public Library

Received

The Psychology of Hardy's Novels

The Psychology
of Hardy's Novels

THE NERVOUS
AND THE STATUESQUE

Geoffrey Thurley

University of Queensland Press

REF
PR
4754
T5
.T5
Cop. 1

© University of Queensland Press, St. Lucia,
Queensland, 1975

*This book is copyright. Apart from any fair dealing
for the purposes of private study, research, criticism,
or review, as permitted under the Copyright Act, no
part may be reproduced by any process without
written permission. Enquiries should be made to the
publishers.*

Printed and bound by Peninsula Press Ltd., Hong Kong
Designed by Cyrelle

Distributed in the United Kingdom, Europe, the
Middle East, Africa, and the Caribbean by Prentice-Hall
International, International Book Distributors Ltd.,
66 Wood Lane End, Hemel Hempstead, Herts.,
England

*National Library of Australia
Cataloguing-in-Publication data*

Thurley, Geoffrey
    The psychology of Hardy's novels: the nervous
    and the statuesque/ by Geoffrey Thurley. —
    St. Lucia, Q.: University of Queensland Press, 1975.
    Index.
    Bibliography.
    ISBN 0 7022 0872 8.

    1. Hardy, Thomas, 1840–1928 — Criticism and
    interpretation. I. Title.

823.8

To Wendy

28P
R

16.50

A variation of the associationist theory contends that judgments of expression are based on stereotypes. In this view, interpretation does not rely on a person's spontaneous insight or repeated observation of what belongs together, but on conventions he has adopted ready-made from his social group. He has been told, for example, that aquiline noses indicate courage and that protruding lips betray sensuality. The promoters of this theory generally imply that such judgments are wrong, as though information not based on first-hand experience could never be trusted. Actually, the danger does not lie in the social origin of the information. What counts is that people have a tendency to acquire simply structured concepts on the basis of insufficient evidence, which may have been gathered first- or second-hand, and to preserve these concepts unchanged in the face of contrary facts. While this may make for many one-sided or entirely wrong evaluations of individuals and groups of people, the existence of stereotypes does not explain the origin of physiognomic judgments. If these judgments stem from tradition, what is the tradition's source? Are they right or wrong? Even though often misapplied, traditional interpretations of physique and behavior may still be based on sound observation. In fact, perhaps they are so hardy because they are so true.

Rudolf Arnheim, Towards a Psychology of Art

Contents

PART ONE

Beginnings

1. The Concept of Typology in Fiction

Ever since Hippocrates postulated two basic types of human being — the pyknic and the leptosomatic — European physicians, philosophers, and psychologists have been impressed with the idea that beneath the apparently inexhaustible diversity of human personality, there run certain recurrent congruences of factors which, if properly understood, would enable us to place any given individual in one of a small number of psychological categories. This view, that there are psychological types, can be called either typological or morphological. A typological theory simply asserts there are distinct and definable psychological types, a morphological theory that such types are definable in specifically physical terms — in terms of body-build or glands or blood, for instance. Hippocrates' dichotomy, which may ultimately prove to underlie all European type-theories, is morphological: it really simply calls attention to the contrast between short-fat and tall-lean people. Galen's theory of the four temperaments is more strictly a psychological theory; but the temperaments are based upon physiological factors — the four corresponding Humours. Both theories are basically therefore morphological: it is my contention that any theory of psychological types either posits a primacy of physical over mental characteristics, or explains mind in terms of body.

Both Hippocrates and Galen were physicians. Hippocrates' interest in typological differences was stimulated by what he felt to be causal relations between physical type and sickness: he found leptosomatics prone to tuberculosis, and pyknics to apoplexy. Galen was concerned with temper. By subdividing Hippocrates' two terms into four, Galen achieved greater precision, and he was interested less in body-build than in colour, pigmentation, and blood. Nevertheless, basically he follows Hippocrates: Hippocrates' apoplectic pyknics are clearly Galen's cholerics, for instance; his tubercular leptosomatics, Galen's melancholics.

This basic structure survived into the nineteenth century when Kant incorporated it into his philosophical system. It was adopted and modified by Wilhelm Wundt, and persists recognizably in apparently purely psychological type-theories like those of C. G. Jung. All that has happened is that, the Humours now being forgotten, the temperaments have been described in terms of both introversion and extroversion and stability and instability. No psychologist or psychiatrist today would own to a belief in the four temperaments themselves, but in fact modern assumptions about the way people habitually behave do follow the broad lines laid down by the mediaeval physicians. Broadly speaking, Galen's melancholics and phlegmatics are introverts, his cholerics and sanguines extroverts. However, if cholerics and sanguines are related by a common extroversion, and melancholics and phlegmatics by a common introversion, cholerics and melancholics are related by a common tendency towards emotional instability, sanguines and phlegmatics by a common tendency towards emotional stability.

So Galen's theory stands up fairly well. Even type-theories of a predominantly literary or philosophical interest tend to follow the broad lines of his account. Nietzsche's Appollonian-Dionysiac dichotomy, for instance, can perhaps be translated into terms of introversion and extroversion, and thence perhaps into Galen's terms. C. G. Jung's four basic psychological types follow the temperaments quite closely: thinking and feeling types being introverted, sensational and intuitive, extroverted. We could, without too much strain, translate Jung's categories, too, into terms Galen would have understood. The more radically morphological approach of Ernst Kretschmer[1] and W. E. Sheldon[2] inserts a third term between Galen's pairs. Kretschmer calls Hippocrates' pyknics by the same term; his leptosomatics he calls asthenics; in between these two types he finds another, the athletic. The

American Sheldon translated Kretschmer's terms first into ectomorphs, endomorphs, and mesomorphs, then into somatotonics, viscerotonics, and cerebrotonics, yielding roughly a division into physical, emotional, and intellectual types.[3]

To the liberal humanist interested in literature, all these investigations seem disturbingly materialist: Kretschmer and Sheldon are concerned with glands, muscles, and body-fat much as Galen was with bile and lymph. But like Galen again, their work yields results which steer us back to familiar territory. After all, Galen gave Chaucer as much, arguably, as Boethius did, and the consistent use of his thought by great writers like Cervantes, Ben Jonson, and Molière suggests that more than sterile categorization is at stake.

There must be some vitality in these notions of character-type for them to have interested so many writers for so long. There is no question of reducing literature to the contents it might have in common with medicine or psychology. Ben Jonson certainly transcends the vision of the Humours psychology; but he does use it, and one can imagine circumstances in which it might have seemed necessary or desirable to bring the fact to general notice. Sometimes it is necessary to describe the terms in an artist's language in order fully to understand what he uses the language to say. I believe that this is true of the fiction of Thomas Hardy. Before we can evaluate his philosophical ideas, we must at least be able to read his language; in his case, this language is framed principally in terms of psychological concepts. Or, as the preceding discussion has already hinted, psycho-physiological. For my argument is, briefly, that Hardy takes his place in a particular fictional tradition, his immediate precursors being the Brontës, Melville, and Scott, his more distant ancestors the great comic writers of the Humours tradition. That is to say, his characters are regularly presented and analyzed in a morphological way, with consistent and significant emphasis on certain typical qualities.

Now, Hardy is commonly — and to a large extent rightly —

reckoned a pessimistic writer, or at least a deterministic one. If we look closely at the whole tradition of typological or quasi-typological literature, we discern certain features characteristic of typological writers. There seems to be some kind of causal connection between the cast of Hardy's philosophical convictions and the typological bent of his characterization. It can be dispiriting to become aware of things happening in familiar and predictable cycles — to see people falling into the same categories again and again. Dispiriting, or simply amusing. It is no accident that among the great typological writers in the European tradition we can count so many of the great comic masters — from Cervantes and Ben Jonson to H. G. Wells and Gogol. The typological writer watches man stumbling through his paces, falling foul of the same few obstacles, all the time convinced that he is the apex of evolution, and a unique tragic victim of Destiny. The reaction may be the chill laughter of Ben Jonson or the profound sympathy of Cervantes; in either case the human enterprise is seen as coming to nothing, as fundamentally absurd. In Hardy's novels, the comic absurdity emerges only in the factitious sequences of fortuitous events the novelist sometimes engineers to convince us of his fundamental case. More characteristic is the sense of hopelessness which attends the careers of his favourite characters. And this seems to me to be inextricably bound up with his penchant for seeing humanity not as infinitely various — as Dickens and Shakespeare saw it — but as restricted to a relatively small number of basic types. A similar fatality envelops the novels of the Brontës and Melville, and some account of their work must be given before the systematic analysis of Hardy's *oeuvre* can be attempted.

Before the nineteenth century, typological literature is dominated by the concepts of the Humours. Ben Jonson is the outstanding instance in English. Cervantes' *Don Quixote,* however, offers a more clarified model of the kind of dichotomy so pervasive in Victorian typological fiction than any work of Jonson's: a long, spindle-shanked leptosomatic wanders in a melancholy fantasy-world, watched over by a fat, sanguine pyknic. If we compare Cervantes' great hero with any of Shakespeare's melancholics, we shall find a perfect contrast between the typological and the non-typological approaches to characterization. Don Quixote's character is his destiny in a very much more profound sense than can be asserted of Jaques or Malvolio, or even Hamlet. Shakespeare is prepared to mock a familiar type until the character begs for serious consideration: when Jaques speaks the great meditative poetry of Hamlet (as he does on a number of occasions), he ceases to be an object of ridicule, and at the same time, also like Hamlet, can no longer be regarded simply as a melancholic. Don Quixote, on the other hand, moons and broods all the time within the cloudy self-engendered universe of the introvert, and Sancho Panza's relationship with him is antithetical: the two characters are polarized by the structural awareness of type-psychology. Sancho Panza is much more than the faithful servant of classical comedy: he is his master's temperamental opposite, and each is defined in terms of the other.

By the end of the eighteenth century, the Humours psychology had been suborned by a subtler tradition of psychological investigation, an introspective tradition engendered out of Rousseauesque romanticism, and empiricist philosophy, with its characteristic attention to the perceptual habits of the mind. In the meantime the modern novel had arisen in England, with its new precision of observation. It is in Scott, I think, that we see the first signs of the typological tradition which Hardy eventually consummated. This new tradition draws heavily upon the fundamentals of Humours psychology, but also upon a mass of folklore, old wives' tales, common knowledge, accepted ways of reading character and of interpreting physical factors to reach psychological and ethical conclusions. This popular underside of the new typological tradition — itself doubtless partly formed by the sedimentation of learned belief into prejudice — survived well into the twentieth century. Reshaped by the art of serious novelists like Emily Brontë, it gave the Hollywood movie and the pulp novel much of their psychology and morality.

In turning our attention to the English novel, we have to make certain adjustments to our terminology. Hippocrates and Galen were Greeks, Cervantes a Spaniard. It is remarkable that their analysis of humanity has so much to offer northern European artists, confronted by often quite different ethnical and physical facts. Certain attributes recur throughout the typological fiction of the nineteenth century in England (and also in Germany), which clearly testify to these differences in racial origin. What we really witness in the English typological tradition is the transformation of the basic Hippocratic dichotomy into northern European terms. New factors are brought into play, factors which could have little meaning for the Mediterranean mind. Among the most important of these is the colour of hair and eyes. In Scott's *Ivanhoe,* for instance, the blond Saxon knight, Athelstane, is contrasted with the dark Norman knight, Sir Bryan. Athelstane's sluggishness, we feel, is meant to seem "typically" Saxon, just as the Norman is meant to be "typically" passionate. At the same time, the blond-and-affable Saxon is "good", the dark-and-cruel Norman "evil". This of course defers to English national myths dramatizing the Saxon struggle against the Normans (Hereward the Wake, Robin Hood, etc.). But it also reveals a layer of purely moral symbolism latent in the terms of the typological dichotomy. Dark people are no more evil than fair people. Scott is here exploiting a simple yet durable popular symbolism which persisted through the sophistications of the nineteenth century into the golden age of Hollywood. Speaking of Hardy's psychological dichotomies, D. H. Lawrence referred to the "dark villain" and "white virgin". Some such ethical symbolism latent in the northern European consciousness lends extra weight and depth to the typological literature of the nineteenth century.

By and large, English novelists paid less attention to this ethical dimension of the fundamental type-dichotomy than American. We have to go to the fanatic puritanism of the

New England consciousness for a full exploitation of its potentialities. The meeting of the fore-top-man and master-at-arms of the *Indomitable* raises the confrontation between the dark villains and the white virgins to the level of a showdown between absolute good and absolute evil. In Melville we witness again the characteristic fatalism of type-consciousness. Claggart is explicitly shown to be doomed out of his own character: "A nature like Claggart's, surcharged with energy as such natures invariably are, what recourse is left to it but to recoil upon itself and like the scorpion for which the Creator alone is responsible act out to the end the part alloted to it?" Melville had come to the conclusion that there is Natural Depravity, "Something invariably dominated by intellectuality", to which "civilisation if of the austere sort, is auspicious". As with Scott, civilization leads in some obscure way to evil. Indeed, Claggart's whole character is presented in terms which testify to the interdependence of his refined intellectuality and his malignancy. The portrait Melville paints is remarkable:

> The face was a notable one; the features, all except the chin, cleanly cut as those on a Greek medallion; yet the chin, beardless as Tecumseh's, has something of the strange protuberant heaviness in its make that recalled the prints of the Rev. Dr. Titus Oates . . . His brow was of the sort phrenologically associated with more than average intellect; silken curls partly clustering over it, making a foil to the pallor below, a pallor tinged with a faint shade of amber, akin to the hue of time-tinted marbles of old.

There are in this passage certain annotational habits which we shall find recurring again and again in the writing of Hardy and the Brontës: the habitual checking-up on regularities (for instance "his brow was of the sort phrenologically associated with more than average intellect"); a general interest in classifying human types; and a tendency to isolate certain physical features as being especially significant signs of character. Contrary to the common belief that it is somehow sterile to "pigeon-hole" people, the habit has a profound fascination for minds of a certain disposition.

Melville had of course already staged another such showdown. Claggart meets in Billy Budd what Ahab had sought in the White Whale. There are significant differences between the two stories. Moby Dick is greater than Ahab, but Ahab is very much greater than anyone else on the *Pequod*. Claggart is a scaled-down villain, of lesser stature than Captain Vere: Ahab is a demonic hero. Now the structure of *Billy Budd* is unquestionably Miltonic; Melville quotes Milton's most pregnant description of Satan to summarize Claggart — "pale ire, envy and despair" — and Satan-Claggart's attack on Adam-Billy is watched over sorrowfully and impotently by God-Vere. In Ahab — Claggart's greater prototype — there is much more of the Satanic power. The fact is that Melville's hero bears a strong resemblance to the dark villains of the Brontës and Hardy. Ahab, Heathcliff, Rochester, and Michael Henchard are arguably the only true heroes in the Victorian novel. Their overwhelmingly obvious origination in Milton's Satan (as interpreted by Blake and glamorized by Byron) goes far to explain the complicated relationship between good and evil in Victorian fiction.

In *Wuthering Heights,* Heathcliff's character is established at once with a gesture:

> I beheld his black eyes withdraw so suspiciously under his brows, as I rode up, and when his fingers sheltered themselves with a jealous resolution, still further in his waistcoat, I announced my name.
> "Mr. Heathcliff?" I said.
> A nod was the answer.

Apart from the "black eyes" and the hooding brows — significant enough details — the character is conveyed through physical movement. If we turn from this to *Paradise Lost,* we cannot help being struck by the way Milton creates the character of Satan by close observation of his tremendous gestures and frowns: "gestures fierce", "mad demeanour", "brows of dauntless courage and considerate pride", "pale ire, envy and despair". The spirit distorts the body, as the physique bespeaks the rebellious spirit within. The point here is not to psychologize Milton, but on the contrary to show how the Miltonic understanding of demonic pride persists into the age of realistic fiction, and how novelists like the Brontës, Melville, and Thomas Hardy explore the Satanic personality through the psychological modes characteristic of their medium. By the time we reach Byron, the powerful inflexible malevolence of Satan has set hard in visual terms that owe as much to Blake's drawings as to the philosophical revelations of *The Marriage of Heaven and Hell:*

> His brow was like the deep when tempest-tossed
> Fierce and unfathomable thoughts engraved
> Eternal wrath on his immortal face
> And where he gazed a gloom pervaded space.

Beethoven? Perhaps. At any rate, the continuous attempt to understand evil through the impression made upon body by thought is impressively persistent, from Milton to Hardy. Thought is destructive of flesh. At least, it is for the Satanic heroes of the nineteenth century, who hug their will and let it distort them into evil. Emily Brontë's physical presentation of Heathcliff is thoroughly typical — "a dark-skinned gypsy, in aspect . . . . rather slovenly . . . yet not looking amiss with his negligence, because he has an erect and handsome figure; and rather morose".

Against this skulking Satan is opposed the novel's fair-haired, blue-eyed angel, Edgar Linton, and the action of the book stems from the division of Catherine Earnshaw between them. But Heathcliff and Linton are more than two men — very much more, indeed, than two psychological types; they are opposed spiritual principles, modes of being, sources of psychic energy. At one level, certainly, *Wuthering Heights* is quite simply the greatest modern example of the Romance myth de Rougemont describes as pervading the whole of Western literature. According to this reading, the passionate lovers, Catherine and Heathcliff, are separated by

Catherine's marriage to Edgar, only to be reunited in death. In this case, Edgar is reduced to the "obstacle" Romance requires to preserve its passion. I should emphasize that I am very far from dismissing such a reading out of hand: Emily Brontë's novel is a truly mystical work, not the debased socialized Romance de Rougemont rightly abhors in most modern fiction and cinema. It is truly mystical because the passionate reunion in death is longed for by the two lovers, as it simply is not in the degraded modern versions of the Tristan myth. *Wuthering Heights* re-enacts the longing for death in the most boldly literal way: Heathcliff, separated from Catherine by her death, simply lets himself de-materialize, ceases to eat. So, the novel ends with the graves under the "benign sky", the reunion in death, and the resurgence of spring. Moreover, there is just a hint that Heathcliff and Catherine are in fact brother and sister: in choosing to make the passion incestuous, Emily Brontë guarantees the passion from soiling fulfilment. And doesn't Catherine proclaim her sexless, narcissistic identity with her lover? "Nelly, I am Heathcliff!" De Rougemont could ask for no more.

But we must push such an account a little further. We simplify the involvements of Emily Brontë's marvellous book if we do not see that Edgar, Catherine, and Heathcliff are fixed in a psychical tension from which they cannot escape, that Catherine's choice of Edgar is neither whimsical, nor motivated simply by the demands of passion. At the end of the book, there are three graves on the moors, not two. On the one hand, we have the passionate love of Catherine and Heathcliff that is usually regarded as the bed-rock of the novel. On the other, the more truly sexual attraction that exists between Catherine and Edgar Linton. Now, Catherine's reaction to Edgar is powerful and decisive. The depths of her being belong to Heathcliff ("I am Heathcliff"); but the spiritual heights remain unappealed to by him. When Linton appears, the more natural (sibling-like) attraction of Heathcliff is neutralized. It is a point frequently missed by romantic readers of the book. To reduce *Wuthering Heights* entirely to the Tristan myth is to distort its real psychical structure. Catherine's love for Heathcliff may be more natural; but the human organism is not merely natural. It is capable of artifice; it needs culture and civilization. So that Edgar Linton, the embodiment of all these things, causes in Catherine Earnshaw a decisive rift. She knows Heathcliff with such animal-like intimacy that he ceases to be the "other", to be outside her. Edgar Linton is precisely this "other". Socially, psychologically and, therefore, sexually, he represents everything that Heathcliff is not. Now Heathcliff, like so many of the readers Emily Brontë encourages to identify with him, simply cannot understand this. The first time we see Edgar, he is "weeping silently". There is, from the first, an air of near-feminine grace about him that translates naturally into sexual attractiveness. Heathcliff is baffled: after all, Linton is a girl — pacific, cultured, soft. Girls are soft, men are hard and tough. And yet Heathcliff miscalculates. He knows nothing of the world of the spirit, of the aura of physical grace generated by the active *and virile* life of the mind, that can make the male body as irresistibly attractive to a woman as rude masculine force. Just as Heathcliff is described by the consistent use of expressions like "sullen" and "skulk", and by reference to his dark, gypsy physique, so Linton is characterized by vocabulary suggesting lightness, delicacy, and a kind of strength to which Heathcliff is utterly blind. Linton gains by his apparent passivity; by yielding to Catherine, by courteously anticipating her wishes, he emerges with a chivalric strength, which is the reverse of the feminine weakness Heathcliff attributes to him. Catherine's two lovers, in fact, begin to change roles: paradoxically, Linton assumes the guise of the courtly lover. He even speaks the language of *cortezia:* "He many a time spoke sternly to me about my pertness", (Nelly Dean reports) "and averred that the stab of a knife could not inflict a worse pang than he suffered at seeing his lady vexed." Thus, the angelic Linton, with his "vacant blue eyes" defeats the demonic Heathcliff. Heathcliff flies the field and, significantly, returns armed with the weapon he acknowledges himself to have been conquered by, civilization. He comes back a gentleman. He is, of course, still the old Heathcliff — even more so than ever in fact, almost a parody of himself: "the cheeks more sallow, and half covered with black whiskers; the brows lowering, the eyes deep set and singular". Nevertheless, he has admitted the superiority of culture over barbarism by himself trying to become civilized. Moreover, in a significant episode, he pays his own tribute to the Linton psyche by taking an interest in, and eventually marrying, Edgar's sister, Isabella. His ulterior design, of course, is diabolic; but it is not purely diabolic. He is keenly aware of her spiritual quality: he speaks too scathingly of her "mawkish, waxen face", and damns her for her blue eyes (which, oddly enough, he imagines turning black), because they "detestably resemble Linton's". Catherine knows what really irks him; " 'Delectably,' observed Catherine, 'they are dove's eyes — angel's.' "

This remark of Catherine's is probably the most overt indication in the book of the spiritual tension that generates the action. It tells us why Catherine made her initial decision to marry Edgar, and also explains why the (supposed) de Rougemont reading of the story must ultimately be abandoned. What is involved here is not perverse waywardness obstructing and thereby facilitating a romantic passion, but an intricate emotional and spiritual drama that must work itself out in its own terms. Seen in this light, Heathcliff's marrying Isabella acquires more significance. The act emerges now not only as a grim parody of Catherine's choice of Linton, but as a recognition of the process that must be completed for the tensions to be resolved: the indirect result of Heathcliff's marriage to Isabella is the reconciliation of the two psyches in the courtship of Hareton and the younger Catherine.

The "universal scowl" Mr. Lockwood observes in Wuthering Heights at the very opening of the book comes from Heathcliff. The ill-temper of the household — Hareton is

boorish and Catherine addresses Lockwood like a virago —
prevails only while Heathcliff himself is kept from what is
most congenial to him, death, and reunion with Catherine
Earnshaw. The jagged roughness of Wuthering Heights must
endure tempestuous conflict, the marriage of opposites, and
the inward dissolution of what seems most natural, before it
is healed finally in the balm of a new spring. Catherine's
refinement achieves release from the "kind of desperation,
singularly unnatural to be there"; Hareton's force is purged of
its uncouthness and made civilized by her influence; wild
currant bushes are pulled up and flower-beds sown. After he
and Catherine have become friends, Hareton's sentimental
education begins to make observable alteration in him: "His
honest warm and intelligent nature shook off rapidly the
clouds of ignorance and degradation in which it had been
bred . . . the brightening mind brightened his features, and
added spirit and nobility to their aspect." A reversal of the
Satanic distortion, in fact. What had been mystic primordial
earth-worship in Heathcliff, in Hareton had appeared only as
crude debasement: it was for the young Catherine, offspring
of Heathcliff's Catherine and Edgar Linton, to bring to
Hareton the light and refinement that raise him above the
level of the boor. So the novel ends with the triumph of
Catherine Earnshaw (both Hareton and young Catherine have
her eyes) in the final union of her twin aspects — the wild
power that united her soul to Heathcliff and the spiritual
grace that drew her to Edgar. The younger Catherine is
released into her true angel-ism, just as Heathcliff is released
into the atmosphere.

Heathcliff and Edgar Linton were real people, rendered
with all the ease bequeathed by an already ripe realist
tradition. Yet they were also spiritual principles, ranged
opposite each other: they were the earth and the ether, the
base and the sublime, the barbarian and the civilized, the
animal and the angel, the Celt and the Anglo-Saxon, the
mystical and the rational, the instinctual and the intellectual.
It is important to bear in mind that the typological tradition

in literature is concerned with more than grouping people and discriminating different psycho-physiological features. As we have seen from the examples from Cervantes, Scott, and Melville the typological vision is a way of understanding the world which explores the racial, spiritual, and economic bases of experience. *Wuthering Heights* offers us a fascinating study of the nature of sexual attraction – at one level. In a sense, it consummates the English typological tradition. A great deal of what was to come is already anticipated in Emily Brontë's great book. Much that is embryonic in her writing is merely brought to birth first by her sister Charlotte, then by Thomas Hardy.

In Charlotte Brontë, the issue is complicated by the writer's own direct participation in the story: *Villete, Jane Eyre, The Professor,* and *Shirley* are all, at one level at least, mere wish-fulfilment. Yet her treatment of the polarities we have already observed active in Emily's novel and in Melville's tales is interestingly matter-of-fact, almost schematized, in a way that makes it easier to discern the springs of the vision. Thus, the psychic energy invested in Mr. Rochester gravitates towards the heroine, Jane Eyre, so that no free play is allowed between the other characters. Miss Ingram's Christian name (Blanche) suggests her alignment with the Linton-psyche; but Charlotte Brontë pillories her so ruthlessly that the love-dance between her and Rochester has little real life. Rochester himself is a more civilized version of Heathcliff, with "broad and jetty eyebrows . . . square forehead, made squarer by the horizontal sweep of his black hair". The portrait is worth quoting in full as wholly characteristic of the typological school: "I recognised – his decisive nose, more remarkable for character than beauty; his full nostrils, denoting, I thought, choler; his grim mouth, chin, and jaw – yes, all three were very grim, and no mistake. His shape, now divested of cloak, I perceived harmonised in squareness with his physiognomy; I suppose it was a good figure in the athletic sense of the term – broad chested and thin flanked, though neither tall nor graceful."

Jane is, to put it bluntly, sizing him up, and it is the franker, if less exalted admiration for the masculine that makes *Jane Eyre* in some ways a more honest book than *Wuthering Heights*. The perceptual habits, we note, are like Melville's. Charlotte Brontë, too, checks up on physiognomical frequencies and congruences. The full nostrils *"denote choler"*, his shape "harmonizes" with his physiognomy "in squareness"; it was a good figure "in the athletic sense of the term" — in no other. Rochester is more ordinary than Heathcliff, and the description places him more indubitably among Hippocrates' pyknics. Unlike Emily, Charlotte Brontë denies us the gratification of a direct conflict between Mr. Rochester and her Edgar Linton, the parson St. John Rivers. The psychic polarization exercises less influence on the course of events. It is, nevertheless, as pointed as it is in *Wuthering Heights:* Rochester's Beethovenish masculinity is contrasted with the cultivated gracefulness of the ethereal intellectual, who is "young, tall, slender", with a face "like a Greek face, very pure in outline". The eyes are "large and blue", the high forehead "colourless as ivory", and — significantly — "partially streaked over by careless locks of fair hair". This sounds like a schoolgirl idealization of Milton, and the influence of such culture-heroes cannot be ignored in Victorian novels written by women. (Casaubon reminds Dorothea of Locke.) Under the other-worldly grace, Jane detects a severity of purpose which makes Rochester seem a gruff old bear by comparison. Rochester's sexuality is suddenly neutralized by Rivers's: Jane finds "something about his nostrils, his mouth, his brow, which indicated elements within, either restless or hard, or eager". Later, his behaviour indicates an "unceremonious directness, a searching, decided steadfastness in his gaze now, which told that intention, and not diffidence, had hitherto kept it averted from the stranger". River's "blue pictorial-looking eyes", therefore, express something slightly different from Edgar Linton's "vacant blue eyes". The two men are different versions of the type: blue-eyed, and spiritual, they are ideal rather than real, detached from rather than dependent on the life of the body. Yet where Linton transcends the body in a nervous grace, Rivers denies it with fanatic intensity. Rivers closely resembles Hawthorne's Arthur Dymmesdale, in fact. Both are examples of what might be called the beautiful vicar syndrome, something obviously important in nineteenth-century rural communities, to which the vicar came as from another world, with a spiritual distinction that exercised an irresistible fascination over the country-women, a fascination as incomprehensible to the village-men as Edgar's attractions were to Heathcliff.[4]

Basically, then, Charlotte Brontë's spiritual world is structured like her sister's. Her canvas is of course much wider, and this gives us plenty of opportunity for watching her go through the insistently typological procedures of her psychological analysis. Again and again, we see her placing the character up against the type-norms, checking up on regularities, or, more interestingly, on the subtle deviations from the expected that help her to grasp the individual in his uniqueness. Mr. Malone, in *Shirley,* is "a tall, strongly-built personage, with real Irish legs and arms, and a face as genuinely national: not the Milesian face – not Daniel O'Connell's style, but the high-featured, North-American Indian sort of visage, which belongs to the Irish gentry, and has a petrified and proud look, better suited to the owner of an estate of slaves than to the landlord of a free peasantry". Type-seeing runs wild here, in fact: Malone is not just a "typical Irishman" (astutely though she can catch this type, too), but *the sort of Irishman that looks like a Red Indian.* We recall Melville's attempts to capture Claggart by comparing his different features with the Indian chief Tecumseh and the celebrated British liar, Titus Oates. An interest in the foundations of national character is an important part of the type-vision, as we have seen in Scott, and shall see again in Hardy.

Elsewhere, Charlotte Brontë reintroduces the concepts of the Humours psychology. Mr. Rochester's brow, we remember, "denoted choler". Other examples are plentiful. Mr. Donne — again in *Shirley* — has "a stilted self-complacency, and half-sullen phlegm", Mr. Sweeting in the same chapter, "a light easy disposition". Mr. Shelstone finally is straight out of mediaeval bestiary: "a personage short of stature, but straight of port, and bearing on broad shoulders a hawk's head, beak and eyes". The expectation implicit in that qualifying "but" seems especially indicative of the natural typology of her vision. A regularity has been disturbed: the progressively finer qualification of type-disturbances may be regarded as the essence of typological characterization.

Before moving on to Hardy himself, I offer a popular instance of the typological tradition. Margaret Mitchell's *Gone with the Wind* reproduces the basic categories of the Brontë psychology with a naive clumsiness that testifies powerfully to the strength of the underlying vision. Scarlett O'Hara is Catherine Earnshaw, Ashley is Edgar Linton ("He moved in an inner world that was more beautiful than Georgia and came back to reality with reluctance"), Rhett Butler is Heathcliff, though heavily adulterated with Hardy's Alec d'Urberville. Like Catherine Earnshaw, Scarlett "impulsively" marries Ashley, living to regret her real love, Rhett. Such popular plagiarizations only serve to confirm the tradition they batten on.

It is plain from the range of these instances alone that in speaking of typological literature we are concerned with something that transcends "mere" psychology. In Cervantes, Scott, Melville, and the Brontës a typological approach seems to throw light on the basic structural relations of their novels. We gain from it a new insight into the inner logic of their art. The terms of this logic derive from psycho-physiological fact: this seems indubitable. But the relations between small *t* and capital *T* truth are in literature not always easy to establish. That is why it might well be better to regard the typological structure of these great novels as elements in an internally cohesive system. That way we can eat our cake and have it too. However, it seems to me only honest to desist from what might be called the structuralist ostrich-act. Yes, it is true that structure is meaning – the position is irrefutable. Irrefutable, yet cowardly, and basically absurd. Meaning is not structure alone, but also use (as linguistic analysis knows), and intention (as phenomenology knows). In the same way, we know well, as human beings, though we may deny it as committed doctrinaires, that there is a vast difference between Honoré d'Urfé's *L'Astrée*, for instance, of which an aesthetic structuralism can seem the only tenable defence, and Racine's *Phèdre* or Corneille's *Le Cid*, in which our structuralism must fade away into the much less satisfactory systems of experience and truth. It is reality – or our unsatisfactory apprehension of it – that confers integrity upon artistic structure, not vice versa.

Thus, in this case, we must, it seems to me, be candid about the rude, unflattering, empirically verifiable bases of typological structure. Much of our respect for Thomas Hardy, for instance, reflects our awareness of his consistently penetrating apprehension of facts about which we are not free to differ. At the same time, we can exploit the structuralist get-out to enable us to see *Billy Budd,* for instance, as a confrontation between good and evil, or *Wuthering Heights* as the last great rearguard action of the Romantic consciousness. These works are about matters which transcend the facts of psychology. But although they may transcend them, they still depend upon them, much as our estimate of the religious doctrines thought to be expressed on some newly discovered stone can only be interpreted if we know the language in which the signs are incised.

Most of the better criticism of Thomas Hardy suffers, it seems to me, from the fatal myopia of inspired guesswork: we have shots in the dark. With few exceptions, the Hardy critics have concerned themselves with relatively ephemeral social matters (the passing of the old England, for instance, or the position of woman in society); or with so-called philosophical matters such as evolutionary meliorism or neo-Schopenhauerian pessimism. That the impact of Darwin upon Hardy was strong is indubitable; nor is it to be questioned that a significant part of his fiction concerns the passing of rural England, and the accession of new modes of mental discomfort and anomy. But both these matters are subordinate to what Pierre d'Exideuil, in one of the best books ever written about Hardy, calls "the Human Pair".[5] Hardy's novels are about relationships, not man in a cosmic void, against a natural background, or unsettled by a changing society, but involved with other men and women. And in my view, until we extricate the factors concerned in these involvements, a mature understanding of Hardy as a novelist is impossible.

The nature of my own conception of this problem has been stated clearly enough: Hardy is one of the most consistent of all exponents of typological characterization. This means that if Hardy's people can be explained only in terms of their relationships with others, these relationships in turn can be understood only in terms of the psychic polarizations they body forth. The most penetrating work yet written about Hardy, D. H. Lawrence's "Study", has already provided me with a dichotomy: in Hardy's novels, the "white virgins" and the "dark villains" are, Lawrence saw, pitched together in a deadly hand-to-hand fight, loving and hating – and in the end seeking to destroy – the principle each is drawn to in the other. Lawrence perceived the general trend in Hardy towards a sympathy with the "dark villains":

> The condemnation gradually shifts over from the dark villain to the blond bourgeois virgin hero . . . It is a complete and devastating shift-over, it is a complete *volte-face* of moralities. Black does not become white, but it takes white's place as good; white remains white but it is found bad. The old, communal morality is like a leprosy, a white sickness: the old, anti-social, individualist morality is alone on the side of life and health.[6]

That is stunningly to the point, an understanding so profound that one must despair of adding anything to it. Yet

Lawrence's particular concern is to identify the white virgin with the "leprous" social morality, the dark villains with the "good" individualism. So that his insight, though it anticipates much that is offered in the following pages, in tangential to my purpose.

Closer to home is Pierre d'Exideuil's discussion of "the mystery of attractions" in Hardy, which assumes a certain affinity between the methods of the artist and those of physiologists such as Ribot. In Hardy's novels, d'Exideuil observes, attraction registers with the "force of a physiological shock". He further observes that "it is perhaps not impossible to find some explanation of this organic fatalism".[7] D'Exideuil's observation is acutely pertinent to Hardy's quasi-mechanistic vision of personality; he seems at any moment about to stumble upon the true secret of Hardy's Linear B. However, he is content to speculate upon "a kind of magic lodged by nature in human beings", and reaches a true Gallic conclusion: "In all that concerns love, therefore, there are many actions for which intelligence cannot account."[8]

Certainly there are. But there are many for which it can. A. J. Guerard goes quite a long way towards providing such an account by picking out some of the recurrent character-types in Hardy's novels. He even provides a table — "The Genealogy of Hardy's Younger Women" — listing the characters under separate headings. Much of what Guerard says shows a deep understanding of Hardy's work. But his discussion suffers from a fatal fault, in my view. The characters are discussed in a physical void, as mental or moral entities, as for instance, "The Vain and the Fickle" or "The Average Intelligent Woman". Now the truth is that until the underlying source of the congruences is discovered, a mere listing of the recurrent character-types in Hardy, though interesting, is really uninformative. Such an account must necessarily blunder back and forth across the truth. Thus, for instance, Guerard's admirable account of *The Mayor of Casterbridge* concentrates upon one aspect of Michael Henchard's character, his self-destructiveness. He relates this to Freudian-Menningerian analyses of the unconsciously deliberate nature of apparent accidents and disasters. (Such a theory of the motivation in Hardy's novels is elaborated at greater length by Roy Morrell in *Thomas Hardy: The Will and the Way*.) Thus, although Guerard acutely remarks that in Henchard's case, "Character is fate", he sheds no light on the bases of that character, and thus fails to understand Henchard's relations with Donald Farfrae, and his significance in the total pattern of Hardy's *oeuvre*. "No doubt it is as a well-meaning man isolated by guilt that he makes his strongest appeal to our sympathy".[9] This seems to have wandered a good distance from Guerard's earlier pertinence, and some such loss of relevance, it seems to me, is the inevitable result of failing to appreciate the typological nature of Hardy's vision.

The novels of the Brontës revolve around the collision of two fundamental spiritual and physical principles: the dark, scowling earth-worshippers and the fair, blue-eyed intellectuals. Initially, Hardy takes over this scheme intact. The first novels habitually contrast blue-eyed angels with swarthy hirsute devils — or, to use Lawrence's terminology, white virgins with dark villains. From the Brontës, too, he inherits what appears to be a feminine vision of sexual relations: the dark villains represent male menace, the white virgins female passivity. I do not wholly endorse Lawrence's view that the development of the next twenty years takes Hardy from a censorious disapproval of the dark villains to a warm sympathy with them. But something of the kind is undoubtedly true. Hardy's fascination with the sexual predator emerges first as fear, only later as a capacity to admire and love. But even in the earliest novels, Hardy is beginning to transform the Brontë polarities into more subtle terms. Already in characters like Edward Springrove, for instance, there are signs of the destructive effect of the act of thinking. Hardy is beginning to assign new values to the old categories. Those who characteristically *think* are radically different in character form those who dance or simply *move* well. Thus, to the basic vocabulary of the Brontës he adds terms like "mobility", "flexibility", "perpendicularity". Words like this — there is a large but limited number of them — have a particular force in Hardy, such as words like "turbulent" and "perturb" have in the poetry of W. B. Yeats.

Gradually, the conception of the two basic types becomes clearer and more subtle. The details of this process must wait their turn. Briefly, though, it can be asserted that a fundamental dichotomy, inherited from the Brontës and roughly parallel with the distinctions of the ancients, remains intact over the whole span of Hardy's work, transfigured by Hardy until it can be described only in his own terms. It is analyzed into numerous drives, principles, and goals. Let us take as an instance the rough distinction foreshadowed above between thinkers and dancers. The thinkers are trapped inside their own mentation, they tend towards abstractedness and un-gainliness, a kind of denial of the body. The type characteristi-cally tends towards a terminal inflexibility, and has obvious affinities with classical melancholia and modern introversion. The dancers, on the other hand, can bend and yield to the requirements of the moment. This gradually becomes the basis for a deep differentiation between character and personality. The Mayor of Casterbridge is "the Man of Character": opposite him is Donald Farfrae, an excellent dancer, flexible business-man, and sunny lover. Character is doomed out of its own strength. At the same time, personality tends towards an equal-ly fatal instability. People like Fanny Robin (in *Far from the Madding Crowd*) break down, like filaments charged with too much current.

It was only in his last major novel, *Jude the Obscure,* that Hardy eventually found the terms to stand for the two principles which, with so many qualifications, modifications, and refinements, had structured his novels from the beginning: the nervous and the statuesque. By this time, this dichotomy had shown itself capable of expressing a wide range of problems. The more sure is his grasp of the psychical facts, the more subtle and flexible is his exploitation of the possibilities inherent in the dichotomy. It can stand for a predilection for the night or for the day, for death or for life, for hope or for despair, for structure or for life, for narrowness or for expansiveness. In the first books, the statuesque threatens the nervous; in the last the nervous mocks the statuesque, as Hellenism might mock Hebraism, or amoralism morality.

It often happens in Hardy's novels that a man who is perfectly contented in his own carefully built-up life suddenly meets a woman who completely destroys his peace of mind. It is Hardy's distinction to have provided something like a comprehensive theory to explain such phenomena. Why, he asks, does this kind of man like this kind of woman, when everyone around can see that it is a futile and pernicious choice? Pierre d'Exideuil cites Darwin and Schopenhauer to support his view that Hardy regarded the matching of pairs of opposites as somehow biologically determined by the needs of the species: "In order that this purpose of procreation may be perfectly realised, it is once more necessary, as with Darwin, that a given type of man should be united with a given type of woman . . . Almost in spite of themselves, the lovers defer to a regard for equilibrium."[10] The habitual mismatching, then, which causes ninety-nine per cent of the unhappiness in Hardy's novels, is required by the species. In point of fact, Hardy's stories support a number of different theories: sometimes people appear to require their own opposite, sometimes their own like. As we shall see, the subject is a little more complicated than d'Exideuil implies. Nevertheless, he has raised the right question: unhappiness in Hardy's world comes not from violating the natural order or from being weak-willed or just from being doomed from the start. It comes from the commitment of the self to others. Our understanding of Hardy's teleology, then, must begin with our attempt to unravel his complicated conception of the laws of human relationship. What is the nature of human attraction? That is our field.

2. The Early Hardy

Desperate Remedies (1871)
A Pair of Blue Eyes (1873)

In trying to define the nature of the typological vision above, I found it convenient to make a rough comparison between Cervantes and Shakespeare. A similar advantage seems to offer itself now in contrasting Thomas Hardy and Dickens. For Dickens appears to be the absolute opposite to Hardy, in almost every respect. He assembled the greatest gallery of characters in fiction without stumbling across the existence of the types — except by chance, through Mr. Grimwig: "I only know two sorts of boys — mealy boys and beef-faced boys." Now Mr. Grimwig is a born pessimist: he is convinced that Oliver will make off with Mr. Brownlow's five pound note, not because of any particular feeling about Oliver but out of his general scepticism about boys. If we can imagine *Oliver Twist* written by Mr. Grimwig, we shall have a shrewd conception of the Hardy novel. It seems that both Dickens's prodigious variety of characterization and his fundamental optimism are equally alien to the typological vision. For all the amazing accuracy of his observation and the phenomenal retentiveness of his memory, Dickens rarely saw beneath the immediate facts. No one in literature, perhaps, has ever equalled Dickens's "extrovert" attentiveness to the appearance of the world.

Hardy himself was aware of the Dickensian genius. He noted its absence in one of his own characters, Edred Fitzpiers: "That quick, glittering, empirical eye, sharp for the surface of things if for nothing beneath, he had not." This very gift precludes the second sight of a Hardy, the ability to hold the subject for longer than it takes to register its retinal impact, and to explore its reality, as it were, in the mind. This introverted speculativeness is the hallmark of Hardy's genius. It is what explains the peculiar quality of his nature-writing — at once so precise and particularized and so thought-over; it is also, of course, what explains his psychological vision. The typological vision belongs to the speculative mind: it is the product of protracted brooding upon the subject rather than immediate response to it. Its conclusions emerge slowly, being formed gradually like the ripples hardening in sand under the soft regular impact of waves.

The studious, subtle realism of Hardy's psychology is the result of his probing interest in such physical data as the colour of the eyes, general pigmentation, carriage, build, and gait. This interest is helped by the decisive work of Scott, Melville, and the Brontës. By the time Hardy came to write, there already existed a literature of elaborate typological definitions, subtly formulated laws of ethnical categorization and moral symbolism: Hardy grew up into an awareness of the significance of typological differentiations. The types themselves of course will be found scattered randomly throughout the works of Dickens or Thackeray, but without an awareness of their significance. Already, as early as *Desperate Remedies,* Hardy on the other hand can be observed setting up the type-polarities and the magnetic fields of attraction, in spite of the distracting web of melodrama that obscures the scene now and then.

Desperate Remedies is by no means as gauche as its title suggests; it is, in places, a more sophisticated piece of work than a novelist so young and inexperienced could have been expected to produce. Consider for example the treatment of the elder Graye at the beginning of the book. The initial characterization suggests youthful casualness: "Graye was handsome, frank and gentle." Hardy seems to have been thinking of a "handsome, frank and gentle" man before any particular individual, so that the phrase does not grip. The vaguely high-class tone of the social writing supports this idea. Meredith seems to have been right to discourage Hardy in the *Poor Man and the Lady* venture; one can sense behind the uncompromising astringency of the satire in *Desperate*

Remedies the embarrassment of the young countryman in the face of class-superiority. But suddenly, after the first Cytherea's rejection of Graye has started some kind of plot-movement, we are precipitated into a thicket of complex and subtle psychological insights which not only betray an astonishing maturity beneath the gaucheness, but a natural bent towards typological observation. After the refusal, Graye's character deteriorates "as emotional constitutions will under the long sense of disappointment at having missed their imagined destiny" (D.R., p. 5). That is immediately arresting, a far more mature judgment than the novel had seemed to promise. A complex psychological fact has been concretely grasped with an instinct for type-distinction ("as emotional constitutions will") that recalls Charlotte Brontë. The vocabulary also suggests the basis of the perceptions in the old Humours psychology: continuing the analysis of Graye's emotional decline, Hardy observes that "the winning and sanguine receptivity of his early life developed by degrees a moody nervousness". The really distinguished touch there seems to me to be the omission of the preposition "into" before the phrase "a moody nervousness". Hardy is even now sure enough of his material to see the enduring substratum of the character beneath the later development. A less scrupulous and subtle writer of perception might easily have rested content with the observation, and slid over into error.

Already, Hardy displays the extraordinary understanding of the decay and decline of character that comes to full fruition in *The Mayor of Casterbridge* and *Jude the Obscure.* Disappointed in his romantic love, Graye marries a woman he does not love and lives off fantasy and expectation until he is emotionally bankrupt: "The practical issue of such a condition was improvidence, originally almost an unconscious improvidence, for every debt incurred had been mentally paid off with a religious exactness from the treasures of expectation before mentioned. But as years revolved, the same course was continued from the lack of spirit sufficient for shifting out of an old groove when it has been found to lead to disaster" (D.R., p.5).

We have here already a sure and supple grasp both of the character and of the character within the type. (In proof of this, we shall be able to trace successively more detached treatments of the Graye type in later novels.)

Graye's daughter Cytherea (romantically named after the old flame) now establishes the novel firmly within the Brontë-Melville tradition. She has blue eyes, like sapphire, but darker than is usual: "they possessed the affectionate and liquid sparkle of loyalty and good faith as distinguishable from that harder brightness which seems to express faithfulness only to the object confronting them" (D.R., p. 8). Again, we note the instinct for checking up on frequencies, for comparing and classifying in a quasi-scientific way, that we have already observed in Charlotte Brontë. Cytherea belongs with the angels of the Brontë-Melville tradition. The fact that she has blue eyes means much more to Hardy than it would, say, to Dickens. Dickens, too, leans unconsciously upon the popular tradition associating blue eyes and golden hair with sweetness and light. Thus, there is a certain simple symbolism at work in *Bleak House,* when Ada, the blue-eyed blonde heroine, is contrasted with the flashing eyes and raven hair of a typically "interesting" villainess like Hortense, Lady Dedlock's French maid. Usually in Dickens to be dark-pigmented is to be the victim of uncontrollable temperament, like Rosa Dartle in *David Copperfield,* "temperament" meaning fire, passion, unpredictability. To be blue-eyed and blonde is to be sweet, open, warm, and trusting. Such symbolism is simple, dramatic, and moralistic, and has only a small part to play in the unfolding of Dickens's fables. It is taken for granted, exploited, and dropped when its immediate purpose is served; it is doubtful if Dickens was even aware of its existence. Certainly, there is an absolute difference between such a reliance upon popular imaginative devices and the conscious explorations of Melville, for example, or Hardy. Even in an immature novel like *Desperate Remedies,* Hardy shows himself to be aware of the psychological possibilities inherent in such physiological facts as Cytherea Graye's sapphire eyes: he not only sees in their hue affectionateness, loyalty, and good faith, but immediately qualifies their quality by contrasting it with another type of blueness, harder, which has "faithfulness only to the object confronting" it. Now this is an observation of extraordinary subtlety: who else in the English tradition would have been capable of such a reservation? Charlotte Brontë, perhaps, Dickens certainly not; and the latter fact is interesting.

The novel only really comes to life, however, when the sapphire-eyed Cytherea comes up against her anti-type – the dark villain, Manston. Manston complicates an emotional situation Hardy seems to have found too banal to develop without introducing a great deal of Victorian plot-machinery to provide reasons why the perfectly natural attraction that exists between Cytherea and the novel's romantic lead, Edward Springrove, should not result in marriage. "Uncontrollable circumstances", we are told, "operated to a certain extent as a drag upon his wishes." There are three ways, it seems to me, we can look at this move of Hardy's: as pure narrative engineering, as a token of Romanticism (in de Rougemont's idiom, Tristan must be kept from Isolde for the love to remain love), or as evidence of Hardy's own innate distaste for marriage. Since the situation occurs in many of Hardy's novels until its apotheosis in the near-farcical marriages, annulled marriages, and remarriages of *Jude the Obscure,* discussion of it can wait. In the present case, Edward Springrove's unconfessable reason for not being able to marry Cytherea makes most sense as sheer narrative carpentry.

Springrove is the first of the Adonises who figure in most of the earlier novels – unusually good-looking sensitives, almost girlish and withdrawn. Before Springrove appears he has been sketched for us by Cytherea's brother as having "dark hair – almost a Grecian nose, regular teeth, and an intellectual face" (D.R., p. 25). Cytherea's interest is confirmed by the reality. It is a significant portrait:

Although the upper part of his face and head was handsomely formed, and bounded by lines of sufficiently masculine regularity, his brows were somewhat too softly arched, and finely pencilled for one of his sex; without prejudice, however, to the belief which the sum total of his features inspired — that though they did not prove that the man who thought inside them would do much in the world, men who had done most of all had had no better ones. Across his forehead, otherwise perfectly smooth, ran one thin line, the healthy freshness of his remaining features expressing that it had come there prematurely. (D.R., p. 32).

Any prolific writer will, of course, repeat himself, or examine more closely his earlier attempts. But the repetitiousness we see in Hardy is different from Dickens's several portraits of his father, or George Eliot's of herself. The insight Hardy is beginning to examine here occurs again and again in his later books, neither accidentally, nor in the absence of anything new to say, but with the considered intentness of a scientist examining a phenomenon from more than one angle. Edward Springrove belongs to a type that, freely varied, includes such later characters as Clym Yeobright, Swithin St. Cleeve, even Jude Fawley; men in whom thought, the act of mentation, visibly and actually shapes, distorts, or stamps the body itself. From one point of view, in fact, the entire Hardy canon can be seen as an investigation of the relationship between the mind and the body. He straddles the Christian-Cartesian dualism and the behaviourism of later thinkers like Gilbert Ryle, and indeed of Stout and other psychologists of his own day. It is, in fact, his dual awareness of the active nature of consciousness, and of the interdependence of the mind and the body, that gives his account its peculiar value. This links up with the typological cast of his vision. It is, as I have remarked above, characteristic of the typological vision to give a physiological basis to personality.

Thus, even in this first published novel we see Hardy at work on his main themes. That "one thin line" that runs across Springrove's forehead is the mark of thought, and Springrove himself with his "air of melancholy", abstracted look, and "fruit of generalities" culled from experience, is the first of Hardy's suffering intellectuals.

Yet in most respects Springrove remains unfulfilled and unfinished, a single insight unlocated in a fully grasped character: it is no accident that in general Hardy's characters fail in so far as they are not totally grasped in their type-essence. Thus, both Cytherea and Springrove embody significant insights which Hardy later developed in the major novels, when the principles by which he instinctively evaluated personality had become clearer in his mind. At the stage of *Desperate Remedies,* he still felt it obligatory to make them good-looking and pure enough to serve as hero and heroine. Hardy could not yet make psychological qualities cohere with another in a consistent whole. Thus, there is no significance in Springrove's Grecian good looks, and it is difficult to believe in his intellectuality. The insight — the inroads made by consciousness into the flesh — is there all right. But for the moment, Hardy can do nothing with it. So he fabricates an "earlier commitment", and keeps the relationship with Cytherea on ice, pending the arrival of Manston.

Manston's appearance is prepared for us by the fourth important character in the novel, Miss Aldclyffe, who turns out in the end to be his mother. Miss Aldclyffe responds to Cytherea with the spontaneous warmth which Hardy often depicts between an older and a younger woman. The masculinity of the older woman, which would be crudely tendentious in a modern novel, is in fact a shade less innocent than the treatment by Dickens of comparable situations. Dickens had made the running with characters like Miss Havisham in *Great Expectations,* Alice in *Dombey and Son,* and even Edith in the same book; and had afforded Hardy a certain familiarity with potentially abnormal relationships. It is impossible to believe Hardy wholly innocent in the otherwise absurd scenes in which Miss Aldclyffe persuades

Cytherea to get into bed with her and kiss her. Here, Hardy follows the dictates of his Victorian readership: novels are about the *haute bourgeoisie,* and involve beautiful people being tangled up with long-lost lovers and illegitimate sons. There is a grain of Hardy's genuine flair for psychological perception in the character, though no more than a grain. He tells us that Miss Aldclyffe has

> clear steady eyes, a Roman nose in its purest form, and also the round prominent chin with which the Caesars are represented in ancient marbles; a mouth expressing a capability for and tendency to strong emotion, habitually controlled by pride. There was a severity about the lower outlines of the face which gave a masculine cast to this portion of her countenance. Womanly weakness was nowhere visible save in one part — the curve of her forehead and brow — there it was clear and emphatic. (D.R., pp. 62–63)

Almost a broken-off piece of classical statuary being turned in the hand of the connoisseur, though without the penetrativeness of Melville's study of Claggart. The typological instinct is stamped on every line of it: like Charlotte Brontë and Melville, Hardy habitually moves from the contemplation of his subject to some remembered parallel, usually drawn from a remote source. The contrast with the Dickensian *thereness* — its insistance on the unique actuality of the immediate personality — could hardly be more marked.

In general, the treatment of Miss Aldclyffe is derivative, too strongly reminiscent of its Dickensian prototypes, and rather too limitingly placed within its type-category. The same cannot, I think, be charged against Manston, who completes the novel's square of tension; and it is the handling of this character that really makes the novel worth reading. In Manston, Hardy offers a more or less complete study of another important type. He significantly complicates the story's hitherto scattered psychological suggestions into something of a genuine plot. If the treatment of characters like Edward Springrove seems inconclusive, Manston

represents a genuine advance by Hardy towards the territory he
later mapped with such completeness. From one point of view,
Manston reflects the Victorian equation of sexuality with evil:

> He was an extremely handsome man, well-formed and
> well-dressed, of an age which seemed to be two or three
> years less than thirty. The most striking point in his
> appearance was the wonderful, almost preternatural
> clearness of his complexion. There was not a blemish or
> speck of any kind to mar the smoothness of its surface
> or the beauty of its hue. Next, his forehead was square
> and broad, his brows straight and firm, his eyes
> penetrating and clear. By collecting the round of
> expressions they gave forth, a person who theorized on
> such matters would have imbibed the notion that their
> owner was of a nature to kick against the pricks; the last
> man in the world to put up with a position because it
> seemed to be his destiny to do so; one who took upon
> himself to resist fate with the vindictive determination of
> a Theomachist. Eyes and forehead both would have
> expressed keenness of intellect too severely to be
> pleasing, had their force not been counteracted by the
> lines and tone of the lips. These were full and luscious to
> a surprising degree, possessing a woman-like softness of
> curve, and a ruby redness so intense, as to testify
> strongly to much susceptibility of heart where feminine
> beauty was concerned — a susceptibility that might
> require all the ballast of brain with which he had
> previously been credited to confine within reasonable
> channels. (D.R., p. 157)

It is strange to think that Melville had not yet written *Billy
Budd* when Hardy wrote this; impossible to deny the
astounding similarity between the working methods revealed
by a comparison of the portraits of Manston and Claggart. In
both cases, the writer holds the face and head before him in
his mind's eye, almost takes its measurements, continually
checking up on expected congruences — "intellectual
brow . . . vindictive determination . . . but ah! interesting . . .
luscious lips . . . "

The resemblance of the passage to the best of Melville,
though, goes beyond the matter of technique. Like Melville,
Hardy clearly suspects Manston of some evil, not because of
any particular insight into the character, but simply because
he is good-looking, and attractively masculine. In most
Victorian fiction in fact, sexual potency is a liability if you
are good and a menace if you are evil. The equivocations in
the portrait of Manston — the suspect femininity, the
sensuality-cum-intellectuality — anticipate perfidy, treachery,
and eventually murder. What is more interesting than the
plot-line itself (archly Victorian melodrama as it mostly is) is
the way Manston coerces the action. In *Desperate Remedies*
there is little or no organic relation between the people and
the things they do. Only Manston's behaviour — arrogantly
sexual and masculine — is consistent at this level: he at least
pursues his own ends and forces people to do what he wants.

The basic structure of *Desperate Remedies* is practically
identical to that of *A Pair of Blue Eyes*. *A Pair of Blue Eyes*
in fact was written in 1873, the year after *Under the
Greenwood Tree*. I am treating it before that novel simply
because of this close parallel with *Desperate Remedies*.

In *A Pair of Blue Eyes*, Hardy contrasts two men, Knight
and Stephen Smith, in relation to the heroine, Elfride
Swancourt. This pattern can be found varied throughout
Hardy's minor fiction. Knight, the older man, is Smith's
"preceptor" (much as Phillotson is Jude's in *Jude the
Obscure*); he is well-off and secure, where Stephen is poor and
struggling; more important still, the two represent different
psychological types, and the novel makes a genuine attempt
to match and contrast them. Even here, where, as in
Desperate Remedies, Hardy thought it necessary to lumber
the plot with an impressive confusion of subterfuge and
mystery, we can see him at work on the distinctions that are
to form the basis of his mature art.

The Knight-Smith contrast strongly resembles the
Brontë-Melville dualisms. Knight is the earliest instance of a
type that was to absorb Hardy until he gave up fiction — the

reflective pedant, who thinks more than he feels, more or less contented, until the imposed equilibrium of his life is disturbed. Once it has been disturbed, it is for good: the type lacks the flexibility to recover balance naturally. A significant detail of the extended portrait Hardy gives us of Knight is the facial hair that hides "the real expression of [the mouth] under a chronic aspect of impassivity" (P.B.E., p. 151). The diction reveals a tendency towards type-characterization of an almost astrological stringency: already Hardy sees little chances for the individual's survival against the limitations of his own constitution. Next, Knight suffers, like Edward Springrove, from the ravagings of thought: his brow and face "were getting sicklied o'er by the unmistakable pale cast". Lastly, the eyes, "though keen, permeated rather than penetrated: what they lost of their boy-time brightness by a dozen years of hard reading lending a quietness to their gaze which suited them well". When this man begins to fall in love with Elfride, he does so "philosophically rather than romantically". Only when Elfride is absent does he become aware of how much space she has come to occupy in his mental world. Hardy observes that she was (strictly) irrelevant to Knight, just as love itself was; but, "the superfluity had become a necessity, and Knight was in love". Most significantly, he comes to love her not through the senses, "by glances of the eye and sympathetic touches of the fingers", but when she had become sublimated in his memory. This disembodied contemplation of the object of love goes so far that Knight does not even "see" her until she is no longer present. Hence it is that Hardy says he loved her "philosophically rather than romantically".

Knight is thus Hardy's first mature essay in the depiction of the contemplative man at one remove from physical experience, and seeking as far as possible to dictate terms to life, and regulate the experience coming his way, so that his preconceived schemata shall be preserved. ("He almost trembled at the possible result of the introduction of this new force among the nicely adjusted ones of his ordinary life"

[P.B.E., p. 223].) Once he has decided to accept the new, it too must become the familiar, it too must become part of the order he constitutionally imposes on the world: "He became restless; then he forgot all collateral subjects in the pleasure of thinking about her" (P.B.E., p. 223). Later, Hardy pushed the study of this type farther than, I think, any of his predecessors or successors: Boldwood in *Far from the Madding Crowd* is the most impressive account Hardy was to give of this aspect of the tragic personality. (In the end, we shall be able to hazard a quasi-psychological hypothesis as to the nature of the tragic personality, based on Hardy's work in this field.)

A Pair of Blue Eyes is really little more than the study of Knight's temperament as it is affected by its tragic catalyst, Elfride Swancourt. The novel's deceptively Gilbert-and-Sullivan-ish title is in fact nicely chosen: a pair of blue eyes — and the intellectual's world is shattered. But what eyes — "blue; blue as autumn distance — blue as the blue we see between the retreating mouldings of hills and woody slopes on a sunny September morning. A misty and shady blue, that had no beginning or surface, and was looked *into* rather than *at*" (P.B.E., p. 2). A superb sentence, as subtle and delicate as Melville's description of Claggart's eyes, though less metaphysical, and more realistic: how finely Hardy suggests that imponderable quality of Elfride's that makes her so much more than a conventional angel: her eyes were "looked *into* rather than *at*". This seems an amazingly subtle observation for so young a writer. Nor is it a passing excellence: there is in Elfride a detached quality that makes her strangely akin to Knight. Later Hardy says of her that "her eyes seemed to look at you, and past you, as you were then, into your future, and past your future, into your eternity — not reading it but gazing in an unused, unconscious way to its original thought". A capacity for abstractedness — hinted at in the earlier beautiful image of the blue distant hills — leavens her whole being with grace. Already the basic quantities of the Brontës have been complicated and refined. Reading this account of the azure angels, we almost feel we know why Claggart had to smash Billy.

The relationship between Stephen Smith and Elfride is pure romance. Smith is the next of Hardy's Adonises, a young architect who has not yet emerged out of adolescent girlishness, with a complexion "as fine as Elfride's own; the pink of his cheeks as delicate, his mouth as perfect as a Cupid's bow in form, and as cherry-red in colour as hers. Bright curly hair; bright sparkling blue-grey eyes . . . "In other words, Billy Budd without the cheerful toughness. His interest (if any) is largely in what he prefigures of future characters. The architecture is of a piece with the excessive sensibility.

Thus, these two novels have closely parallel plots, layout, and psychological structure. In most respects, the earlier book is inferior to the later. Nothing in *Desperate Remedies* approaches the maturity of the treatment of Knight, which is indeed a significant achievement in its own right. The conception of later characters like Boldwood in *Far from the Madding Crowd* owes much to the work done on Knight here. In one respect, however, *Desperate Remedies* goes beyond the later novel. In a crucial passage, Hardy says of Cytherea that "motion was her speciality, whether shown on its most extended scale of bodily progression, or minutely, as in the uplifting of her eyelids, the bending of her fingers, the pouting of her lip. The carriage of her head — motion within motion — a glide upon a glide — was as delicate as that of a magnetic needle. And this flexibility and elasticity had never been taught her by rule, nor even been acquired by observation" (D.R., p. 7). Later he speaks of her "apt lightness in the dance". Something new has entered English fiction here. No earlier writer would have placed that sort of emphasis on that sort of fact. Hardy displays extraordinary delicacy and skill in getting at Cytherea's centre of gravity: it will hardly be possible to find anywhere else in literature that kind of extended fragility of probe, establishing so surely and strongly so intangible a thing. It is possible now to appreciate anew the significance of the entire tradition within which

Hardy was working. New areas of experience and knowledge had been opened up to exploration. For the time being, Hardy could only get out the facts themselves. It was for later novels to examine the implications in terms of relationships. Bearing in mind Cytherea's "flexibility", we can pass on to Fancy Day in *Under the Greenwood Tree* in possession of the first wholly original element in Hardy's psychological vocabulary. We must wait a little for the other implicit complexities to spell themselves out, most notably the attraction that exists between the fair, distant purity of Elfride and the dark brooding power of Knight.

3. *Under the Greenwood Tree* (1872)

Under the Greenwood Tree is the first real Hardy in the way that Sibelius's Third Symphony is the first real Sibelius. Just as Sibelius had to throw off a lot of spurious Tchaikowskian rhetoric to get at his real material, so Hardy had to jettison the pseudo-glitter of his social satire and the kind of irrelevant plot-mongery which Dickens had managed to convert into genuine artistic elements. In fact it took a decade more for Hardy to rid himself wholly of the idea that a serious and important novel had to concern titled ladies, wills, forgeries, and secret alliances: even after major achievements like *The Return of the Native,* he could relapse into the artificial stilted vein that vitiates almost half his published fiction. The unremittingly satirical manner of the early novels betrays Hardy's own social position: while he felt the world of the manor-house to be the real locale for serious literature, he still could not bring himself to fawn upon it. The serious country intellectual reveals himself in the boringly hostile satirist. So that it is poignant to see him hankering after the humble rusticity he really loved in such episodes as those concerning Springrove's father in *Desperate Remedies* – a real Hardy yokel, complete with public-house cronies and dialect comedy. The whole novel is thereby undermined, of course: such belief as we ever entertained in the young Springrove is destroyed in a flash when we are asked to credit his parentage. We realize that he is just a literary convention.

In the circumstances, then, *Under the Greenwood Tree* is an astonishing breakthrough, a wholly successful novel totally unmarred by the flaws of taste and tone that disfigure the two novels considered in the previous chapter. It usually passes for a slight book that manages to delight everybody. In fact, it is an impressive comedy, subtle and well-structured. Its peculiar strength derives from its sound union of three separate elements: the passing of the old rustic life (the book's subtitle is *The Mellstock Quire*); the revolving of the natural cycle; and the tensions and resolutions of the psychological elements. The three strands combine with such simplicity that one is at pains to recollect afterwards how the final pattern was achieved.

Like all of Hardy's best fiction, the novel closely follows the rhythm of the natural year. In a sense, Hardy replaced the life-cycle of the Dickens novel with the nature-cycle. Instead of pursuing the arc of a single life, as Dickens does in *David Copperfield* and *Great Expectations,* Hardy's fables rise and fall with the seasons. In fact he tends to lose control when he loses contact with the rhythm of nature: most of the minor novels at a certain stage stop dead, and flail around helplessly in factitious complications of action. His people begin to behave like marionettes at the mercy of a whimsical master because their inner nature has ceased to provide enough motivation to keep the plot going. As we have seen, in *Desperate Remedies* only Manston really coerced circumstances and thereby got things going: the authenticity of the action then derived from the genuine interaction of personalities. Cytherea was afraid of Manston and attracted by him at the same time. Hence, their characters (which is to say their types, also) were genuinely engaged in the energic process of attraction-revulsion which drives Hardy's best fiction along. Similarly, in *A Pair of Blue Eyes,* only when Hardy begins to follow out the implications of Knight's character do we experience the quality of mature art. Invariably in Hardy's fiction, it is this kind of psychological authenticity that provides interest and engagement.

Under the Greenwood Tree takes place in a much sunnier, less intense world. The basic comedy situation, however, is still geared to the psychological qualities of the characters. At the end of the previous chapter I suggested a link with *Desperate Remedies:* the central character in *Under the Greenwood Tree* is Fancy Day, who may be seen as a more fluently realized version of Cytherea Graye. The action of the novel concerns her courtship by Dick Dewy, harassed by parental disapproval and the attentions of the vicar and a churchwarden. Through the classic comedy-mechanism runs the consistent psychological reasoning glimpsed only intermittently in *Desperate Remedies* and *A Pair of Blue Eyes*. Here, the mechanism is designed to join, separate, and finally reunite Fancy and Dick. It is especially important to be right about the nature of the characters and their involvement. For without proper understanding of the plan behind the story, it can seem to degenerate into the merely pleasant fantasy it is often taken to be. As so often in Hardy, the conflict derives from the vacillation in a woman's mind about the man she really wants. In Hardy this situation springs from the inner complexity of one of two fairly constant types. Fancy is an example of the "nervous" type, closely following in general contours her predecessor, Cytherea Graye. Women of this type in Hardy always have names symbolizing lightness or grace or ethereality. Fancy Day is dark, like Sue Bridehead of whom she is an earlier version. Hardy's initial description, as always, is decisive. After a glimpse which discloses her as "comely, slender and prettily dressed", we get a careful portrait:

> She belonged to the taller division of middle height. Flexibility was her first characteristic, by which she appeared to enjoy the most easeful rest when she was in gliding motion. Her dark eyes — arched by brows of so keen, slender, and soft a curve that they resembled nothing so much as two slurs in music — showed primarily a bright sparkle in each. This was softened by a frequent thoughtfulness, yet not so frequent as to do away, for more than a few minutes at a time, with a certain coquettishness; which in its turn was never so decided as to banish honesty. Her lips imitated her brows in their clearly-cut outline and softness of curve. (U.G.T., pp. 60–61)

This is a little schematic towards the end: the vacillation

comes rather too easily to be totally convincing, so that the coquettishness begins to take on a conventional tone that tends to blunt the incisiveness of the initial conception. Darkness and softness are there, as with Cytherea. But the "flexibility" is what really matters. Hardy's real quality — his penetrating shrewdness of eye — emerges in this single detail: flexibility is, indeed, the basic factor in Fancy's constitution. As her name suggests, her spirit is peregrine, migratory, flamelike.

A mind of strange insight is at work here, compact of a strange, sometimes frightening, mélange of sophistication and primitivism. Critics are perhaps over-fond of the big elemental words in describing Hardy. I, for one, confess to an initial disappointment on first reading his novels. Where was the elemental power, the primal savagery, I had been led to expect? Well, it was there; but as with Nature itself it was a very delicate, sophisticated power. Hardy teaches us, indeed, that Nature is never simple and rarely straightforward.

In the present case, the weird acuity reveals itself in the insight into the relations between dancing and the occult. No one else, in my experience of fiction, has ever approached Hardy's understanding of the intoxication of the dance, the power of music to express and release the demonic. Now, we are very close here to the essence of Hardy's art. The evidence piles up: Fancy Day is coquettish, errant, and apparently unpredictable. Like Cytherea Graye, she is most at rest in movement: she glides. Later she consults a witch. She is, therefore, wayward in her nervousness. Now, the devil also is a spirit. Perhaps Hardy's major contribution to our knowledge of the human mind is just this insight into the nature of the demonic, the spirit of darkness, that is not yet evil. The demonic associations of music are ancient. Hardy explores the theme again and again, most brilliantly in a couple of early stories, which I must here break off to describe.

The Fiddler of the Reels (in the story of that name) is too crude a demon to engage our interest very deeply. The whole story, like a number of Hardy's shorter pieces, is schematic rather than imaginatively realized. But the theme it schematizes is absolutely central in Hardy's work. Mop Ollamor, the fiddler who seduces girls with his demonic playing, has a "power which seemed sometimes to have a touch of the weird and wizardly in it". The portrait Hardy paints has curious undertones; the fiddler — "un-English", swarthy, and oily — had a curious unmasculine air about him. He smelled of "boy-love" and had a double row of curls. The long hair completes a picture calculated to arouse the average Englishman's contempt — a vaguely effeminate foreigner, irresistibly attractive to women. "All the devil's tunes were in his repertory", Hardy remarks. The story follows his seduction of Car'line Aspent ("weak-mouthed" and pretty, peevish now and then). Its main interest lies in Hardy's evocations of the demonic possession of music: "Mop was standing in his door-step, as was his custom, spinning the insidious thread of semi-and-demi-semiquavers from the E string of his fiddle for the benefit of passersby, and laughing as the tears rolled down the cheeks of the little children hanging about him." The effect on Car'line Aspent is catastrophic — convulsions and thrills of ecstasy seize her. Her body becomes a vessel for the holy (or unholy) spirit: "presently, the aching of the heart seized her simultaneously with a wild desire to glide airily in the mazes of an infinite dance". She glances up, finds to her relief that he plays with his eyes closed — steals closer, only to discover with a shock that *one* of his eyes is open "quizzing her as he smiled at her emotional state". Later in the story, after she has persuaded stolid, manly Ned Hipcroft to give her (and Mop's) child a name, and acquired a new London dignity, Car'line returns to her old haunts, and again helplessly falls to Mop's fantastic fiddling. The story ends, disturbingly, with Mop, having abducted Car'line's child, rumoured to be living off her dancing in America, he "an old scamp verging on three-score-and-ten, and she a woman of four-and-forty".

The second of the stories, "Absent-Mindedness in a Parish Choir", concerns the same Mellstock Choir as provides the subplot to *Under the Greenwood Tree*. One Christmas, the members of the band drink too much brandy on their rounds of the village, doze during the sermon, and, on waking abruptly, launch into "The Devil among the Tailors" instead of the hymn tune. The ironical end to the tale is interesting. To replace the disgraced choir, the Squire sends for a new barrel-organ "that would play two-and-twenty new psalm-tunes, so exact and particular that, however sinful inclined you was, you could play nothing but psalm-tunes whatsoever". Now *Under the Greenwood Tree* also concerns the dismissal of the same choir. Music is associated with the devil: what is interesting is not that the players doze in church and forget where they are, but what it springs into their heads to play when they wake up. But music is also associated simply with joyous possession. The music of the devil belongs to the past: the choir must be dismissed. The final link in the chain is that where in "Absent-Mindedness in a Parish Choir" it is replaced by a dreadful, psalm-playing machine, in *Under the Greenwood Tree* it is replaced by Miss Fancy Day. At one stroke, in fact, Hardy has fused all the elements of his story together. The implication is that Fancy Day's organ-playing is tidy, mediocre, and dull – the day, indeed, as opposed to the night of the soul that expresses itself through the old music. Yet she herself has been shown as eminently susceptible to music, as being all motion and flexibility.

Fancy is proposed as a candidate to play the organ instead of the choir by a churchwarden, Shiner. Shiner provides one of the complications in the story's emotional web. Both he and Maybold, the new young vicar, became suitors of Fancy's and this it is – though there is never any serious doubt in the reader's mind about Dick Dewy's chances – that provides the material of the action. Already, it has become obvious that it is neither a lightweight nor a perfunctory mechanism that Hardy has contrived. Shiner, "a character principally composed of a crimson stare, vigorous breath, and a watch-chain, with a mouth hanging on a dark smile but never smiling", doesn't really get near Fancy, though she lets Dick think he is in the running. His masculine force exercises a certain attraction over her, and this is his function in the novel. His comparative wealth, his bodily vigour, and his sneering boldness make a beautiful contrast with the vicar, Mr. Maybold (May-pole, May-be-bold). All the elements have now been enumerated. For religion — both as a social and as a spiritual resource — often figures in Hardy's psychological polarities. We have seen Charlotte Brontë's St. John Rivers and Hawthorne's Arthur Dymmesdale as earlier examples of what I have called the beautiful vicar syndrome. Both socially and sexually, the cleric must have exercised a tremendous fascination over the girls and women of country districts in the nineteenth century. The vicar of the Victorian novel brings light, and a new kind of sexual grace, into a world dominated by rude extrovert masculinity. Mr. Maybold hovers indecisively over Fancy, disconcerts Dick, but sheers off at the first hint of an earlier understanding between the two. The two strands — Fancy's flirtations with Shiner and Maybold — never converge, and are indeed handled separately in two main phases. The first culminates in the dance at the house of the Tranter (Dick's father). Hardy's intimate knowledge of country mores and his weird intuition into the nature of musical possession here coalesce. The dance is taken over by the demonic spirit: the fiddlers play asleep as "humming-tops sleep by increasing their motion and hum" (U.G.T., p. 68). Shiner's overtures, accompanied by the flashing of his watch-chain, fail to shake Dick's hold. During the dance, significantly, she belongs to Dick. The music and movement grip her a level deeper than that of the merely physical attraction exercised by Shiner. In the possession of the music, her real self gravitates towards Dick.

Maybold disturbs Dick's tenure more seriously. The air of idealism and learning, of superior fineness, temporarily eclipses Dick's rustic straightforwardness. Fancy's letter to him confides precisely what has been the source of his attraction for her:

"It is my nature — perhaps all women's — to love refinement of mind and manners; but even more than this, to be ever fascinated with the idea of surroundings more elegant and luxurious than those which have been customary!" (U.G.T., p. 244)

It is the feeling that the counter-attractions will never really shake Dick's hold over Fancy, probably, that gives *Under the Greenwood Tree* its light tone. Yet the elements of Hardy's mature art are all — or nearly all — there, and at all times handled with a wry realism.

What is perhaps the most disturbing scene in the book I have left till last. Apart from the flirtations with Maybold and Shiner, Hardy has up his sleeve that oldest of comic cards, parental opposition (one of the many respects in which the book anticipates *The Woodlanders*). Dick isn't good enough for Fancy's father. To overcome his opposition, Fancy consults the village witch — named, with subtle simplicity, Elizabeth Endorfield. (There is an interesting parallel with Hawthorne here: Mistress Hubbard in *The Scarlet Letter* has a similar comic-evil aura.) Elizabeth Endorfield is paring potatoes for her husband's supper when Fancy calls; she calls out before Fancy knocks, for she was "an exceedingly and exceptionally sharp woman in the use of her eyes and ears" (U.G.T., p. 212). She is, of course, the local witch, or, as the locals had it, "a Deep Body, who was as long-headed as she was high" (p. 213). Interestingly, Hardy suggests that under the old vicar — Mr. Grinham, who was popular and liked for preserving the old ways — witches thrived. Hardy implies that Maybold — all light and modernity — will sweep away all this old religion, together with the old music, the possession — *and the zest for life*. The witch's advice to Fancy is simply that she refuse to eat, until her father agree to the marriage. The shrewd device works and Maybold loses Fancy — as the new light of reason, in important respects, loses out to the old.

Thus, Fancy calls upon the dark powers to help her save herself for Dick. As I have noted above, the affinity with

Dick is itself guaranteed by their common genius for the dance: in the dance she belongs to Dick, just as in the dance they both belong to a lower instinct associated with possession, the demonic and the old. The seemingly innocent subplot, the Mellstock Quire, is, therefore, centrally relevant to the whole fable: in a strangely paradoxical way, what relates Fancy to Dick (her aptitude for music) is also what relates her to Maybold, since she is chosen by him to replace the old choir. Music associates her at once with the old, demonic "knowledge" — the knowledge, undercutting reason and light, that Maybold's predecessor wisely allowed to persist — and with the bright new world of efficiency and day. Both elements are rather beautifully fused in her name — Fancy Day.

On the typological plane, Hardy distinguishes three main threads: neither the spirituality of Maybold nor the physical sexuality of Shiner can claim Fancy. She is marked down for Dick Dewy in virtue of a different quality — her "flexibility". This is of course vastly to oversimplify, and to present in too schematic a fashion what is conveyed naturally and without identifying labels. But this, in essence, is the structure underlying a deceptively simple fable.

4. "A Reciprocity of Influence"

Minor Novels:
The Hand of Ethelberta (1876)
A Laodicean (1881)
Two on a Tower (1882)

The minor works of a great writer often reveal the sinews of the art that are hidden beneath the flesh and skin of his accomplished masterpieces. One thinks of *Timon of Athens,* too nakedly tragic a statement to be tragedy. The minor novels Hardy wrote in the later seventies and early eighties – *The Hand of Ethelberta, A Laodicean,* and *Two on a Tower* – all divulge extraordinary glimpses of his imaginative principles and sometimes plain statements of method. This is perhaps less true of *The Hand of Ethelberta* than of *Two on a Tower* and the weird *A Laodicean.* Yet even there the handling of Christopher Julian, the musician hero, is in places more explicit and conscious of itself than that of, say, major characters like Clym Yeobright and Jude Fawley.

Basically, the novel is something of a relapse. It returns to the remorseless satirizing of the rich that marks Hardy's earliest novels. There are effete gentlemen ("sportsmen") with names like Ladywell and Neigh; a seedy old aristocrat who ogles the models in London fashion catalogues; a lady's maid called Manlove. The whole atmosphere suggests Restoration comedy without the *savoir faire* needed to leaven the satire with urbanity. Just how keenly Hardy felt about urban high society could be illustrated from Mrs. Hardy's biography,[1] but there is a beautifully naked tremor of indignation in *Far from the Madding Crowd* that will serve our purposes as well. When Gabriel Oak – good honest yeoman – calls on Bathsheba Everdene to ask for her hand, he tells Bathsheba's aunt to let her know that "somebody" wants to see her. Lest we should misunderstand, Hardy parenthetically assures us that ("Calling oneself merely Somebody without giving a name, is not to be taken as an example of the ill-breeding of the rural world: it springs from a refined modesty, of which townspeople, with

their cards and announcements, have no notion whatever.")
Such susceptibility could hardly be expected to give a fair or
even rational account of the urban middle class, and it is not
for Hardy's attempt to do so that *The Hand of Ethelberta*
deserves to be read, but for his treatment of Christopher
Julian.

Julian, an impoverished musician, continues Hardy's
investigation into the thinking type. He is described as a
"thinker by instinct", a man "whose countenance varied with
his mood, though it kept somewhat in the rear of that mood"
(H.E., p. 18). Although Hardy refers to "repressing
experiences" which had helped make Julian reticent, the real
truth is that he characteristically sees through a network of
internal images, and only occasionally breaks through to the
present. Hardy offers here one of his subtlest accounts of
introversion. Out walking with Picotee, Ethelberta's
apple-cheeked sister, Julian has suddenly ceased to listen to
her: "He was a man who often, when walking abroad, and
looking as it were at the scene before his eyes, discerned
successes and failures, friends and relations, episodes of
childhood, wedding-feasts and funerals, the landscape suffering
greatly by these visions, until it became no more than the
patterned wall-tints about the paintings in a gallery. Nothing
but a special concentration of himself on externals could
interrupt this habit" (p. 26). We can easily recognize here
kindred traits of other Hardy introverts: Boldwood's inability
to "see" Bathsheba until she has inserted herself between him
and his habitual preoccupations; Knight's inability to
contemplate Elfride properly except in her absence; the
abstracted look of Edward Springrove.

Apart from such passages as this, the novel moves in the
unreal social world of Hardy's most jejune fiction. All that is
really characteristic of Hardy in the story is the attraction
that exists between Julian and Ethelberta, and the choice of
the two temperaments. Again, the intellectual introvert
attracts the flexuous woman. Our first glimpse of Ethelberta
is her gathering up her skirts impulsively and running

excitedly to watch two birds. The portrait itself is not very penetrating. She is "a plump-armed creature, with a white round neck as firm as a fort — altogether a vigorous shape, as refreshing to the eye as the green leaves" (H.E., p. 40). The details of her manner of speaking tell us more — "rapid but not frequent, an obstructive thought causing sometimes a sudden halt in the midst of a stream of words". And even more instructive, clearly relating her to such early heroines as Cytherea Graye, is the "peculiar gaze into imaginary far-away distance when making a quiet remark to a partner — not with contracted eyes like a seafaring man, but with an open full look" (H.E., p. 40). Such details, together with the emphasis on her movement, on her free dancing, create the image of an impulsive, physically orientated creature readily drawn to Julian's in-turned quietude. A final detail confirms the almost scientific bent of Hardy's mind: "One may say of a look that it is capable of division into as many species, genera, orders, and classes, as the animal world itself" (H.E., p. 41).

Almost ten years — from 1878 to 1886 — separate *The Return of the Native* from *The Mayor of Casterbridge*. No artist develops regularly and smoothly all the time. The process is more likely to be jerky and erratic. In the case of Hardy the three novels he produced between these two great works handle characteristic themes with occasional subtlety and slightly more frequent bathos and absurdity. None of them is a real success. I shall therefore treat them briefly and schematically.

Schematic is exactly what the novels are, in fact — often rather fascinating ideas frittered away in arbitrariness for want of an overmastering drive. *Two on a Tower* — disowned by Hardy's preface as "a slightly built Romance" — begins with the Tower, moves on to the Two, and after some passing excellences, rambles listlessly yet irritatingly among most of the possible ways of keeping two lovers from marrying when there is no reason whatever why they shouldn't. The novel has its own key — a chaste minor — established with intricate skill by subtle observation of the terrain. It begins "on an early winter afternoon, clear but not cold, when the vegetable world was a weird multitude of skeletons through whose ribs the sun shone freely" (T.T., p. 1). As often in Hardy, the basic collocation of personalities interests us more than anything they actually do. Symptomatically, the relationship between Swithin St. Cleeve and Lade Viviette Constantine combines a good many of Hardy's basic preoccupations.

In the first place, Swithin St. Cleeve belongs with the intellectual-spiritual idealists of the Hardy scheme, as his saint's name should by now enable us to guess without our knowing anything more about him. The Tower itself — somewhat absurd in the context of this century's remorseless Freudianizing — cannot clearly be made sense of without at least emblematic interpretation. And in fact, Hardy not only makes this easy, he does the job for us. For St. Cleeve uses the Tower for his astronomical studies: Lady Constantine, who owns the land the Tower stands on, mounts the Tower and finds there a pretty youth "to disperse an almost killing ennui" (T.T., p. 3). Hardy himself seems to have experienced some embarrassment in the company of upper-class women, and in his fiction upper-class women are invariably consumed with boredom and a destructive purposelessness. He also had little real sense of their manners: Hardy's ladies seem to dress for dinner at ten in the morning and lie around all day languidly expressing the tedium of their existence, after the fashion of Dickens's Lady Dedlock.

Viviette Constantine is certainly no exception to this part of the rule. But the *de-haut-en-bas* element of the relationship expresses its sexual basis, and this is perhaps a key to all Hardy's bored ladies. Their wealth or prestige gives them a sexual initiative Hardy found at once attractive and embarrassing. At any rate, he continues to hedge for the rest of the novel, inventing reasons why the two should not get married, including a bequest of Swithin's uncle forbidding him to marry, and a long-lost husband of Viviette's, who returns from the wilds of Africa. Most of Hardy's lesser novels, in fact, turn on impossible, false, quasi- or postponed marriages.

(Even in the major novels whole tracts, plots, and subplots revolve around earlier pledges, and unforeseen obstacles. Only with *Jude the Obscure* did Hardy admit that all this hesitant drawing back from marriage concealed, or rather expressed, something like a deep distaste for the relationship itself.)

This time, again, as in *The Native,* the voyeurism is reversed: the woman "espies" the man, as befits the more aggressive part she is to play in the relationship. Hardy dithers coyly over the looks of the young man "who might properly have been characterized by the word the judicious chronicler would not readily use in such a connection, preferring to reserve it for raising images of the opposite sex" (T.T., p. 6). Only the straightness of the features, indeed, corrected "the beholder's first impression that the head was the head of a girl" (T.T., p. 6). Viviette perceives St. Cleeve to be like something out of Raphael, with "very light shining hair" and a clear complexion. Interestingly, Hardy makes the comparison of their different types more explicitly than he has ventured to hitherto. Perhaps it is the freedom of the consciously lightweight work that enables him to do this; perhaps the gradual surfacing of his awareness of his own methods and meaning. Viviette, he states right away, is "herself of a totally opposite type" from the youth. We have here some explicit pointers to Hardy's entire psychological methodology. The fair hair and the hint of Raphael immediately put us in mind of the Brontës' English angels. Now, Hardy tells us that Viviette's hair was "black as midnight, her eyes had no less deep a shade, and her complexion showed the richness demanded as a support to these decided features" (T.T., p. 7). The point is made quite definitely that the complexion and hair colour denote their deeper spiritual difference of type. For immediately after this description of dark-and-rich Viviette, she is shown physically responding to ascetic-spiritual-abstracted Swithin St. Cleeve, who is so engrossed in his telescope that he does not notice her: "As she continued to look at the pretty fellow before her, apparently so far abstracted into some speculative world as scarcely to know a real one, a warmer wave of her warm temperament glowed visibly through her, and a qualified observer might from this have hazarded a guess that there was Romance blood in her veins" (T.T., p. 7). A little later, the relationship — or at least the attraction — is under way, and the event is conveyed in equally explicit type-vocabulary: "He continued to look at her and forget the sun, just such a reciprocity of influence as might have been expected between a dark lady and a flaxen-haired youth making itself apparent in the faces of each" (T.T., p. 7).

In the post-Freudian world, a straight account could be given of the episode in sexual terms: the hungry lady ascends the Tower and gets a glimpse of the sun: "She assented, and looked through the shaded eye-piece, and saw a whirling mass, in the centre of which the blazing globe seemed to be laid bare to its core. It was a peep into a maelstrom of fire, taking place where nobody had ever been or ever would be" (T.T., p. 8).

The youth is a sun-worshipper all right, but he lives up on a Tower; the lady has to persuade him to come down. The astronomy provides Hardy with exactly the right imagery for the love-dance, leading up to the final consummation. It symbolizes St. Cleeve's unreality — his excessively sublimated libido, which is the source of his attractiveness, as far as Viviette is concerned. At the same time, it enforces an awareness of the powers ruling human behaviour. In the phrase, "reciprocity of influence", the latter word bears its astrological and astronomical meaning. Thus, the types now emerge as themselves determinants of behaviour: we cannot help being dark and passionate or fair and ethereal. This, bluntly, and in a very small nutshell, is my theme, and, I believe, Hardy's.

As I have been arguing all along, Hardy's main discoveries in the realm of psychology concern the fundamental dispositions of mind, and the main interest in his novels lies in the interaction of contrasting, conflicting, or neutralizing characters: in other words, in the laws of attraction and repulsion, that obtain among people of opposite or adjacent character-types. In the meeting between Swithin St. Cleeve and Viviette Constantine, Hardy defines the "reciprocity of influence" that arises between a certain type of fair intellectual and the Romance-blooded sensualist. Eustacia Vye, of course, has both the Romance blood and the passion of Viviette. But the characters are distinct, though Eustacia's attraction towards Wildeve to some extent parallels Viviette's passion for Swithin. Swithin, in fact, is a strike-back to the Adonises of the earlier Hardy. It is his astronomy that most interests us about him. Astronomy is the most abstract, the most exalted, the most awesome, yet the coldest of the physical sciences. Hardy's early heroes are either musicians (like Christopher Julian in *The Hand of Ethelberta* — note the saints' names again), architects, sculptors, or astronomers. Thus, his idealists pursue abstract science-arts, elevated and intellectual, which are at the same time deprived of the warmth, colour, and blood of so-called real life. If we think of "the warmer wave of her warm temperament" that glowed through Viviette (*vivre-vivante*-vivid), the nature of the polarity is immediately apparent. So is the relationship of Hardy's investigations to those of the Brontës.

St. Cleeve's astronomy, therefore, symbolizes unearthly idealism. It also, as I have suggested, serves not as a background but as a kind of planetarium, whose roof Hardy slides back now and then to make the mistaken purposes, confusions, inheritances, and returns of long-lost husbands down below appear the silly clowning they really are:

> "You would hardly think, at first, that horrid monsters lie up there waiting to be discovered by the moderately penetrating mind — monsters to which those of the oceans bear no sort of comparison."
> "What monsters may they be?"
> "Impersonal monsters, namely, Immensities . . . monsters of magnitude without known shape . . . There is a size at which dignity begins," he exclaimed: "further on there is a size at which solemnity begins; further on, a size at which

awfulness begins; further on, a size at which ghastliness begins. That size faintly approaches — the size of the stellar universe. So am I not right in saying that those minds who exert their imaginative powers to bury themselves in the depths of that universe merely strain their faculties to gain a new horror?" (T.T., pp. 34–35)

Viviette is chastened, her flesh and blood thoroughly subdued. But the young intellectual hasn't finished yet:

"And to add a new weirdness to what the sky possesses in its size and formlessness, there is involved the quality of decay ... Imagine them all [the stars] extinguished, and your mind feeling its way through a heaven of total darkness, occasionally striking against the black, invisible cinders of those stars ... If you are cheerful, and wish to remain so, leave the study of astronomy alone." (T.T., p. 36)

Compare this, with its air of indubitably grasped horror, with the grandiose vaguenesses of Joseph Conrad's "Inscrutables" and "Ineffables", and it is obvious that where Conrad half-relishes the frisson, Hardy genuinely fears the insight. And without that sober fear, his work would lose its integrity.

Yet, as Hardy points out often enough, the movement of the stars confers significance on human life by exactly the same token as it appears to remove it. How tremendous to be part of *that!* And how tremendous to be *aware* of it! If Hardy did not have this ineradicable belief that what people value *is* valuable, he could not claim our attention as a novelist: the stoicism of the stars comes easily to a certain kind of self-dramatizing immaturity, as F. R. Leavis long ago pointed out apropos of Bertrand Russell.

George Somerset of *A Laodicean* is an architect, and if it is doubted that Hardy's use of his heroes' professions has the significance I am attributing to it, we may turn to Dickens or to Ibsen for comparison. Pecksniff is an architect, so is Martin Chuzzlewit. The fact has no bearing whatever on either the character (the very idea of Pecksniff, any more than Micawber, or Falstaff, having a job — as if it were not enough of a job being himself!) or on our understanding of him. Dickens presents no problem. Ibsen on the other hand devoted a lot of care to the selection of his heroes' professions: they had a lot of symbolic work to do. The obvious comparison with Hardy is *The Master Builder*. Architects, with their erections and projections, have long been a source of easy Freudian symbolism. (William Golding's *The Spire* shows how unresonant the symbolism can be when used facilely.) Solnes's final destruction — he falls off his own erection — consummates, or rather fails to consummate, a powerful sexual allegory, which also works on the ontological plane: Solnes's very existence and purpose are at stake. To this extent, Ibsen successfully exploits the symbolic potentialities in architecture. But the symbolism is also to some extent arbitrary — it is, in the end, allegoric rather than symbolic, in the modern sense of the word. Hardy uses architecture so subtly and precisely that it expresses part of his character's psychological being. It is not really psychologically significant that Solnes is an architect: architecture simply afforded Ibsen a convenient allegoric pattern. But in *A Laodicean*, George Somerset's very personality is set forth in his pursuit of architecture. Which does not — it should hardly need saying — mean that it is a book about architects, any more than *Two on a Tower* is a book about astronomers. It just means that Hardy's use of architecture, astronomy, and music is elaborately involved in the presentation of his basic psychological schemes.

I have already indicated how he does this with St. Cleeve's astronomy, how the saintly, Raphaelesque young man fails the warm-blooded lady, who has to die ("of too much Joy", "joy after despair had touched an overstrained heart too smartly" [T.T., p. 332]) because of his tardiness and incorporeality. George Somerset's name prepares us for a less ethereal character. Yet, like Clym Yeobright's, "his face bore contradictory testimonies to his precise age". And this, Hardy observes, returning to one of his *idées fixes,* was because of a

> too dominant, speculative activity in him, which while it
> had preserved the emotional side of his constitution, and
> with it the significant flexuousness of mouth and chin,
> had played upon his forehead and temples till at weary
> moments, they exhibited some traces of being
> over-exercised. A youthfulness about the mobile features,
> a mature forehead — though not exactly what the world
> at large has been familiar with in the past ages — is now
> growing common; and with the growth of juvenile
> introspection it probably must grow commoner still.
> Briefly, he had more of the beauty . . . of the future
> human type than of the past; but not so much as to
> make him other than a nice young man. (L., p. 5)

The deflationary measure of the last clause operates
throughout the novel, in fact, and Somerset doesn't really
come to much. He stands as a rather brilliant study in failure.
(Hardy handles his vacillations with an extraordinary wry tact;
he manages to give the metaphor of "breaking in" a genuine
relevance to the given case.) Yet the reader will have noted in
the description not only the trademarks of Hardy's
psychological methods, but the ease and maturity he now
commands. Key-words like "flexuousness" (a favourite of
Hardy's) and "mobile [features]" work precisely and
concretely, and the entire approach is saturated with
type-consciousness: Hardy turns, for example, to the
"emotional side of him" with the assurance of a skilled
surgeon. Note how his eyes, finally, were, "of the dark deep
sort" with "*that* ray of light which announces a heart
susceptible to beauty of all kinds" (my italics).

Somerset stands with Knight (of *A Pair of Blue Eyes*) who
had a soft shapely mouth "under a chronic aspect of
impassivity" and a brow and face "sicklied o'er by the
unmistakable pale cast". The relative lightness of the
treatment of Somerset allows one perhaps to call him a link
between Knight and Clym Yeobright. At least, the constancy
of the preoccupation behind all three characters is evident: in

all three cases, different combinations of sensuality (or susceptibility) coexist with intellectuality. Knight's face wears experience like a mask; Somerset's only the marks of too much thought, like Clym Yeobright (who, however, entirely lacks the sensuality).

The rest of *A Laodicean* concerns not Somerset but the weird father-son duo of Dare and de Stancy, and their attempts to get hold of Paula Power and her millions. In passing, one detail reveals spectacularly how thorough and consistent Hardy's techniques of psychological interpretation had become. Before he has met Paula — Hardy gives her the usual build-up — Somerset passes through her room, and notices the decoration: " 'She affects blue', he was thinking, 'Then she is fair' " (L., p. 41). Hardy could scarcely have made himself plainer: Somerset's perception is pure typology, and testifies to a ready stock of such beliefs (derived partly from common wisdom, but more from Hardy's own evolving theories) as would allow an unknown person's coloration and general constitution to be deduced from the way she chose to decorate her bedroom. Somerset's prediction could not even make sense without the assumption of a system of ideas relating behaviour to psychological type.

This explicitness concerning working methods is even more striking in another remark of Somerset's. During a casual conversation turning on the likeness of Paula Power's quasi-lesbian companion Charlotte to Dare, Somerset observes, "People's features fall naturally into groups and classes . . . To an observant person they often repeat themselves; though to a careless eye they seem infinite in their differences" (L., p. 82). By now we have excellent reasons for accepting this as nothing more or less than Hardy's own view. And even the relative failure of characters like Somerset himself to advance on earlier models such as Springrove only serves to emphasize the point. There is no casual or lazy repetitiousness in the similarities that occur again and again in Hardy's novels. On the contrary, they only demonstrate the unfailing seriousness of his probing of the phenomena of human typology. It is

even true to say that after a relatively early stage there is no
real extension of his range of characters. As the reader will
already have observed, it becomes a question of the further
exploration of already known types. The narrowness of
Hardy's range, it can hardly be emphasized too often, seems a
puzzle and a limitation only when we fail to grasp the
principles of his psychology.

Dare and de Stancy emerge as a comedy team, though
etched with the usual concern for establishing particular
temperaments. Dare, an unreal rogue with Italian blood and
most un-English sexual swagger, is his illegitimate father's
straight man. For simple economic reasons, he manoeuvres de
Stancy into position and lets Paula Power's optical poem (the
pink-flannel routine in the gymnasium mentioned later) play
across his susceptibility, so that, salaciously foaming at the
mouth, he is ready to do everything Dare wants him to. The
episode is certainly the most ridiculous in Hardy. Like all the
de Stancy-Dare material, it amounts to nothing more than a
rather bad unintentional satire on the Victorian horror of
aggressive sexuality that vitiates so much of Hardy's minor
fiction: the sexual predator is either an outright criminal, like
Manston in *Desperate Remedies,* or a Pavlovian clown, like de
Stancy, his concupiscence on tap to the adroit manoeuvrer.

Hardy's only historical novel, *The Trumpet-Major,* set in
the Napoleonic period later so powerfully dramatized by
Hardy in *The Dynasts,* offers what can only be described as
negative support for the typological thesis: it seems to have
absolutely no trace or vestige of the types or of Hardy's usual
methods of characterization or presentation. One can only
surmise that he simply assumed the Scott mantle, and
completely disconnected his normal awareness of people to
indulge in the pleasures of historical charade. The portrait of
Anne Garland, the heroine, bears the odd typological touch —
"her mouth was clearly cut and yet not classical" — and the
shortness of her upper lip casually anticipates the detail so
skilfully exploited to conjure up Tess Durbeyfield. Yet she
amounts to nothing but a nice girl, fit to be the heroine of a

historical romance. Which is probably where one should leave the book. Anne's mother similarly is "festive and sanguine"; and the great big Shakespearean character, Festus Derryman, "red-haired and of florid complexion". Yet there is nothing whatever to suggest the usual typological methods. The two brothers who court Anne are distinguished on vaguely contrasting lines, Bob gay and spontaneous, John withdrawn and cautious. But nothing of significance accrues from this in either action or character development.

PART TWO

The Pentagonal Novels

Introduction

Under the Greenwood Tree was built upon three characters — Fancy Day and her two suitors, Dick Dewy and Maybold-Shiner. In the earliest novels and in the minor novels of the late seventies and early eighties, there was a tendency towards a more complicated structural skeleton. *A Laodicean,* for instance, never a wholly serious work, really explores the differences and affinities, attractions and revulsions, among five people — Paula Power, her companion Charlotte, George Somerset, and Dare and de Stancy. This is not simply a question of greater maturity producing greater complexity: on the contrary, *A Laodicean* (1881) is a very much less mature work than *Under the Greenwood Tree* (1872). It is a question rather of what sort of thing Hardy wants to say. *Under the Greenwood Tree* is structurally closer to Hardy's last (and greatest) novels, *The Mayor of Casterbridge* and *Tess of the d'Urbervilles.* In all four novels, attention is maintained upon one character. In the great novels that precede the tragic phase of Hardy's fictional career — *Far from the Madding Crowd, The Return of the Native,* and *The Woodlanders* — Hardy establishes a quite different structural basis, consisting of five contrasting characters. The remarkable family resemblance obtaining among these three novels justifies — necessitates, indeed — the violation of chronological sequence here: *The Woodlanders* was published the year after *The Mayor of Casterbridge.* An artist's inner development does not, obviously, always proceed by the calendar.

5. *Far from the Madding Crowd* (1874)

The main characters of *Far from the Madding Crowd* fight out, endure, or stumble blindly through a struggle of psyches and hesitantly grasped destinies, which can only be understood when the psychological quantities engaged are themselves understood. We saw in Fancy Day the first attempt at a type Hardy remained obsessed with until he stopped writing fiction; we have seen as well her real gravitation towards Dick Dewy, and her no less real awareness of a different order of masculinity in Shiner, and still another in the pure-minded, idealist parson, Maybold. This was a mere sketch of the battles that were to come. The first is the one that starts with Gabriel Oak and Bathsheba Everdene. As always, the names set forth the qualities; Gabriel Oak's, in fact, does so even misleadingly. Its suggestion of lovable solidity oversimplifies the character and sends us off on a false trail — especially as the book begins with the celebrated description of his smile. Hardy's openings are usually marvellously atmospheric. He begins here with a character-sketch, fails to establish rhythm, and rather confuses us, I think. We don't quite know how to take Oak: he seems too broadly simple a character to engage serious interest. Evidently, this is going to be a sufferer, an enduring "stalwart", and a foil, if nothing else, for Bathsheba Everdene. Here the name is more astutely chosen. We think of the Old Testament story, as we are meant to. When Oak first sees her she is looking admiringly into her mirror: "Vanity" is what he sees in her. On the first three occasions she appears in the book, she is glimpsed unawares, spied on almost, in a manner typical of Hardy. The peeping-Tom situation is generally used by Hardy to present a certain type of woman: the type who likes in fact to be looked at, but would prefer to know it, so as to be able to put her best face forward. Hardy and Oak enjoy looking at her without her knowing it: first through the hedge; then through a chink in a hut-wall, when she is sitting up helping her aunt tend a calf; and lastly, from inside Oak's own hut, when Bathsheba goes through a strange, rather exciting performance on horseback. Hardy relishes the situation: "Here he ensconced himself, and peeped through the loophole in the direction of the rider's approach" (F.M.C., p. 17), and she "looked around, for a moment as if to assure herself that all humanity was out of view" (F.M.C., p. 18). In that preposterous but interesting novel, *A Laodicean*, two men, Dare and de Stancy (father and illegitimate son) peep through a knot-hole in the wall of a gymnasium to watch "a sort of optical poem. Paula, in a pink flannel costume, was bending, wheeling and undulating in the air like a goldfish in its globe, sometimes ascending by her arms nearly to the lantern, then lowering herself till she swung level with the floor" (L., p. 19). When one considers that the son has brought his father there to inflame his desire for Paula (surnamed Power), and that this gymnastic performance is given before an audience of two women, a maiden aunt and a young companion who cherishes a quasi-Lesbian affection for Paula, the whole episode, in so far as it is not absurd, clearly expresses a curiosity about women that puts Hardy's well-known fastidiousness in another light. The dirty old man smacking his lips over his new catalogue of fashion models from London (Mountclere in *The Hand of Ethelberta*) can be set aside as crude satire on pornography and semi-perversion. But Hardy is a little too often to be found elaborately rigging up opportunities to spy on a certain kind of woman. (There is an interesting parallel in Keats here: the *Ode to Psyche*, *Endymion*, and *The Eve of St. Agnes* all contain over-intense voyeuristic episodes or scenes.)

The real point of interest is that the particular type of woman he chooses to spy on is usually engaged in a certain kind of athletic performance. Like Paula Power (gyrating like a goldfish), Bathsheba performs an ecstatic physical ritual:

dexterously dropped backwards flat upon the pony's back, her head over its tail, her feet against its shoulders, and her eyes to the sky. The rapidity of her glide into this position was that of a kingfisher — its noiselessness that of a hawk . . . The performer seemed quite at home anywhere between a horse's head and its tail, and the necessity for this abnormal attitude having ceased with the passage of the plantation, she began to adopt another, even more obviously inconvenient than the first . . . Springing to her accustomed perpendicular like a bowed sapling, and satisfying herself that nobody was in sight, she seated herself in the manner demanded by the saddle, though hardly expected of the woman, and trotted off in the direction of Twenell Mill. (F.M.C., p. 18)

Oak is only "amused, perhaps a little astonished" by the performance, and certainly the episode could hardly be expected to appeal to such a naive character. The performance, we feel, was for Hardy's benefit.

Yet, this is the anchor-relationship of the novel. What is it based upon? Just as he is largely unaffected by a kind of performance which thrilled de Stancy almost to the point of rapine, Oak often hardly seems apt material for Bathsheba's attractiveness. He is, on the face of it, altogether too bland and slow-moving. Yet this is only partly true, the over-simple impression created by Hardy's initial description of him. Subsequent details form a slightly different kind of character, or rather a character of whom we can predict different things. When Bathsheba, having turned down his proposal of marriage, leaves the neighbourhood, we are told that "Oak belonged to the even-tempered order of humanity, and felt the secret fusion of himself in Bathsheba to be burning with a finer flame now that she was gone — that was all" (p. 37). An earlier image describes his sigh as "a deep, honest sigh — none the less so in that, being like a pine-plantation, it was rather noticeable as a disturbance of the atmosphere". This accords with his name and asserts a straightforward identification of goodness with the "course of Nature". For Oak *is* the good man, of course, with "'one-and-a-half Christian characterisations too many to succeed with Bathsheba". This is the kind of conclusion John Holloway tries to persuade us to accept.[1] But the conclusion cannot be accepted. For Bathsheba likewise is defined in terms of Nature. She is like a "bowed sapling". So the case is a little more complicated. Everyone grew out of the earth, Hardy argues; a naive back-to-Nature solution is the last thing to fool *him*, of all men.

Bathsheba's pliancy, like Fancy Day's flexibility, indeed is presented as a quality superior to Oak's slow stolidity. "Oak's motions, though they had a quiet energy, were slow and their deliberateness accorded well with his occupation" (F.M.C., p. 11). More, "his special power, morally, physically and mentally, was static, owing little or nothing to momentum as a rule" (F.M.C., p. 11). We recognize at once here the terms of what is beginning to emerge as Hardy's own peculiar vocabulary. Like Fancy's "flexibility", Oak's "quiet energy" evinces Hardy's interest in the basis of character in movement, the possibility of exploring and understanding people and their behaviour through their psycho-physiological cast or rhythm. Bathsheba's strange ritual takes on a new significance, then, and places her in a particularly interesting relationship to Oak.

Only after Oak has watched her equestrian routine does Hardy treat us to a full-face portrait of Bathsheba. The handling of the portrait betrays from first to last Hardy's peculiar involvement with typology. Bathsheba turns out to be less tall than Oak had thought (feared?): "She could have been not above the height to be chosen by women as best" (F.M.C., p. 19). One by one, Hardy checks for her flaws. "All features of consequence were severe and regular." This observation entails a short disquisition on English women among whom "a classically-formed face is seldom found to be united with a figure of the same pattern, the highly-finished features being generally too large for the remainder of the frame". Moreover, among English women, "a graceful and proportionate figure of eight heads usually goes off into random facial curves" (F.M.C., p. 19). The odd finesse of observation testifies to an extraordinary interest in the subject. Hardy must have watched a lot of women a long time to be able to discourse so minutely and with such a degree of confident generality. No one, not the most moon-struck Silver sonneteer, ever devoted more curious attention to the subject of English women and their beauty than Thomas Hardy.

This opening phase of the novel really ends with Oak established in Bathsheba's farm as shepherd. In passing, the natural imagery should be mentioned. A rather exquisite bleakness prevails; not the awful grandeur of *The Return of the Native,* or *Tess,* but an almost Japanese delicacy, with recurrent imagery of the waning moon and dry leaves. Bathsheba flits away, like "the flitting of a dead leaf upon the breeze" (F.M.C., p. 21). The last leaves on the winter trees "in falling rattled against the trunks with smart taps". Then, "the thin grasses, more or less coating the hill, were touched by the wind in breezes of differing powers and almost of differing natures — one rubbing the blades heavily, another raking them piercingly, another brushing them like a soft broom" (F.M.C., p. 9). There are more profound intimations: the trees chanting to each other "in the regular antiphonies of a cathedral choir"; and the stars seeming "but throbs of one body, timed by a common pulse". (The words "sob" and "throb", occurring close together here, give the entire passage a particularly plangent intensity.) But predominantly, the natural participation is delicate, hushed, and remote. The best example perhaps is the nocturne when Oak loses his flock of sheep:

> By the outer margin of the pit was an oval pond, and over it hung the attenuated skeleton of a chrome-yellow moon, which had only a few days to last — the morning-star dogging her on the left hand. The pool glittered like a dead man's eye, and as the world awoke a breeze blew, shaking and elongating the reflection of the

moon without breaking it, and turning the image of the
star to a phosphoric streak upon the water. All this Oak
saw and remembered. (F.M.C., p. 41)

The description comes at the appropriate moment, at the
nadir of Oak's fortunes. Yet the final sentence — "All this
Oak saw and remembered" — lifts it above the level of mere
pathetic scoring: Hardy points out how the scenery enters
whole into Oak's mind precisely *because* he has just been
shattered.[2]

The actual sequence of events is somewhat heavy-handed.
Immediately on the heels of Oak's proposal comes the disaster
of the sheep; to be followed in turn by the fire at Bathsheba's
farm, and Oak's being taken on by her as shepherd. The
psychological tension between them is exhausted for the
moment. And Hardy now introduces his next important
character, Fanny Robin.

Characterization begins at once, and in a way which
prepares us for a more interesting foil for Bathsheba.
Bathsheba has been delineated throughout in terms of a rather
exciting autocracy of spirit: she is one of Hardy's goddesses,
flirtatious, like Fancy Day, but, unlike Fancy, dangerously
beautiful, and capricious. There seems no reason whatever at
this stage of the novel to like her, although one is meant to
admire her, and does. She rather mocks Oak, though she
openly admits she doesn't love him, and enjoys his reversal.
By contrast, Fanny is introduced as a "timid girl", "a slim girl
rather thinly-clad". More strikingly her voice is "unexpectedly
attractive, it was the low and dulcet note suggestive of
romance". When Oak by chance touches her wrist, he finds
that the pulse is beating "with a throb of tragic
intensity . . . It suggested a consumption too great of a vitality
which, to judge from her figure and stature, was already too
little" (F.M.C., p. 58).

In the context created by Hardy's habitual mode of
psychological analysis, the idea of "intensity" in this passage
acquires considerable import: the notion of the slim vessel
having to bear an excess of emotional intensity has to be

construed after Hardy's own fashion, that is, in terms of a psycho-physiological conception of the character. "Vitality", too, in the context designates a certain quality much more precisely than it would seem such an over-used abstraction could. These observations are important. For we gradually become aware of how rapidly Hardy is developing his emotional, psychological language, a language consistent within the dynamic context of the words, though showing forth truths obtaining outside it. Our understanding of Hardy's novels is likely to depend very largely on our understanding the structure and anatomy of his psychology. In the given instance, for example, not only do words like "intensity" and "vitality" possess an unforeseeable precision and weight; we know that they denote qualities which specifically could *not* occur in connection with certain other characters — Gabriel Oak, for instance. And this is something different from mere consistency of characterization. The artist uses his vocabulary — or rather the system of laws that governs his vocabulary — as an instrument, a mode of discovery. What obtains within the single novel, obtains also, with interest, within the whole canon. It would be an empty critical aphorism — an unimpeachable but not the less vacuous article of faith — to assert that one must read all Hardy's work to understand any single part of it fully. In fact, some of his works merely instantiate the laws, without adding to them or qualifying them. What is true, however, is that one must read a certain (fairly large) number of the major works to fully comprehend any one of them.

A criticism of Hardy's fiction frequently heard is that the actual motivation of the characters' actions sometimes seems arbitrary, too little related to their psychological need, even when this is powerful enough to justify a tragic tone. *Under the Greenwood Tree* avoids this pitfall by sheer simplicity. *Far from the Madding Crowd,* an obviously greater book, does not. Until the arrival on the scene of Boldwood, the actions of the personages are either arbitrary or the results of bad luck. Oak's only positive venture fails when Bathsheba turns down his proposal of marriage. From that point, his career is merely passive: Fate takes over, in the familiar formulation. (One that can hardly be gainsaid here: it is *just* bad luck that Oak loses all his sheep. He would not have got Bathsheba at that stage if he had not lost his sheep, certainly; but he becomes a figure of suffering only when he does.) Bathsheba determines the course of the novel from this point by an act of pure whimsy: she throws a book up into the air to decide whether she should send a Valentine to a small boy, Teddy, or to Farmer Boldwood. Hardy's meaning is plain enough. The Valentine if sent to Teddy not only would have no consequences; it would *be* a different thing from what it becomes when it is sent to Boldwood. And the episode cannot be otherwise explained. To say that Boldwood had it in his power *not* to react as he did (the kind of interpretation Roy Morrell favours)[3] is not only to rewrite the novel: it is to misread it as it stands. It is inescapably part of Boldwood to react as he does. I think, moreover, that much as he risks the integrity of his narrative by making so much depend on so little, Hardy succeeds thereby in cornering something no other novelist quite could have. This something is primarily invested in Boldwood's character, and again springs from the tight psychological scheme obtaining throughout. It is neither factitious nor bathetic that so much suffering springs from so slight an occasion as Bathsheba's teasing Valentine. In putting Boldwood in this situation he subjects him to just the kind of pressure (tiny, but excessive) he is unable to withstand. That the capricious act sorts well with Bathsheba's character we know; Hardy has now what is perhaps the more difficult task of making Boldwood an appropriately explosive recipient. He must, in other words, do what he has failed to do with Oak — draw him into genuine polaric interaction with Bathsheba. On this kind of success depends the integrity and validity of the entire novel. And this is not a question of mere credibility, or convincingness. The inner structure of the novel is at stake. Thus, again, the psychological tension is crucially important.

On all scores here Hardy succeeds magnificently: the

"relationship" between Bathsheba and Boldwood marks an epoch in Hardy's maturation as an artist. Boldwood's gradual insinuation into the texture of the novel equals the best that Dickens could achieve by way of artful preparation. But these successes can by now be taken for granted, together with the excellence of the nature-writing. We are now concerned with a major artist somewhere near the peak of his powers, and can go direct to the portrait Hardy now has us as eager to hear as Bathsheba is to see its subject: "A gentlemanly man, with full and distinctly outlined Roman features, the prominence of which glowed in the sun with a bronze-like richness of tone. He was erect in attitude, and quiet in demeanour. One characteristic pre-eminently marked him — dignity" (F.M.C., p. 104). In the context, that final word falls like the black spot in *Treasure Island*. With it, Hardy has pronounced a kind of death sentence on Boldwood. And again, it works solely in terms of the presiding psychological scheme. Bathsheba has picked on just the wrong man — just the one man in Wessex, perhaps, on whom her joking "Marry me!" could act, like a finger's pressure moving an ocean liner, and change — unalterably — the course of his life. Oak might have been hurt: Boldwood is undermined. "A large red seal was duly affixed", Hardy writes of Bathsheba's joke, "Bathsheba looked closely at the hot wax to discover the words. 'Capital!' she exclaimed, throwing down the letter frolicsomely, 't'would upset the solemnity of a parson and clerk too!' Liddy looked at the words of the seal, and read — 'Marry me' " (F.M.C., p. 111).

The seal functions beautifully: what begins as a playful red blob in a childish prank becomes to Boldwood "as a blot of blood on the retina of his eye" (F.M.C., p. 112). Hardy anticipates the narrative means of cinema here. Imagine Bathsheba stamping the wax; a close-up of the words "MARRY ME" as seen (playfully) by Liddy, then, without break, solemnly by Boldwood. Only what the cinema could not convey is the key metaphor — the seal as "a red blot of blood on the retina of his eye".[4]

Hardy almost invariably pauses at his axial points, and discourses philosophically on the meaning and origin of the event in question. It is against the rules, of course; just as it is against the rules to talk to the reader over his characters' heads: "The letter must have had an origin and a motive. That the latter was of the smallest magnitude compatible with its existence at all, Boldwood, of course, did not know" (F.M.C., p. 113). That is an impropriety Dickens would never have committed; though Thackeray or George Eliot might have, and have given offence thereby. Hardy does not give offence. His diction hereabouts is at first sight awkwardly abstract, yet it succeeds. For Hardy is handling here the most delicate, yet weighty subject matter. In general, in fact, we must be wary of rushing to judgment on Hardy's "style". The mixture he habitually employs of abstract Latinism and Anglo-Saxon concreteness, of idea and image, often succeeds in articulating the fragilely significant. We have here, I think, one of Hardy's greatest gifts, the coexistence within the same mind of the most fragile intuition with the most profound and "weighty" thought. His capacity for abstract thinking is as impressive as George Eliot's. Unlike George Eliot, though, he exploits naturally, with a poet's sensibility, the full resources of metaphor and figure to present meaning. "The disturbance was as the first floating weed to Columbus — the contemptibly little suggesting possibilities of the infinitely great" (F.M.C., p. 113).

Perhaps the point that Hardy is most at pains to underline in this disquisition is that "reality" depends more or less totally on the conditioning mind of the subject, that truth is, as Kierkegaard has it, subjectivity. Thus, Bathsheba's words "Marry me" change under our own eyes, as the red seal becomes a blot of blood on Boldwood's retina: "The pert injunction" (a beautiful example of the stylistic feature noted above, both abstract and simple) "was like those crystal substances which, colourless themselves, assume the tone of objects about them. Here, in the quiet of Boldwood's parlour where everything that was not grave was extraneous, and where the atmosphere was that of a Puritan Sunday lasting all the week, the letter and its dictum changed their tenor from the thoughtlessness of their origin to a deep solemnity, imbibed from their accessories now" (F.M.C., p. 112).

Dickens's treatment of homicidal neurosis, particularly the case of Bradley Headstone in *Our Mutual Friend,* has influenced Hardy's writing here: "Boldwood looked, as he had a hundred times the preceding day, at the insistent red seal: 'Marry me!' he said aloud" (F.M.C., p. 114). Less brilliant, less insistent than Dickens, Hardy's sober handling works no less effectively to make plausible the transition from equanimity to possession. And, of course, we do not need to be told that, once possessed, Boldwood is possessed for good. Like Dickens also, Hardy orchestrates the scene richly. The moon is there — for Oak — a "wasting moon, now dull and greenish-yellow, like tarnished brass" (F.M.C., p. 115). Boldwood now also notes the scene "listlessly". Almost as by an unconscious association, Oak comes back into Hardy's mind and into the pages of the novel by means of a letter now brought to Boldwood and mistakenly opened. One can follow here, I think, the actual processes of the artist's mind: possibly, he had no intention of reintroducing Oak, until the similarity of the scene with the much earlier one after Oak's disaster by degrees suggested the move to him. As it happens, the introduction leads nowhere in particular and somewhat laboriously informs us that Fanny Robin is to marry Sergeant Troy. At this stage, indeed, Oak's role is entirely passive. He must merely endure until the end of the book, when Bathsheba will marry him. The phenomenon is common in Hardy and is consistent with his general psychological scheme. Some people act, he intimates, others merely endure. In *Far from the Madding Crowd,* Oak doesn't act at all; Bathsheba — until now — has acted capriciously, with an almost deliberate absence of intention; Boldwood has been set in motion, against his will, but unstoppably; Fanny Robin has flitted in and out of the book, frail and passive, at the mercy of a man whose voice has been heard, but who has not yet been seen:

Sergeant Troy, the last major character of the novel, a soldier and a rake.

Curiously, Troy's first part in the story is purely passive. By one of Hardy's wildest improbabilities, he is left standing at the altar by Fanny Robin, who — of all people — gets the church wrong. The unlikely scene is brilliantly carried off in fact — Troy's military vigour making the immobility of his wait at the altar-rail almost resonant. In Hardy, the military man is usually a sexual predator, as he so often was in the Victorian novel. An officer is a seducer, an other rank (a "man") a near-rapist. Troy's spurs and uniform are sexual insignia, like a cock's comb and plumage. His masculinity, again, differs from Oak's passive, rooted solidity, and Boldwood's "dignity". Now Bathsheba's character is in the process of being more sharply defined by her reaction to Boldwood's proposal. So that Troy's appearance at this juncture is well conceived. Where Oak really failed to engage Bathsheba's interest, Boldwood forces her to change: his very existence, after he has been made aware of *her* existence, compels her into action. Hardy writes, "But a disquiet filled her which was somewhat to her credit, for it would have affected few" (F.M.C., p. 150).

Hardy himself seems now to have found something more in Bathsheba than he had thought was there. He is moved to reconsider her: "Bathsheba's was an impulsive nature under a deliberate aspect" (F.M.C., p. 150). The phrasing and diction here are interesting: it is the language and tone of the horoscopist, the astrologer, and it springs from the well of Hardy's fundamental fatalism. Words like "impulsive" and "deliberate", too, assume the tone-colour of the total psychological scheme. They reflect the gradual hardening and clarifying of the basic concepts. In this respect, as in many others, *Far from the Madding Crowd* is decisively important in Hardy's *oeuvre*. It is the culmination of the first phase: at the end of this chapter it will be possible to describe the continuity and evolving firmness of the methods of characterization, and see how the fragmentary insights of the first three novels have strengthened into consistent and original concepts.

Far from the Madding Crowd is Hardy's first major novel. In one way, it seems to be the prototype of all of his later novels. Essentially it is a dialectic of two psychical principles, and these two principles are Hardy's poles, his version, if you like, of the basic Hippocratic dichotomy. This statement can only be appraised when Sergeant Troy has been considered: everything indeed that has been said about Bathsheba, Boldwood, and Fanny Robin remains incomplete without Troy. The passivity and lightness of Fanny Robin, for example, scarcely at first seem to qualify her for serious consideration. What was initiated in her "dulcet" voice, the vague romanticism attaching to her, is never perhaps fully realized. She certainly seems inadequate to Troy; yet their association is significant. For in spite of her lightness, Fanny Robin throbs with a nervous intensity that strongly appeals to the strange temperament of Sergeant Troy.

The description of Troy is one of the longest character-studies in Hardy. (Almost the whole of chapter 25 — running to almost fifteen hundred words — is devoted to it.) The difficulty for the critic is to abstract any "drift" or content from something so sustainedly absorbing and informative. As with most of Hardy's portraits, it is impossible, ultimately, to use any other words to communicate its content. Without going all the way with the Organic Form incantations, it really is difficult to leave out much of what Hardy says about the Sergeant without a feeling of having impaired the whole. That this should be so underlines again the nature of Hardy's writing: these portraits of his are at the farthest possible remove from the quick sketches of Dickens and the detailed studies of the Naturalists. They reflect the deep brooding introspectiveness of his mind, the tendency to meditate long, in the subject's absence, on the subject's essence.

Almost the first words Troy had uttered to Bathsheba at their accidental meeting by night were, "I am a man." The proud boast reminds us of the classical association of his name. He is a Trojan, a Cretan, and a Corinthian, by turns, and is not quite wholly ironically referred to as a Philosopher — a Stoic, we may be sure. The attention Hardy concentrates on him suggests what I think is true, that in some sense he is the pivotal character in the novel: the other characters, in retrospect, are seen to revolve about him. For the essence of his character is "impulse", and impulse has already become a key-concept in Hardy's psychology. Bathsheba has been described as "an impulsive nature under a deliberate aspect". Boldwood, on the other hand, is the man in whom impulse does not exist: a thing has to become a familar part of his own introverted universe to be acceptable, whence of course the disastrous affect of Bathsheba's Valentine.

Fanny Robin's "throb of tragic intensity" adds to the complex psychological pattern. I will not pretend to be able to assign the various elements precisely defined and labelled roles in this pattern: that is impossible, not merely because of my own inability, but because Hardy's intricate precision makes any attempt to "label" the qualities invalid. What we can with safety assert is that analysis of the psychological constituents of the novel reveals an intricate interrelatedness: Bathsheba, Troy, and Boldwood are conceived as shades in a spectrum of vitality, ranging from the impassivity of Oak to the "tragic intensity" of Fanny Robin. A diagram may help:

Oak   Fanny Robin
    — Boldwood — Troy — Bathsheba —

At one end stands the rooted tree — Oak; at the other, the frail bird — Fanny Robin. Reading from Oak to Fanny, we pass first through the "dignity" of Boldwood: "that dignified stronghold", with his "square-framed perpendicularity", his flat-footed walk ("his foot met the floor with heel and toe simultaneously"), his "still mouth and well-rounded but rather prominent and broad chin". Oak has been shown to be almost completely well-adjusted, as the psychiatrists would say: he meets every set-back with equanimity and trudges on. This of course is his role in the book: he is its sheet-anchor. But we remember also his inability to respond to Bathsheba's strange performance on the horse; and reflect that Boldwood might not have been so unaffected. There is in fact a radical difference between Oak's impassivity and Boldwood's stillness, which seemed, Hardy observes, "so precisely like the rest of inanition", but "may have been the perfect balance of enormous antagonistic forces — positives and negatives in fine adjustment. His equilibrium disturbed," Hardy goes on, "he was in extremity at once. If an emotion possessed him at all, it ruled him; a feeling not mastering him was entirely latent" (F.M.C., p. 137). There is, I feel, something of Wordsworth in Boldwood. Like Wordsworth, Boldwood had no "light and careless touches in his constitution, either for good or for evil. Stern in the outlines of action, mild in the details, he was serious throughout all. He saw no absurd sides to the follies of life" (p. 137). This disquisition on the farmer's character sounds ominous notes for Bathsheba: "Bathsheba was far from dreaming that the dark and silent shape upon which she had so carelessly thrown a seed was a hotbed of tropic intensity" (F.M.C., p. 138).

Thus far along the spectrum, we have had varieties of stolidity: Oak's placidity and Boldwood's "dignity" may be seen in the psychologist's terms as stable and unstable versions of similar types. What about Troy? Physically, Troy continues the movement towards flexibility. Boldwood's unstable equilibrium indicates greater mobility than there is in the immovable Oak. Troy, on the other hand, "was full of activity". Hardy's immediate qualification is interesting to the point of enigmaticism: "but his activities were less of a locomotive than a vegetative nature". I am still not quite sure what this means, though it seems extraordinarily interesting. It appears to refer to that absence of perspective in Troy's mind that goes far toward placing his particular impulsiveness. For Troy emerges finally as a superb satire on "living in the present". Because he has never made any basic decisions about the conduct of life, Troy lacks character. In fact, he and Boldwood beautifully exemplify the Freudian distinction between personality and character, personality being somehow lively and creative, character square and ugly. Troy has absolutely no character at all. For character is built upon the expectation that we should be prepared to answer for our actions, and to do as we are done unto. Now the whole point about Troy is that his world has neither past nor future. "That projection of consciousness into days gone by and to come, which makes the past a synonym for the pathetic and the future a word for circumspection, was foreign to Troy. With him the past was yesterday; the future, tomorrow; never, the day after" (F.M.C., p. 192). Hardy's discussion of this quality of Troy's needs quoting in full: the modern mind, especially as it has been conditioned by D. H. Lawrence and by certain aspects of existentialism, is likely to envy Troy his philosophy and even to admire him for it. Hardy anticipates the possibility: "On this account he might, in certain lights, have been regarded with great plausibility as one of the most fortunate of his order. For it may be argued with great plausibility that reminiscence is less an endowment than a disease." In return for his blitheness, though, Hardy points out that Troy necessarily suffers a "certain narrowing of the higher tastes and sensations", and though Troy cannot regret this, the limitation is there. It makes him that much less sympathetic: there is after all a degree of sheer stupidity in Troy that is at variance with his degree of education. Hardy's analysis of this stupidity is philosophically exact and original: speaking of Troy's "activities", Hardy observes that, "never having been based upon any original choice of foundation or direction, they were exercised on whatever object chance might place in their way" (F.M.C., p. 194). Thus, in spite of "quick comprehension and a considerable force of character" his mind became "engaged with trivialities whilst waiting for the will to direct it, and the force wasted itself in useless grooves through unheeding the comprehension" (F.M.C., p. 194). Hardy grants Troy "considerable force of character". At first sight this seems to contradict my own assertion that Troy had no character at all. In fact, the two statements are perfectly compatible. For the whole of Hardy's analysis turns upon the fact that being unanchored in long-term decisions committing him to what would be in fact a morality, Troy sinks to the level of the banal. Hence, the only use he can find for his intelligence is seduction. His success as a philanderer directly reflects the "principles" by which he lives: he flatters — with great skill and plausibility and no thought for the consequences. He is enormously successful. Like many philanderers, Hardy remarks, Troy "jauntily" continued indulging his skill "with terrible effect". In a way, the whole novel turns upon the revenge the world takes on him. At a later stage in the story Hardy describes him as "sanguine by nature", with a "power of eluding grief by simply adjourning it" — a superbly logical derivate from the postulates set down in the study in chapter 25. At last Troy's intelligence, which is in fact his fundamental *stupidity* about people, gets its deserts: unexpectedly life calls in its debt, and Troy finds himself shattered, entirely against his own code, by the death of Fanny Robin.

Troy's careless treatment of Fanny — that it is carelessness and not blackhearted villainy says much for Hardy's freedom from Victorian prejudice — is beautifully balanced both in motivation and consequence by Bathsheba's whimsical treatment of Boldwood. The equilibrium obtaining throughout the book indeed is remarkable. For Bathsheba's irresponsible tangling with Boldwood's latent emotionalism brings about a sordid violence inversely proportionate to the muted pathos of Fanny Robin's death in labour. Where Troy passes on without a thought (initially at least) from what has been for him nothing but the exercise of his art, Bathsheba immediately regrets her lightheadedness. Boldwood is able to work upon her — extracting by duress promises which a man like Troy would have scorned — precisely in virtue of her fundamental superiority both to Troy and to Boldwood himself. Bathsheba's maturation begins with the badgering Boldwood subjects her to, or rather with her prior perception of the terrible change she has wrought in him. (The loyalty of

Oak, by contrast, had left her cold.) Thus, endowed with some of Boldwood's *probity* — "all features of consequence were severe and regular" — and a heavy-limbed build, Bathsheba's "bowed sapling" pliancy marks the next stage along the morphological spectrum, of which the centre is the sanguine but impulsive Troy, the left wing the quietly energetic Oak, and the right the nervously intense Fanny Robin. If Boldwood is strength crushed by the infinitely small (the joke Valentine), Fanny is weakness smashed by the incomparably great (death in labour). She is like a filament overloaded with current, and lacks Bathsheba's flexibility and resilience. We are left at the end with Oak and Bathsheba. I do not think Hardy wants us to draw morals from this, offering a lesson for us all in Gabriel's manly stoicism and Bathsheba's contrition: in fact, I am fearful of having already trespassed too far along this path of cliff-top moralizing in my efforts to compress what I see to be the structure governing the incidents and episodes of this deceptively leisurely story.

The fact is that in art the value is born out of the conflict of constituent elements, not out of any preconceived moral pattern into which the artist pours dosages of ethical chemicals. For the moment, it will be enough to point out the elements themselves. At the end perhaps, some general conclusions may be drawn. So far, we have watched the emergence of a distinctive and characteristic dichotomy in Hardy's characterization: a type of human being based upon flexibility, movement, rhythm, balance,[5] is confronted, opposed, or attracted by one based upon solidity, rootedness, rigidity. The diction is beginning to settle into certain patterns: words like flexible, intense, and mobile being contrasted with words like dignified and stately.

6. *The Return of the Native* (1878)

Straightaway, I think, it must be emphasized that Hardy was attempting something unprecedented in these pentagonal novels. I can think of no other example of a novelist's trying to bind five characters together not commercially, as Dickens does in *Copperfield,* nor politically, as Dostoyevsky does in *The Devils,* but simply out of their own psychological qualities. The emergent pattern (which might be called the eternal pentagon) is first essayed in *Far from the Madding Crowd.*

In that novel, Gabriel Oak had the function of sheet-anchor, and only participated passively in the action. Fanny Robin remained only partially realized. The main action was fought out by three characters who represented Hardy's first serious efforts to explore the archetypes of human personality, as he saw them. Thus, the importance of *Far from the Madding Crowd* can hardly be exaggerated. Before it, only the odd character had been fully defined in what now becomes Hardy's habitual psychological language. In *Far from the Madding Crowd* the psychology is wholly consistent, and the characters are defined in terms of each other. Fanny Robin's "intensity", Boldwood's "dignity", Bathsheba Everdene's "heavy-limbedness" — these are terms in a carefully thought out psycho-physiological vocabulary. From now on, it is true to say, all Hardy's major characters will be described and presented in such terms. And they will be drawn irresistibly into relationship with each other on the strength of the qualities so defined.

In *The Return of the Native* there is a new advance in depth and clarity, an advance that is often obscured by the extraordinary power of the writing in which the Heath itself is presented: Egdon Heath *is* a character. Yet it generally escapes notice that the air of fatality imparted by the Heath — which there is no sense whatever in seeking to deny — is present also in the characterization and in the tensions that grow among the personages of the drama. It is generally assumed in some way that the Heath "symbolizes" Nature or Fate, or that the Heath shows "man's helplessness in the face of Nature and Time", etc. In fact, there is no sense of the over-used word symbol that can possibly be applied to Egdon Heath in *The Return of the Native*. It isn't a symbol; it isn't — in any acceptable sense of the word — a setting, either. Clearly, Hardy isn't scene-painting in those tremendous opening pages. It is probably the almost oppressive meaningfulness of the Heath that drives critics to "interpret" it. Yet it really needs no interpreting. It does not, in the first place, stand for or symbolize anything but itself. Like the Hintock woods in *The Woodlanders,* Egdon supports the whole narrative, neither as symbol nor background, but simply as a presence. A presence moreover which means different things to different people: it is alternately prison, redemption, and destroyer.

From the very title of the opening chapter, a strange and very characteristic idea takes hold: Egdon is called "A face on which Time makes but little impression". Behind the phrase are two notions Hardy explores in the following pages and, incidentally, in his later poetry. The first is that consciousness is a disease, the second that the Greek conception of physical beauty as a spiritual ideal belongs to the past. Speaking of the impressiveness of Egdon itself, Hardy observes:

> Indeed, it is a question if the exclusive reign of this orthodox beauty is not approaching its last quarter. The new Vale of Tempe may be a gaunt waste in Thule: human souls may find themselves in closer and closer harmony with external things wearing a sombreness distasteful to our race when it was young. The time seems near, if it has not actually arrived, when the chastened sublimity of a moor, a sea, or a mountain will be all of nature that is absolutely in keeping with the

moods of the more thinking among mankind. (R.N., p. 5)
So powerful is the presence of the Heath in these opening
pages that Hardy himself begins to explore its nature in terms
which suggest the habitual mode of his psychology: "Only in
summer days of highest feather did its mood touch the level
of gaiety. Intensity was more usually reached by way of the
solemn than by way of the brilliant, and such a sort of
intensity was often arrived at during winter darkness,
tempests, and mists. Then Egdon was aroused to reciprocity;
for the storm was its lover, and the wind its friend" (R.N.,
pp. 5–6). This recalls *Wuthering Heights,* of course, and its
especial animistic romanticism; but there is a particularity in
the psychological vocabulary that makes it Hardy's own. The
tension between "intensity", "the solemn", and "the
brilliant" reminds us strongly of Hardy's techniques of
characterization. In describing Egdon, Hardy might almost be
describing Clym Yeobright, the native whose return the book
concerns. In passing, one may observe that some of the
differences between the basic psychological data of Hardy and
the Brontës may perhaps be referred to their different
historico-geographical backgrounds. I have mentioned the
historical schism – almost a race-trauma – that lies behind
the Brontës' light-dark, angel-demon dichotomies. The clash
between the English and the Picts that created the North –
the emergence of Northumbria out of Strathclyde Scotland –
is in a sense, re-enacted in the conflict between Linton and
Heathcliff. In Wessex, the British held out much longer
against the West Saxons, and were never, indeed, wholly
eradicated. Thus, Hardy's warp and woof is as much British,
perhaps, as English: he has fewer fair-haired angels, although
his exploration of the intellectual-spiritual type surpasses that
of the Brontës in range and subtlety. The whole situation begs
to be represented also in terms of the supersession of the old
British gods by Christianity; or, alternatively, of the Roman
invasion, for the Roman element provides a further strand in
the weave that cannot be found in the Brontës' Yorkshire.
The Mayor of Casterbridge is the book of the Roman, just as,

in a sense, *The Return of the Native* is the book of the old British way. Yet the Roman traits can be found everywhere, subtly mingled with the British and the English in Hardy's novels. We have already noted Boldwood's "dignity" and his "Roman features". Somehow, in the people of Wessex there is a Roman probity insisting down through the shadowy British wildness, just as the Roman roads cut through the countryside like rulers, and set square towns like Casterbridge symmetrically upon the least symmetrical terrain in Europe. Hardy's vocabulary at all times expresses the paradox, and nowhere more so than in *The Native,* with its more than ever precarious balance of abstract Latin and tough Anglo-Saxon. He speaks of "an old vicinal way"; the Heath's "coat" is a "satire on human vanity"; "swarthy monotony"; a "barrow" — "intelligent"; "circumference" — "ballast", the antitheses multiply endlessly. Sometimes, indeed, Hardy runs close to bad taste; his diction jingles and jangles with flashy loan-words or with bits of Latinate jargon: he speaks of "the facade of a prison"; "the heath wore the appearance of an *instalment* of night" (my italics). Yet this *is* Hardy — a strange mélange of naivety and sophistication, ancient soul and modern consciousness, awkwardness and refinement.

It is probably the portrait of Thomasin Yeobright that combines most studiedly these disparate elements of Hardy's style. Thomasin's superiority over Fanny Robin reflects a general advance in organization. Similarly, Diggory Venn, who takes over the role of Gabriel Oak (though his psychological model is Dick Dewy) is much more suavely handled. But it is important at this stage to be wary of identifying the types from book to book, giving the impression that Hardy merely rings the changes on unvarying elements. No major Hardy novel repeats any of its predecessors. If characters do repeat themselves, it is invariably in a different situation, with different import. Compare Fanny Robin — "a slim girl, rather thinly clad" with a "romantic tone" to her voice — with Thomasin Yeobright, and it is apparent that where Fanny acts largely as a foil to Bathsheba's impetuosity, even as a source of pathos, Thomasin is fully grasped, and meaningfully involved in the action. Sergeant Troy's relationship with Fanny was almost peripheral — it only really existed when Troy kissed her in her coffin, and the purpose of that scene was really to galvanize Bathsheba. Hardy expends a great deal more care on Thomasin. The first glimpse of her in Venn's caravan — a beautiful example of what I have spoken of as Hardy's "cinematicism" — does a great deal to establish her role and nature:

> A fair, sweet, and honest country face was revealed, reposing in a nest of wavy chestnut hair. It was between pretty and beautiful. Though her eyes were closed, one could easily imagine the light necessarily shining in them as the culmination of the luminous workmanship around. The groundwork of the face was hopefulness; but over it now lay like a foreign substance a film of anxiety and grief. The grief had been there so shortly as to have abstracted nothing of the bloom which had as yet but given a dignity to what it might eventually undermine . . . She seemed to belong rightly to a madrigal — to require viewing through rhyme and harmony. (R.N., pp. 43–44)

It is remarkable, it seems to me, first that the word "dignity" as used of Thomasin has none of the precise force it had when used of Boldwood in *Far from the Madding Crowd,* a point which strengthens (negatively) the whole argument being offered about the type-basis of Hardy's vision. Applied to Boldwood, "dignity" designated a psycho-physiological property; here it rather tamely asks us to admire Thomasin a little bit more. Almost, but not quite. The idea behind that sentence in the Thomasin description is close to the heart of the whole book. It refers back to the description of the Heath appealing to the higher modern mind because of the increasing depth and melancholy humanity is acquiring. The same notion arises with Diggory Venn and Clym Yeobright, and might almost be described as the key-notion behind the novel. (I shall return to this idea later.)

The portrait is also rich in the combinations of concrete and abstract words mentioned above as being so central to Hardy's style. Sometimes the abstract word is used with a concrete meaning — as in the case of "an instalment of night". Here, a strong, everyday Anglo-Saxonism is invested with the maximum of abstract reference: "Though her eyes were closed, one could easily imagine the light necessarily shining in them as the culmination of the *luminous workmanship* around. The *groundwork* of the face was hopefulness" (my italics). "Luminous workmanship", of course, is the masterstroke: only a very original mind could have known that the teutonic ring of "workmanship" (with its clanging echoes of Norse myth and saga) could be combined with the unearthly glow of a word like "luminous". "Groundwork", used in describing a girl's face, is not far behind in verbal daring. When Thomasin's eyes open, "an ingenuous, transparent life was disclosed; as if the flow of her existence could be seen passing within her" (R.N., p. 44). Hardy never, I think, surpassed these sentences in their reverence for the human soul and the almost religious delight in women. These qualities are rare enough in art as in life. "Respect for life" has become a cliché nowadays among psychiatrists and lay-preachers. Hardy here demonstrates what the phrase can really mean.

This is, of course, Thomasin Yeobright, and only Thomasin Yeobright. Yet even here, where Hardy manages so delicately to transmit the pulse of a unique human spirit, we see him at work analyzing the bases of character. "The groundwork of the face was hopefulness": in the context the phrase tells us a great deal more about what Thomasin Yeobright's destiny will be than the mere postulation of "hopefulness" would in a Dickens character. In Hardy, the identity of the character is inextricably involved with the psycho-physiological basis of the personality. From this, I have said, we can deduce, perhaps, the pessimism, the predestinarianism, the whole tragic cast of the mature novels. In both types of art, to say it again, the functions overlap: in Dickens of course we see the relevance, the universality of the characterization; in Hardy and the Brontës, we see not stereotypes, but real, breathing, unique human beings. And yet, the two modes are utterly different; and the difference is not concerned with techniques but with purpose, meaning, and content.

The pathos of Thomasin Yeobright is of a kind different from that of Fanny Robin. We are asked to feel sorry for Fanny: with Thomasin we see a human being utterly exposed, her very purity and openness the source of the pathos. It is Hardy's refined sense of the essence of his creations that makes this possible. Hardy's characters are always shown at their psychic centre: their typicality is their psycho-physiological centre of gravity. Hence, the inevitable collision of people, the fore-plotted pathos of attraction. Hence, also, the despair which is not gloom, the detachment which is not indifference.

In the treatment of all main characters, the procedure is the same. The diction insists on type-conception. Mrs. Yeobright was "a woman of middle-age, with well-formed features of the type usually found where perspicacity is the chief quality enthroned within" (R.N., p. 37). Still more generally, Hardy observes that "persons with any weight of character carry, like planets, their atmospheres along with them in their orbits" (R.N., p. 37). Yet the case doesn't rest upon such isolated verbal evidence, but upon the gravitational swing among the major characters involved in the action.

We have already noted the "dignity" conferred upon Thomasin by grief, and the relation of this to the earlier observations about Egdon. We can trace the notion throughout the book. Diggory Venn, the Reddleman, is "young, and his face, if not exactly handsome, approached so near to handsome that nobody would have contradicted an assertion that it really was so in its natural colour" (R.N., p. 10). This echoes the earlier equivocations about the Heath, "a place perfectly accordant with man's nature — neither ghastly, hateful, nor ugly: neither commonplace, unmeaning, nor tame; but, like man, slighted and enduring; and withal singularly colossal and mysterious in its swarthy monotony" (R.N., p. 6). And later, Thomasin is described as "between pretty and beautiful". A curious affinity exists between the Heath, Venn, and Thomasin. Venn appreciates this, vanishing into it, and emerging from it, like an animal part of it. Thomasin, however, cannot "see" Venn at all. Again, we may compare Bathsheba's ignoring of Gabriel Oak, neither very strange nor very surprising. Oak simply would not attract her. Thomasin, similarly, is attracted not by the moralizing goodness of Venn, but by the destructive grace of Damon Wildeve.

Venn and Thomasin, subtended by the Heath, are therefore significantly "in a situation" with each other. They are related as much by Thomasin's blindness to Venn, as by Venn's love for her. The technical advance over *Far from the Madding Crowd* reflects the increase in psychological clarity. Both Venn and Thomasin are fully realized, both individually and in relationship. Venn's main feature is his eye, "which glared so strangely through his stain", and is "in itself attractive – keen as that of a bird of prey, and blue as autumn mist" (R.N., p. 10). The eye interestingly differs from the characteristic blue eyes of the Brontë angels, which suggest the sky. Venn is one of the angels of the piece, in fact – though his trade to the contrary suggests the devil – as in the scene round the bonfire at the beginning, when he emerges "out of the shadows like a spirit". Yet this function puts him closer to Giles Winterborne in *The Woodlanders*: both are subtly related to the soil, and both are slighted by fair-haired angels. But Hardy works more precisely than this, and the resemblance should not be pressed too hard. The characters are different: we should in general classify Hardy's characters on the strength not of the *things they do,* but of the psychological groundwork of their personalities. It would not be helpful to tot up lists of slighted lovers, sufferers, flirts, and so on, even if the final "groupings" were correct.[1] It is the basis of the groupings that is important.

Besides the "mist" blue of Venn's eyes, Hardy makes a

careful note of "the soft curve of the lower part of his face", and the lips, "thin, and though, as it seemed, compressed by thought", with a "pleasant twitch at their corners now and then" (R.N., p. 10).

Passivity does not necessarily make for a lower order of importance — some of Hardy's great characters, Tess Durbeyfield and Giles Winterborne, for example, by and large do nothing positive or purposeful with their lives. In *The Return of the Native,* however, it is the other three major characters who generate most of the interest and nearly all of the action. They deepen Hardy's conception of psychological motivation to body forth a situation more complex and "fated" than any he had hitherto achieved. The names again are significant, especially in the case of the first of the three, Damon Wildeve. His antithetical status to the later Angel Clare is obvious: he stands in relation to the darker aspect of spirituality, as Clare does to the light. He is, as his Christian name tells us, a daemon, and also, as his surname tells us, capable of abandon and recklessness. The first description of Wildeve is not only conclusive, but itself a landmark in Hardy's work, showing how far he had advanced in assurance and definition from *Under the Greenwood Tree:*

> He was quite a young man, and of the two properties, form and motion, the latter first attracted the eye in him. The grace of his movement was singular: it was a pantomimic expression of a lady-killing career. Next came into notice the more material qualities, among which was a profuse crop of hair impending over the top of his face, lending to his forehead the high-cornered outline of an early Gothic shield; and a neck which was smooth and round as a cylinder. The lower half of his body was of light build. Altogether he was one in whom no man would have seen anything to admire, and in whom no woman would have seen anything to dislike. (R.N., p. 49)

The "flexibility" of Fancy Day had been given its place in a loose psychological groundwork. Now, every detail is significant in the total psychological scheme. Damon Wildeve is Hardy's first real essay in the demonic. Immediately, the portrait we have been given of Thomasin Yeobright takes on a fresh significance: her fundamental fairness and her hopefulness at once become polar opposites to Wildeve's "motion", his grace, dark smoothness, and manifest unreliability. So precise and definite is the work here, that Hardy can trust as worn a cliché as "lady-killing" to do its work, with no more than a passing remembrance of Sergeant Troy.

Until Wildeve appears in *The Return of the Native,* the real nature of Hardy's psychological principles could hardly have been guessed at. As it is, of course, one can reconstruct it from a knowledge of the entire canon. But the glimpses vouchsafed hitherto have been fragmentary, the approach still "blind", even in *Far from the Madding Crowd.* Gabriel Oak's static-ness, Troy's impulsiveness, the obviously significant nature of Bathsheba Everdene's flexibility, these were definite insights, but I doubt if one could have understood them very fully without a knowledge of the novels that came after. Together with the greater certainty of the psychological methodology in *The Return of the Native,* moreover, runs an increase in animus and dynamism. In simpler words, people get a little nastier and a little more energetic. It may be Hardy's real pessimism beginning to assert itself, it may be a souring with experience. (Although at the time of writing *The Return of the Native* Hardy was only thirty-two it was an old thirty-two.) It is more likely to be a greater certainty about things, about the way people really are made. For all its cohesiveness, there is an air of moral timidity about *Far from the Madding Crowd.* The introduction of Damon Wildeve – by a long way the most daring and modern contribution made to the study of sexuality in its time – reveals Hardy's greater confidence and penetration.

The scene that follows the description of Wildeve deepens the lines sketched in it: he treats Thomasin's aunt with a curt superciliousness. This is not mere incivility: "Think what I have gone through to win her consent; the insult that it is to any man to have the banns forbidden; the double insult to a man unlucky enough to be cursed with sensitiveness, and blue demons, and Heaven knows what, as I am", he says himself, adding to our impression of his self-involved petulance (R.N., p. 51). This is not the whole truth, however. For Hardy goes on: "Seeing that she was really suffering he seemed disturbed and added, 'This is merely a reflection, you know. I have not the least intention to refuse to complete the marriage, Tamsie mine — I could not bear it.' 'You could not, I know!' said the fair girl, brightening. 'you, who cannot bear the sight of pain in even an insect, or any disagreeable sound, or unpleasant smell even, will not long cause pain to me and mine' " (R.N., p. 52). (This last statement of Thomasin's reminds us of how indebted to Hardy D. H. Lawrence was, especially in his handling of the Paul Morell-Miriam relationship, which could scarcely have been so fully and confidently grasped without Hardy's mediation.)

The conception of Damon Wildeve may well have been suggested to Hardy by the character of Thomasin herself. For the relationship between them is antithetical: they are polarized, and this new magnetism in the relationships obtains in the novel in a more logically coherent way than in *Far from the Madding Crowd*. For Eustacia Vye and Clym Yeobright are fixed by a similar axis of attraction. One is defined in terms of implicit reference to the other. Eustacia Vye's entrance into the novel is held back chapter after chapter. She is glimpsed, as the spike on the helmet in the third chapter of the book. When we get closer to her, Hardy gives us glimpses of her build — "tall and straight"; her movements — "ladylike"; her profile — "as though Sappho and Mrs. Siddons had converged upwards from the tomb to form an image like neither but suggesting both". Then a bound up a bank reveals her youthfulness. The words "wayward" and "petulant" finally prepare us for what we get, a full-scale study in the Bathsheba Everdene style of one of Hardy's goddesses. Almost involuntarily, Hardy returns to the

Greeks. Treating Bathsheba (with her Old Testament aura), he had confined himself to praising the classically formed features. Eustacia, having been held back even longer and glimpsed more impressively than Bathsheba, gets the full treatment. She is "the raw material of a divinity. On Olympus she would have done well with a little preparation" (though there is satire in the tone here). From beginning to end of the extended portrait — a whole chapter long — it is not only classical mythology, but the Mediterranean origination of that mythology that helps to define the basis of the character. The Latin-Teuton antithesis is more familiar in German than in English literature: the Germans tour Italy more than any other nation, reflecting not only the "attraction of opposites", but a will to understand themselves. Thomas Mann's Tonio Kröger gets his dark fineness and sensibility from his Italian mother, and conversely adores the blue-eyed, fair-haired angels of the North. From this alone, it is obvious that the kind of dichotomy I have been describing in English fiction expresses a general northern European consciousness of psycho-physiological polarities. The differences are as interesting as the similarities: in Mann the South represents dark-haired sensibility, an almost feminine delicacy of structure and refinement of feeling. In the Brontës, dark pigmentation tends to represent Celtic mysticism, and, at the same time, animal earthiness, while the blue-eyed angels tend, like young Linton, to vaporize into the ether. Hardy's terms differ from both, though they are related. For all her southern Romanticism — Hardy doesn't use the word but it can be applied to Eustacia Vye with a precision guaranteed by the fullness and richness of the writing — Eustacia Vye belongs to a different species from Tonio Kröger. She has, in fact, not the fineness of the South, but its sensuality. The fact forces us again to remember that for all that they have their roots in reality, these psychological terminologies do at the same time function symbolically. Thomas Mann's perceptions of the Southern temperament are not invalidated by Hardy's or vice versa; there is no clash or collision of findings. In each case, the artist is narrowing down the field of vision to express a coherent theory of the human organism.

Eustacia Vye can be called a study in the Romantic sensibility in a much more meaningful way than Emma Bovary. There are no binding psychological reasons why Emma Bovary should behave the way she does. Nor is there any particular reason for Flaubert to provide them. He didn't provide them simply because he was not aware of that stratum of meaning. In fact, of course, *Madame Bovary* is not a study of the Romantic temperament, because it is not a study of a temperament at all, but simply of boredom, and the sense of meaninglessness that lies behind it. *The Return of the Native* does provide one of the great studies of a particular temperament — a temperament that if it is not Romantic is nothing. Unlike Flaubert, Hardy revels in the sustained descriptive portrait. Is this naivety? Should the character just emerge, through what he says and does? No. The literary "description" is dangerous, since no amount of verbal labour can really suggest a likeness. What happens, in fact, is that we find an equivalent for the character from among our own acquaintance; so that the verbal artist's work is, often, so much wasted effort. But in fact the Flaubert-Tolstoy-James doctrine (or the aspect of it which deplores such things as the visual portrait) serves and rationalizes a different kind of art. The Hardy set piece less establishes a likeness for us to carry in our minds, than it explores an operative psychological category. Hardy's interest in what people look like has its roots in his habit of assessing and evaluating their temperament or type. In the case of Eustacia Vye, the most significant single sentence in the portrait is this: "She was in person full-limbed and somewhat heavy; without ruddiness, as without pallor; and soft to the touch as a cloud" (R.N., p. 77).

Following this, Hardy focusses attention on her hair — its intense blackness, of course, but also its neurasthenic significance: "Her nerves extended into those tresses, and her temper could always be softened by stroking them down.

When her hair was brushed she would instantly sink into stillness and look like the Sphinx" (R.N., p. 77).[2]

The full-limbed heaviness immediately relates her by contrast to Wildeve ("the lower half of his figure was of light build"), with whom she is emotionally involved. She hates Egdon Heath, and is oblivious to its beauty and grandeur. So the antithesis is not between the rooted and the rootless. Her heavy beauty contrasts with Wildeve's grace and lightness: yet her hair contains a strange electricity, associating her with the demonic by way of nervousness. Thus, in spite of her own admission that her infatuation for Wildeve happened merely in the absence of anything better, the affinity between them is real and strong. Pagan, imperious, captious (all Hardy's words, or grammatical derivates of them) — she is too wayward for the comfort of those around her, and waits for something big enough to arrive on the scene, and pull her into its orbit.

Which brings us to the last, and possibly the most important character in the novel, Clym Yeobright. The long build-up suggests a significant collision of the two characters — an elemental drawing together of titanic forces. The great irony of the book, in fact, is that Clym turns out to be a human form of Egdon itself: in recognizing Yeobright, Eustacia recognizes some unanswerable myth, and flees in disorder to a fatuous death-by-drowning that places her with Emma Bovary, Hedda Gabler, and Anna Karenina. To get into Yeobright's company — Eustacia's excitement affects the reader in a way that the writer's mere assurance of the fact never could — she dresses up as a boy in a mumming performance. (Here, Hardy picks on a significant psychological fact — the occasional impulse in the most feminine of women to appear as a youth.)[3] Concealed by the disguise, she savours Clym at her leisure in a curious inversion of Hardy's usual voyeuristic situation. Hardy first associates Yeobright with Rembrandt portraits: "The spectacle constituted an area of two feet in Rembrandt's intensest manner" (R.N., p. 167), then postulates "a strange power" that focusses the observer's attention only on his face. When his face is finally described, the vacillation noted above as being somehow central to the whole novel reasserts itself. Yeobright seems neither old nor young — oldish to the young, youngish to the old. "But it was really one of those faces which convey less the idea of so many years as its age than of so much experience as its store", for "the age of a modern man is to be measured by the intensity of his history" (R.N., p. 161). Again Hardy suggests that in the modern age beauty is of less interest than mental experience. The corollary, that consciousness is a disease, now receives its fullest statement:

> The face was well-shaped, even excellently. But the mind within was beginning to use it as a mere waste tablet whereon to trace its idiosyncrasies as they developed themselves. The beauty here visible would in no long time be ruthlessly overrun by its parasite, thought, which might just as well have fed upon a plainer exterior where there was nothing it could harm. Had Heaven preserved Yeobright from a wearing habit of meditation, people would have said, "A handsome man." Had his brain unfolded under sharper contours they would have said, "A thoughtful man." But an inner strenuousness was preying upon an outer symmetry, and they rated his look as singular. (R.N., pp. 167–68)

The abstract is here made concrete, the nature of the act of thinking described precisely in physical terms. Yet the vocabulary Hardy uses at this stage of the book is general in its applicability. What Hardy is doing here is describing "the thinking type". Possibly no other single passage in his novels gets so close to expressing his central theory of consciousness. He speaks explicitly of "the mutually destructive interdependence of spirit and flesh", and of thought as "a disease of the flesh". As in his description of Thomasin, his cousin, Hardy takes great risks in combining the over-abstract and the clumsily concrete, and again succeeds: "placid pupilage", "a full recognition of the coil of things", "mental luminousness must be fed with the oil of life" — such phrases create the type, superbly. Clym's is basically a bright disposition: he had a "natural cheerfulness striving against depression from without, and not quite succeeding". "As is usual with bright natures," Hardy concludes," the deity that lies ignominiously chained within an ephemeral human carcase shone out of him like a ray" (R.N., p. 168).

Hardy only assumes this Cartesian-Christian dualism of mind and body with characters like Clym and his cousin, both of whom are lighted from within by "the light of the spirit". Compare Thomasin's "luminous workmanship" with Clym's "mental luminousness"; Clym explicitly has a "deity within", Thomasin "an ingenuous, transparent life". Such expressions simply could not occur in connection with Eustacia Vye or Damon Wildeve, with their nervous-physical basis. Already, Hardy's investigations have revealed an intricacy we could hardly have suspected. For Wildeve's "grace" — his demonism, in fact — is translated directly through the body into physical movement. One remembers Fancy Day's "flexibility" again, and, in contrast, Farmer Boldwood's "dignity" — the careful premeditation of behaviour that precludes such organic psycho-physical routines as dancing, and, what is more to the point, making love.

Now, clearly, whatever form Eustacia's "smouldering rebelliousness" will force itself out into, it is hardly going to have much in common with Clym Yeobright's "browsing". Perhaps Hardy runs the risk of short-circuiting his thought here by too abrupt an identification of Clym with Egdon. "Take all the varying hates felt by Eustacia Vye towards the Heath, and translate them into loves, and you have the heart of Clym" (R.N., p. 213). Yet this is very much a part of Hardy's peculiar integrity — straightforwardness that can risk any disclosure because its ultimate effect does not depend upon rhetoric or drama at all. Ultimately, perhaps, he fails to find adequate motivation for the relationship between Clym and Eustacia. Clym's puritanism resists corruption and even at the height of the affair, at the superb noon-eclipse scene, he can soberly censure her sensualism: "You are ambitious, Eustacia — no, not exactly ambitious, luxurious. I ought to be of the same vein, to make you happy, I suppose. And yet, far from that, I could live and die in a hermitage here, with proper work to do" (R.N., p. 245). The mortar of the relationship is Eustacia's projection of her own intense need to be loved. Hardy needed to convince us a little more than he is able that Eustacia had found, or thought she had found, something more solid in the objective facts to sustain her own projection. There is no need for the death of Mrs. Yeobright to bring Eustacia to the point of saying to Clym after their marriage, "I almost wish you would kill me". This incident, though powerful and moving in itself, is really a red herring: it suggests a decisive motivation for a disintegration which required only its own inner working to come about. As sometimes happens in Hardy, the inner thrust of the psychological quantities eddies away, and a spurious direction is imposed through factitious plot-mongering. Thus, there is only a vague appropriateness about the drowning of Eustacia Vye and Damon Wildeve. If this should be doubted, compare the last chapters of the novel with the sweep of *Wuthering Heights* or of Hardy's own later masterpieces. (Or, still more pertinently, with the closing chapters of *The Mill on the Floss,* which seems to have given Hardy much by way of character-gravitation and symbolic resolution. Eustacia Vye owes something in conception to Maggie Tulliver, with her profuse black hair and her need to be loved.)

Perhaps a clue to what one feels to be the final unsatisfactoriness of *The Native* can be found in D. H. Lawrence's irritated judgment on Clym: "By nature a passionate violent product of Egdon, he should have suffered in flesh and in soul from love long before this age. He should have lived and moved and had his being whereas he had only his business, and afterwards his inactivity."[4] Lawrence pays Hardy the compliment of treating Clym as though he were a real man and not a figure in a book. Yet there is something irritating about Hardy's attitude to Clym, and Lawrence's "should" is, of course, really directed at his creator: Hardy expects us to respect what we merely despise, Clym's sobersided disapproval of Eustacia (which amounts to a rejection), and his settling to a life of quiet good-doing as a blind teacher.

Clym plays an important part in sustaining the tension of the psychological scheme. He is the first wholly achieved essay in one of Hardy's fundamental types: introverted and intellectual, scored by too much thinking, and held by a tension between an "inner strenuousness" and an "outer symmetry". Precisely what Clym cannot have is the kind of mobility Wildeve excels in, just as Wildeve is incapable of Clym's ruminative good character. Where there is nothing separating the conception of his desire from its prosecution, Yeobright allows a veil of mentation to fall between himself and the world, himself and action. Hence, in the end, Clym is for morality, Wildeve for himself. It is significant that for Hardy this means for evil. Yeobright thinks, Wildeve acts. And these statements are derived (or could be) from the initial portraits of the characters rather than from the actual incidents of the story. The essential information is conveyed by Hardy in terms of build, of constitution. By contrast with such early *esquisses* as Edward Springrove, with his meaningless Grecian good looks, Clym Yeobright is totally consistent in conception. Hardy now understands that Springrove's introversion — signalized by that "one thin line" running across his otherwise clear brow — cannot be housed in a neutral or conventionally attractive body. Everything partakes of the one organic cast. Clym's fundamental handsomeness has gradually been suborned by the disease of thought. More, his whole conduct of his life is determined by it, where Springrove, the thoughtfulness noted, simply drifted about at the mercy of Hardy's plot-mongering. Not only does Clym's "return" express a basic spiritual decision about life, the relationship with Eustacia also derives from and develops the psychological qualities involved.

Yeobright has a "bright deity" within; Wildeve has "form and motion", and a "grace of movement". Eustacia's "full-limbed and somewhat heavy" person — "soft to the touch as a cloud" — nevertheless moves with an athleticism that contrasts with Clym's slowness. We remember her leap up the bank at the beginning of the book, which revealed her youthfulness, and which aligns her with the grace of Wildeve rather than the inner brightness of Yeobright. She is really a new addition to Hardy's type-vocabulary, though she owes much to Bathsheba Everdene. The words he uses to define her — "lymphatic", "luxurious", "full-limbed" — are characteristic of Hardy's mature methods, and further increase the stock of psycho-physiological terms he is gradually building up to replace the expressions of the Humours psychology. The words in Hardy's own vocabulary refer to physical qualities with precise psychological connotations. We have seen him gradually develop the notion of "flexibility" to define a quality which is neither mental nor physical, but organic. Similarly, the "dignity" of Boldwood, the "quiet energy" of Oak, the "impulse" of Troy, all denote precise psycho-physical quantities. *The Return of the Native* presents the most direct confrontation Hardy had yet engineered between the types. Complex as were the entanglements of the characters in *Far from the Madding Crowd,* they scarcely amounted to a confrontation. Which means that Hardy was that much less sure and clear about what he was doing. The quite explicit treatment of Damon Wildeve is the first sign in *The Native* that Hardy is prepared to pit the psyches against each other in open conflict.

This conflict concerns only the inner triangle of the novel — Clym, Wildeve, and Eustacia. Outside are Venn — his eye "keen as that of a bird of prey, and blue as autumn mist" — and Thomasin Yeobright with her "ingenuous, transparent life": two angels, almost Brontëesque in their purity. Put schematically, the demonic and the ethical compete for the soul of Eustacia Vye. Thomasin is drawn by Wildeve's dark grace, but is saved by Venn, largely by playing the devil at his own game: the lunatic game of chance on the Heath has a strange effectiveness. Eustacia is claimed by the demon in virtue of her lower half, the half of her that belongs to movement and action ("below is all the fiend's"). The trouble is that one cannot regret her escape from Clym and a life of quiet purpose on Egdon. For the real tension of the book should have been provided by the struggle for her soul: Wildeve is interesting enough to represent the devil fighting for her body, but Clym does not do justice to the principles of light and the mind. The book directly foreshadows *Tess of the d'Urbervilles,* where Tess herself owes much to the lymphatic softness of Eustacia, and Angel Clare directly inverts Damon Wildeve. Only in *Tess* the man of grace and motion rejects the soulful offering on behalf of the principles of light (Clare: *clair*), and the fiend claims his own by default.

The Return of the Native shows Hardy's strengthening power of presentation, and testifies to the greater clarity of vision achieved since *Far from the Madding Crowd.* Between the two books falls *The Hand of Ethelberta,* and between *The Native* and *The Mayor of Casterbridge* a whole decade of minor fiction. Some account of the psychological *aperçus* in these lesser books has already been given. In them Hardy was found experimenting, losing his way, then getting clear just what it was he had achieved. Meanwhile a brief survey will not be out of place.

Beyond any reasonable doubt, the inner triangle of *The Native* anticipates in exact detail the three basic categories of Kretschmer and Sheldon: Eustacia Vye is viscerotonic, Clym cerebrotonic, and Damon Wildeve somatotonic.[5] While we do not wish to praise Hardy simply for anticipating the pragmatically tested findings of the psychologists, the fact is impressive in itself, and confirmation of the basic thesis being argued here. It is not simply the occurrence of the types that is important — the types would be found by a psychologist in any random sample of individuals, whether in real life or in fiction — *it is the way their qualities and drives provide the action of the moral tale* that counts. Hardy was clearly aware of carefully distinguishing different personalities, and drawing out their implied destinies by pitting them against other contrary or adjacent types. The attention to physique, build, temper — in its more precise sense — of course brings to mind the whole typological tradition from Galen to Kant. And as the parallel with Sheldon underlines, Hardy's fundamental types do follow the broad lines laid down by Hippocrates. There is no reason to distinguish between the methods of science and those of art: it is only the final aims and purposes, the ultimate *Weltanschauungen,* that serve to differentiate the insights of science and psychology from those of art. Hardy's perceptions and his understanding are those of a great psychologist, and, whether or no any direct influence can be shown, materially contributed to the understanding of the mind and its workings in the twentieth century. In *Far from the Madding Crowd* we saw him in the process of isolating degrees of mobility, flexibility, and inflexibility. *The Native* shows the hardening of these categories. *The Woodlanders* (written nine years later) finally brought the pentagonal form to perfection, by eliminating the passional element associated with the "lymphatic, luxurious" Eustacia Vye almost entirely, and concentrating attention upon the slow, enduring energy of Diggory Venn.

7. *The Woodlanders* (1887)

The precise function of the Hintock woods in *The Woodlanders* is no easier to determine than that of Egdon Heath in *The Return of the Native*. They do not symbolize anything: symbolism is a diadic relation, and any attempt to replace with a single term the complex and shifting participation of the woodland in this narrative must be more than usually arbitrary and uninformative. Yet equally obviously, it is not just scoring, or background. It is perhaps more like a key-centre. Certainly, the different characters in the novel define themselves as much in relation to the woods as to each other.

The gloomy atmosphere of the woodland alternates with the breathtaking beauty of the cider-country, where "the air was blue as sapphire — such a blue as outside that apple-region was never seen. Under the blue, the orchards were in a blaze of pink bloom" (W., p. 164). The air itself seems to change: the "spongy" Hintock woods give way to a clear ethereal radiance. Giles Winterborne moves between these worlds in two different capacities; he plants trees (Hardy devotes some of his most penetrating writing to describing this skill of Winterborne's), and in season moves around the countryside with a cider-press. Like Diggory Venn in this role, he wears the insignia of his trade — pips and flecks of apple-flesh. These two functions of Winterborne's serve to define him. In a material sense, Winterborne carries the novel on his back; any account of it must begin with him, as the narrative ends with him.

It is significant, therefore, that the Hintock woods have so little of the pastoral, Ardenesque magic of *Under the Greenwood Tree*. The contrast with the cider-country insists itself: the Hintock woods enclose a world more stagnant and unhealthy than still and mystical. Hardy was never one to mysticize Nature, of course, even when, as in *Return of the Native,* he wrote of it with awesome power. The Hintock woods are pervaded with mist and fog, and divulge hints of Nature's ruthlessness and bungling:

> They went noiselessly over mats of starry moss, rustled through interspersed tracts of leaves, skirted trunks with spreading roots whose mossed rinds made them like hands wearing green gloves; elbowed old elms and ashes with great forks, in which stood pools of water that overflowed on rainy days, and ran down their stems in green cascades. On older trees still than these huge lobes of fungi grew like lungs. Here, as everywhere, the Unfulfilled Intention, which makes life what it is, was as obvious as it could be among the depraved crowds of a city slum. The leaf was deformed, the curve was crippled, the taper was interrupted; the lichen ate the vigour of the stalk, and the ivy slowly strangled to death the promising sapling. (W., p. 62)

This is a long way from Richard Jefferies, from the sylvan paradise of *Under the Greenwood Tree,* and Nature-mysticism; a long way too, from the all-powerful determining system John Holloway finds in Hardy; mankind is a part of Nature, in Hardy's view, neither cleverer nor stupider, neither infallible nor hopeless. Nature, like man, follows blindly not a pattern, but the lines of least resistance towards nothing but futurity.

Giles Winterborne, the man in the novel most attuned to this great organism, the Natural Universe, ought, by Holloway's criteria, to be a well-adjusted, well-balanced being. In fact, he pursues doggedly a downward path to a miserable grave. Yet Hardy could hardly have praised more highly Winterborne's natural genius. Of his tree-planting Hardy says, "there was a sort of sympathy between himself and the fir, oak, or beech that he was operating on; so that the roots took hold of the soil in a few days" (W., p. 76). And a little later, with an almost Lawrentian sensuousness, "Winterborne's fingers were endowed with a gentle conjurer's touch in spreading the roots of each little tree, resulting in a sort of caress under which the delicate fibres all laid themselves out in their proper directions for growth" (W., p. 77). It is Marty South, not Giles himself, who is really conscious of his gift:

> "How they sigh directly we put 'em upright, though while they are lying down they don't sigh at all," said Marty.
> "Do they?" said Giles. "I've never noticed it."
>
> She erected one of the young pines into his hole, and held up her finger; the soft musical breathing instantly set in which was not to cease night or day till the grown tree should be felled – probably long after the two planters had been felled themselves. (W., p. 77)

Yet, Winterborne could not have died more wretchedly. Clearly, the common conception of Hardy's Nature-mysticism, of being in tune with Nature in some way that somehow promotes happiness and well-being, will, in the face of this novel, simply have to be abandoned. As always in Hardy, the tenor of the character's lives expresses their type. Giles's surname tells us something about him straightaway, perhaps: "borne-toward-winter" or "born-by-winter". At any rate, winter predominates in his soul's year, as it does often in the novel as a whole. Winterborne has nothing of Gabriel Oak's equanimity, yet he falls the same side of the type-transversal, like all Hardy's sufferers. The treatment never, I think, falters, from the initial hesitancies on: "a man, not particularly young for a lover, not particularly mature for a person of affairs", and "there was reserve in his glance, and restraint upon his mouth" (W., p. 22). He had (towards Marty South) "a kindly manner of quietly severe tone" (W., p. 22). It is significant that all these details which establish Winterborne so subtly come from his first scene in the book, a scene that takes place at dawn, amid mist, in the company of Marty South. To say that Giles is here "at his best" does not quite suit Hardy's methods. Yet he is certainly at his most easy and natural: his

temperament shows itself in its better aspect, for the qualities
he displays when he is alone with Marty South will express
themselves later, with Grace Melbury, in a completely
different light. Yet they are the same qualities, it is the same
temperament expressed, always with a total absence of
falseness. Hardy shows us two Winterbornes, in fact, one with
Marty, another with Mr. Melbury and his daughter Grace.

What Hardy has shown as "reserve and restraint" and a
"kindly manner of quietly severe tone" emerges in the
company of Melbury as "absence of alacrity", a guardedness,
a "somewhat rare power", as Hardy calls it, "of keeping not
only judgement but emotion suspended in difficult cases" (W.,
p. 39). When he is selling his trees in Sherton Abbas
Market-place, Hardy remarks that "he was, in fact, not a very
successful seller either of his trees or of his cider, his habit of
speaking his mind when he spoke at all militating against this
branch of his business" (W., p. 42). The admirable honesty
soon begins to be seen as a species of defeatism. Later, Hardy
ascribes to him "a certain causticity of tone towards himself
and the world in general" which has prevented him seeing to
it that he is presentably dressed when Grace finally meets him
in the market-place: "her momentary instinct of reserve at
first sight of him was the penalty he paid for his laxness" (W.,
p. 43). The earlier absence of "alacrity" with which he
responded to Melbury's suggestion that he meet Grace for him
is obviously related to that "causticity of mental tone" which
prevented "any enthusiastic action on the strength of that
reflection".

It is more than Grace's new education that causes the
darkening of what had appeared to be Winterborne's strength.
I have described in the earlier novels the "reciprocity of
influence" Hardy sees in sexual or emotional attraction. This
always explicitly concerns the psycho-physical constitution —
the types, in a word — of the characters involved. Grace
Melbury's attraction for Giles springs, inevitably, from her
own character-type. Grace, as the name warns us, introduces a
new quality into the novel. She appears first as a "flexible

young creature". The portrait that follows a little later (presented in pure type-terminology) establishes a small-scale creature:

> In simple corporeal presentment she was of a fair and clear complexion, rather pale than pink, slim in build and elastic in movement. Her look expressed a tendency to wait for others' thoughts before uttering her own; possibly also to wait for others' deeds before her own doing. In her small, delicate mouth, which had hardly settled down to its matured curves, there was a gentleness that might hinder sufficient self-assertion for her own good. (W., p. 14)

Nothing now is left to chance; everything is conveyed in terms of psychological chemistry. This is the girl Hardy plays off against Giles. Already it seems a dangerous situation. Marty South and Giles, in that first important scene, had appeared surrounded by mist. Other mythological references sealed the impression of an ancient rightness between them; on the evening when Marty overhears the conversation between the Melburys that blasts her hopes of Giles, she appears as an archaic figure, timelessly dressed, completely unanchored in the historical period the novel is set in: "She wrapped round her a long red woollen cravat and opened the door. The night in all its fulness met her flatly on the threshold, like the very brink of an absolute void, or the ante-mundane Ginnung-Gap believed in by her Teuton forefathers" (W., p. 15). After the mist-dawn scene in which Giles is introduced into the book, another important scene confirms the drift. Grace's father warns her off Giles. Shortly after, Giles is working high up a tree, lopping off its boughs. While he works, Grace passes by on the ground. It is a shrewdly planned scene; Giles up in his "skyey field" (where he belongs), shrouds the tree, watched by Marty, and by her father "sitting motionless with a hand upon each arm of the chair" (W., p. 115). Grace cuts him, "too full of the words of her father to give him any encouragement". A sudden fog descends, "completely cutting Giles off from the ground

Only the stroke of the bill-hook, and the flight of a bough downwards, and its crash upon the hedge at intervals" tell of his presence at all.

Grace at once regrets the cut and goes back: it is important that, small-scale prettiness and all, she has the emotional reserves to love Giles. Her basic rootedness in the old ways can break up with time the thin crust of education which has kept her aloof from him. But Winterborne, significantly, entirely fails to respond to her overture. "Had Giles, instead of remaining still, immediately come down from the tree to her, would she have continued in that filial, acquiescent frame of mind which she had announced to him as final?" (W., p. 117). Hardy suggests that she would not: "The probabilities are that something might have been done by the appearance of Winterborne on the ground beside Grace . . . But he continued motionless and silent in the gloomy Niflheim or fogland which involved him, and she proceeded on her way" (W., p. 117).

Hardy's speculation here, the weighing-up of the probabilities, must, I think, be taken entirely in good faith; it is part of the correct reading of his entire canon to do so, indeed. No single passage better demonstrates the precise nature of his conception of personality. The "responsibility" for his life could not have been planted more firmly on Winterborne's shoulders; yet he is what he is, and he cannot respond.

It is difficult not to feel that Winterborne belongs up there in Niflheim, with the old Norse gods of the forest and sea, with Marty South and the old life, rather than with Grace (all light and flexibility) and the new. A key-passage involves Grace's father — himself a superb study — in the same sad scheme. Just before Grace's return from school, Melbury takes a lantern out to look at a sentimentally preserved imprint of his daughter's foot in the garden. Hardy comments:

> Melbury perhaps was an unlucky man in having within him the sentiment which could indulge in this fondness about the imprint of a daughter's footstep. Nature does

not carry on her government with a view to such feelings; and when advancing years render the opened hearts of those that possess them less dexterous than formerly in shutting against the blast, they must, like little celandines, suffer "buffeting at will by rain and storm". (W., p. 2)

That seems to me one of Hardy's plainest and profoundest statements about life itself in general and the life of the emotions in particular. It makes it clear beyond doubt that the inevitability informing his novels cannot be equated with any abstract Law of the Universe. It suggests also that his novels are to be regarded as descriptive rather than prescriptive. Thus in one sense it is foolish, ultimately, to say that Giles could have come down and spoken to Grace: and in general this mode of criticism — watching the characters go through their paces until they trip up — is misguided. If the "errors" of the heroes were never made, tragedy would never be written. So, we may take it that Sophocles and Aeschylus and Shakespeare were perfectly aware that it is possible to live without sleeping with one's mother, murdering one's husband, or assassinating one's king. Yet there is a school of criticism which asks us in effect quietly to congratulate ourselves for not having committed the heroes' errors: tragedy on this theory teaches us how to spot and avoid the tragic flaw.

That is not only misguided — it is corrupting. Tragedy does not teach us to hug our own safety and virtue. Hardy does not imply, "If Giles had slid down the tree and made it up with Grace, everything would have been all right". In a sense, it is true, as I have said, that Giles could not respond, because of the man he was; and in the same sense, the novel does retail Giles's character in such a way as to make it obvious why he could not be happy. But put in that form, it does not really seem worth doing. Why bother to tell us that men cannot be happy? Yet isn't this what Hardy's novels do? His greatest works show us that people like Winterborne seem made to suffer. In the character of Marty South, he shows us someone who so closely understands Giles that they are hardly separate beings. And we can scarcely resist the temptation to think that they should have had each other. Hardy avoids saying this — not out of delicacy, but out of the depth of his understanding of the nature of suffering and character. But the entire structure and substance of the novel seems to say so, from the first exquisite dawn-scene where, alone with her in the world, Giles lifted her "like a doll as she was about to stoop over the bundles, placed her behind him, and began throwing up the bundles himself" (W., p. 24). The work of art, in fact, neither instructs us how to avoid pain, nor tells us it cannot be avoided. It is rather an enactment, a sacrificial performance in which we are persuaded to join.

The other of the two overlapping triangles of which the book is constructed has for its pivot the young doctor, Edred Fitzpiers. The Arthurian-Norman name signifies, in the context of Hintock, superior refinement and culture, and Fitzpiers serves to catalyze the innocent aspiration of Grace Melbury. As often in Hardy, the social superiority translates directly into sexual or emotional attraction. One does not, perhaps, take Fitzpiers as seriously as one should: the gentlemanly character was not one Hardy knew well, at least in its caddish variety. Edred Fitzpiers never quite loses the air of public-school rake Winterborne detects in him as he watches him observing Grace: "The stranger appeared as a handsome and gentlemanly personage of six or eight and twenty, and he was quizzing her through an eyeglass" (W., p. 79).

The philosophical veneer — beautifully satirized by Hardy — suggests superficiality; so does the portrait:

> A finely formed, handsome man. His eyes were dark and impressive, and beamed with the light either of energy or of susceptivity — it was difficult to say which; it might have been a little of both. That quick, glittering, empirical eye, sharp for the surface of things, if for nothing beneath, he had not. But whether his apparent depth of vision were real, or only an artistic accident of

his corporeal moulding, nothing but his deeds could reveal . . . the classical curve of his mouth was not without a looseness in its close. (W., pp. 125—26)

Lastly, he had a "readily appreciative mien" and "reflective manner", which "bespoke the philosopher rather than the dandy" (W., p. 126). But dandyism is there somewhere, Hardy hints. Everything goes to create something like Winterborne's anti-type — above all the "susceptivity". Fitzpiers's sensuality is welcome after Winterborne's dourness. So is his affair with Suke Damson, a kind of sluttish prototype of Arabella Donn. And it is by contrast with Fitzpiers, naturally, that Giles most suffers. On Midsummer Eve, when Giles and Fitzpiers turn out with the rest of the village bachelors to catch their future wives, Winterborne's doggedness repels us as an almost surly negativism. This scene conjures up the pixie magic of the woods almost in the manner of *A Midsummer Night's Dream*. Fitzpiers seems more natural in the setting than Giles, though Giles is almost part of the woods, and Fitzpiers hitherto had seemed improbably urbane in the Hintock setting. The point is important, for it reveals again the functional nature of Hardy's "settings". What makes Fitzpiers more than just a dandy, and a real force in the emotional action, emerges only perhaps when we see him lurking in the woods, waiting for a girl on Midsummer Eve. At this moment Winterborne, the man of the trees, is paradoxically out of his element. He is eclipsed by the intellectual dandy with a weakness for women. A Faustian air has hovered uncertainly around Fitzpiers ever since the first mention of his light burning through the night in the first chapter of the book, when one of the locals says, "A very clever and learned young doctor lives in the place you be going to — not because there's anybody for'n to cure there, but because they say he is in league with the devil" (W., p. 5). Fitzpiers has already shown himself to be a bored dandy with too many ideas. Yet here, at Midsummer Eve in the forest, he makes sense as a minor demon, while Winterborne just is not "with it". We see Giles "walk slowly to the bend in a leafy defile, along which Grace would have to return", at the instigation of Grammer Oliver, Melbury's servant. Mrs. Melbury betrays Winterborne by suggesting to Fitzpiers that he move near to Giles's station to give him a better chance to catch Grace. Winterborne reacts characteristically, with the "offhand manner of indifference which had grown upon him since his dismissal". The two men are now openly competing for Grace, and Giles fails, in the dourness of his character, to rise to the occasion: "Fitzpiers had quickly stepped forward in front of Winterborne, who disdaining to shift his position, had turned on his heel" (W., p. 186).

Fitzpiers captures Grace unopposed, and succeeds in his purpose of establishing himself on a new level of seriousness with her. But it is what happens after the (not disingenuous) kiss he gives Grace that really reveals Fitzpiers for what he is. When Grace has gone, together with the rest of the respectable population of the village, the sluttish Suke Damson mistakes Fitzpiers for her boyfriend, Tim Tangs, and lets him pursue her. The result is one of the wryest, richest episodes in Hardy, culminating in a corn-field seduction of great beauty. Hardy succeeds in riding the line between enhancing the scene out of all reality (it is a beautiful nocturne), and relishing its impropriety — for Suke has long since realized that it is not Tim Tangs in pursuit.

Thereafter it seems natural that Fitzpiers should exercise a strong fascination over Grace — an almost psychic influence. She is not in love with him, but she admits to herself at once, on being told by her father that Fitzpiers has approached him about her, "that Fitzpiers acted upon her like a dram, exciting her, throwing her into a novel atmosphere which biased her doings until the influence was over, when she felt something of the nature of regret for the mood she had experienced" (W., p. 200). The guilt is exciting: "A premonition that she could not resist him if he came, strangely moved her."

Thus, all three relationships so far considered — Marty and Giles, Giles and Grace, Grace and Fitzpiers — rest on quite different affections. (They also, incidentally, quite regularly ascend the social scale.) Only Marty really knows what she wants. Grace is of the four the least sure what she needs. But her part in the novel can hardly be adequately comprehended without the participation of her father. I have mentioned already the incident of the footprint. It would require a detailed account of each of Melbury's scenes to do justice to the excellence of Hardy's workmanship. His pride in Grace; his secret enjoyment of being made to feel inferior by her; the stiff dutifulness of his attitude to Winterborne; the fumbling, amazed incredulity with which he receives Fitzpiers's proposal — every gesture and speech shows Hardy at his best. And it is the influence Melbury exerts at various points in the novel, notably when he discourages Giles and persuades Grace to accept Fitzpiers, that makes the central action so plausible. Indeed, Fitzpiers's social superiority and her father's social ambition work together to make Grace's vacillating indecision credible and poignant. Her uncertainty is beautifully symbolized by the ghastly thaw that holds the woodland in its grip on the morning when she finally, hesitantly, commits herself. The situation is thoroughly typical of Hardy's methods: a character defers coming to a decision, and exploits an incidental eventuality to let himself slide into what he always wanted, without ever taking responsibility for it.[1] In this case, Grace Melbury uses the pretext of Grammer Oliver's fear of Fitzpiers to facilitate the commitment to him she really desires. The old lady has entered into a (suitably Satanic) pact with the doctor, agreeing to let him have her skull after her death. Grace welcomes the chance to intercede, and the horror of the grey morning, turning reluctantly from winter to miserable spring, seems dismally appropriate to her state of mind:

> The battle between frost and thaw was continuing in mid-air: the trees dripped on the garden plots, where no vegetables would grow for the dripping, though they were planted year after year, with that curious mechanical regularity in the face of hopelessness; the

moss which covered the once broad gravel terrace was swamped; and Grace stood irresolute. (W., p. 153)

The same icy dreariness holds Fitzpiers himself in a destructive *ennui*. They are both determined by the evil dampness of the woodland: his boredom welcomes her uncertainty, and decides it. Notice that no distinction is made between the exile townsman and the country girl. The woodland means different things to each of them, but they are equally oppressed by it. Hardy indicates, admittedly, that the locals find some interest in the dreariness:

> To people at home there these changeful tricks had their interests; the strange mistakes that some of the more sanguine trees had made in budding forth before their month, to be incontinently glued up by frozen thawings now . . . and other such incidents prevented any sense of wearisomeness in the minds of the natives. (W., p. 157)

Yet although this suggests that Grace is brought down by stepping out of the contented life of the woodlanders, and letting her father's social ambition deracinate her, still it is a dreary form of adjustment to ask her to accept — a kind of spiritual coma well suited to Marty South and Giles, but not to the "Daphne-esque" Grace.

The icy silence of the woodland and the leaking dampness of its winter pervade these pages; and Hintock House, the home of the last major character of the book, Felice Charmond, seems more at its mercy than the village itself. A curiously graphic oddity of location establishes its nature: "It stood in a hole. But the hole was full of beauty. From the spot which Grace had reached a stone could easily have been thrown over or into the birds'-nested chimneys of the mansion" (W., p. 69).

The luxuriance of vegetation consequent on its low damp site only augments its oppressiveness. One becomes aware here, in fact, of the vegetative nature of the entire novel. If *The Return of the Native* celebrates the earth itself, *The Woodlanders* celebrates (if that is the word) the vegetable orders: "The situation of the house, prejudicial to humanity, was a stimulus to vegetation, on which account an endless shearing of the heavy-armed ivy went on, and a continual lopping of trees and shrubs" (W., p. 70).

That strikes me as being rather horrible; like certain other passages in the novel — I think of the "green gloves" of the trees in an earlier passage — it is vaguely frightening because it is *no longer metaphorical*: "heavy-armed" seems quite literally applicable to the ivy.

The world of Hintock, in fact, seems to strive after a union of vegetation and water in a prehistoric swamp: "He went on foot across the wilder recesses of the park, where slimy streams of fresh moisture, exuding from decayed holes caused by old amputations, ran down the bark of the oaks and elms, the rind below being coated with a lichenous wash as green as emerald" (W., p. 248).

Of Felice Charmond herself, it does, I think, have to be confessed that she adds little or nothing to earlier models: Hardy has allowed himself to lose sight of the psychological basis of the character in a mist of class-glamour. This is Lady Dedlock grafted on to Eustacia Vye: "Inside the carriage a pair of deep bright blue eyes looked from a ripely handsome face, and though behind those bright eyes was a mind of unfathomed mysteries, beneath them there beat a heart capable of quick extempore warmth — a heart which could indeed be passionately and imprudently warm on certain occasions" (W., p. 44).

In spite of a few characteristic epithets — "Olympian", "lymphatic" — there is nothing that goes beyond the characterization of Viviette Constantine or Eustacia Vye. The entire affair with Fitzpiers fails to hold up its end:

> "Nameless, unknown to me as you were, I couldn't forget your voice!"
> "For how long?"
> "O — ever so long. Days and days!"
> "Days and days! *Only* days and days? O, the heart of a man! Days and days!" (W., p. 239)

The adolescent flirtation they are speaking of is, indeed, intentionally down-graded by Fitzpiers; but later, the Cleopatra-act works: "He gazed at her in undisguised admiration. Here was a soul of souls!" (W., p. 240).

There is no point in prolonging the agony. It is enough to say that this is not what we read Hardy for. What we do read him for is manifested in an episode so powerful, natural, and original that it almost of itself consummates the fable.

It takes us out of Hintock to the Vale of Blackmoor. Giles here appears in his other role, as the travelling cider-maker, transfigured by the mush of the "aphrodisiac" out of that "bitter placidity" of his into a kind of grace, rooted, apparently in older and deeper intoxications than Fitzpiers can know of:

> He had hung his coat to a nail of the out-house wall, and wore his shirt-sleeves rolled up beyond his elbows, to keep them unstained while he rammed the pomace into the bags of horse-hair. Fragments of apple-rind had alighted upon the brim of his hat — probably from the bursting of a bag — while brown pips of the same fruit were sticking among the down upon his firm arms, and in his beard. (W., p. 221)

Winterborne at once undercuts and transcends Fitzpiers's magic influence. A later passage tellingly shows Fitzpiers, worn out by the affair with Felice he has now begun, riding obliviously through a landscape of amazing beauty and fecundity, "the gorgeous autumn landscape of White-Hart Vale, surrounded by orchards, lustrous with the reds of applecrops, berries and foliage, the whole intensified by the gilding of the declining sun". Into this landscape again, and again watched by Grace, comes Winterborne, this time still more allegorical:

> He looked and smelt like Autumn's very brother, his face being sunburnt to wheat-colour, his eyes blue as corn-flowers, his sleeves and leggings dyed with fruit-stains, his hands clammy with the sweet juice of

apples, his hat sprinkled with pips, and everywhere about him that atmosphere of cider which at its first return each season has such an indescribable fascination for those who have been born and bred among the orchards. Her heart rose from its late sadness like a released bough; her senses revelled in the sudden lapse back to Nature unadorned. The consciousness of having to be genteel because of her husband's profession, the veneer of artificiality which she had acquired at the fashionable schools, were thrown off, and she became the crude country girl of her latent early instincts. (W., p. 260)

This is as plain a statement of what is often held to be Hardy's view of civilization as anyone could wish. It is impossible, moreover, to find any reason in the passage that follows, for any reversal of the upward thrust set in here. Winterborne climbs back into the novel: "Impersonating chivalrous and undiluted manliness, he had risen out of the earth ready to her hand".

At this point one simply feels inclined to follow Lawrence's example, and rewrite Hardy's novel for him. There seems no reason to negate the general trend of the tale here towards a deeply meaningful relationship between Grace and Giles. Everything in the book cries out for it. Winterborne has suffered enough; Grace's marriage to Fitzpiers has cured not only herself but her father of the longing for refinement. The profound natural basis of the relationship has now been established in these scenes where Winterborne returns, transfigured by the season. The genius with the trees stands revealed for what he is — a satyr, a creature of ancient lineage, part of Nature, and in contact with deeper springs of knowledge than Grace's finishing school or Fitzpiers's demonic dabbling could claim awareness of. Giles is a pagan, a Dionysiac worshipper of the earth and the seasons, associated profoundly with growth and fruitage.

Yet he belongs also of course to the fog-bound Niflheim of the woodland, the Ginnung-Gap where Marty South is at home. If this side of him was grounded in the negative qualities revealed in the surly refusal to compete on Midsummer Eve, the cider-merchant episodes show quite unmistakably that there is a divinity in him. Giles Winterborne is of course strongly related to Diggory Venn. Venn's blue eyes were "keen as a hawk's", Giles's are as "blue as corn-flowers". Both are ritualistically associated with the earth in virtue of their perennially practised professions. Both of them, finally, endure passively, though Venn's dogged patience is rewarded, where Winterborne is crushed. Both certainly have an indisputable attractiveness within their orbit, though Giles reveals an anti-life sullennness when asked to compete outside it. The books have a curiously inverted relationship to each other in fact. The attention which in *The Return of the Native* is focussed upon Eustacia Vye is here switched to the equivalent of Diggory Venn, while Eustacia's (approximate) equivalent, Felice Charmont, is on the edge of things. We are now in a position to make a general comparison of all three pentagonal novels, for *Far from the Madding Crowd* contains the same or parallel elements.

The psychological quantities are the same as ever. The lymphatic, luxurious Felice draws Fitzpiers; the dour Winterborne draws stolid Marty South; the flexible Grace draws Winterborne; and the intellectual, diabolic Fitzpiers draws Grace. This is the roundabout of *The Woodlanders*. There is a spectrum that might be represented thus:

Marty — Winterborne — Felice — Fitzpiers — Grace

Again, as in *Far from the Madding Crowd,* we can read from left to right along a scale of increasing "elasticity" — to use an expression Hardy adds to his vocabulary in this novel. Marty South, like Gabriel Oak, is the sheet-anchor (beginning and ending matters), almost entirely unleavened in spirit, but mystically at one both with Winterborne and her own world. Winterborne's main characteristic is his reserve, guardedness, absence of alacrity (all Hardy's terms), which serve him badly outside his natural orbit. Psychologically speaking, it is this joylessness Hardy is at pains to reveal. He has a mystical orbit that seems to mark him out for Marty South. Or rather he has two, and this is the trouble. For the second brings him to Grace Melbury. Quite simply, neither can satisfy him. If he had taken one, he would really need the other. And this is a point made again and again in the Wessex novels.

Hardy has distinguished in Giles Winterborne an abstracted, inwardly turned man, a kind of unthinking, nature-oriented introvert. Earlier versions are Diggory Venn and Dick Dewy. They are marked negatively by a silent, taciturn absence of initiative and impulsiveness, and positively by a natural identification with the earth and its processes. They are all blue-eyed, incidentally, indicating their alignment with the Brontë-Hardy angels. It is remarkable how Hardy often inverts the structure of his books: *Under the Greenwood Tree* is told from the point of view of the capricious and unfulfilled girl. Lawrence laconically noted that "Dick will probably have a bad time of it". He does — in Giles.

In the present case, positive indications suggest a natural liaison between the "elastic" — though timid — Grace Melbury, and the dogged Giles, with his slow-moving taciturnity. Dick Dewy may perhaps be Hardy's first sketch of the Winterborne type: certainly Grace links up with Fancy Day (identical types, beyond doubt),[2] and enough is revealed in Dick's silent acceptance of Fancy's changeability to suggest his similarity to Giles. (In the dance, Dick was Fancy's: *The Woodlanders* is one of the few dance-less Hardy novels. A pity.) Anyway, Hardy refuses to allow the possibly harmonious resolution. Quite arbitrarily, it seems, the wealth and abundance of the apple-harvesting turns into the lethal gloom of the Hintock woods in winter: "The woods seemed to be in a cold sweat; beads of perspiration hung from every bare twig; the sky had no colour, and the trees rose before him as haggard, grey phantoms whose days of substantiality were passed" (p. 232).

The dampness in the Hintock air freezes the life-marrow of everybody in the book, including Fitzpiers and Grace. Yet the behaviour of Giles in his long-drawn-out martyrdom derives logically enough from his psychological basis: it amounts in fact to a judgment on his taciturn refusal to take the initiative, his tendency to let life take a course if it shows the slightest inclination for it, even if that course runs counter to his own desires.

The relative failure of the novel — its final lack of consummation — stems, I think, from Winterborne's position as central character: some version of Arnold's judgement on his own Empedocles seems relevant. Where *The Return of the Native* swings unstably between two centres of energy — Eustacia-Wildeve and Eustacia-Clym — *The Woodlanders* depends entirely upon Winterborne for its tragic impact. As I have suggested, the unpredictable, luxurious Felice Charmond is shifted too far from the fulcrum of the book to have any powerful influence on its resolution. So that we are left with the "passive suffering" (justified as we have seen by the psychological facts) of Giles Winterborne, the martyr.

What the martyrdom lacks is brought out sharply by contrast with the magnificently macabre incident of the man-trap Tim Tangs sets for Fitzpiers. Man-traps had occurred earlier in the novel, when Grace visited Felice Charmond in her role of aspiring lady's companion. When Grace notices the traps on the walls of her mansion, Felice observes, "playfully, 'Man-traps are of rather ominous significance where a person of our sex lives, are they not?' " (p. 71). Grace fails to appreciate the joke, since "that side of womanliness was one which her inexperience felt no great zest in contemplating". The incident throws some useful light on both women, in fact: first, it reveals the timid priggishness of Grace (witness her rejoinder to Felice's quip, "They are interesting, no doubt, as relics of a barbarous time happily past" — no wonder Felice did not take her on as companion!) a quality that unites her with the dourness of Giles. Then, it anticipates many of the most interesting insights we get into Felice herself, as one of the women "who lingeringly smile their meanings to men rather than speak them, who inveigle rather than prompt, and take advantage of currents rather than steer". If this smacks rather too much of the more novelettish aspects of Eustacia Vye, it also more seriously reveals the fundamental similarities of both with Tess Durbeyfield. This point is made even more clearly in Felice's following remarks. "I think sometimes I was born to live and do nothing, nothing, nothing, but float about, as we fancy we do sometimes in dreams. But that cannot really be my destiny, and I must struggle against such fancies" (W., p. 72). The significance of this combination of floating fantasy and sensuality will emerge more fully when we come to Tess herself. For the moment, it will be enough to note the common basis of all three characters, Eustacia, Tess, and Felice, in strong, soft sensuality. It is in contrast with Felice, too, that Grace herself is defined most clearly. "There was always something so sympathetic, so responsive in Grace's voice, that it impelled people to overstep their customary reservations in talking to her" (W., p. 64). It is in this way that Hardy's characters are habitually defined — in contrast to each other.

The man-trap comes into its own at the end of the book, as Hardy's symbols always do, naturally and realistically. Tim Tangs, the pathetic gull who marries Suke Damson, gets wind of the old liaison with Fitzpiers, and, on the eve of leaving with his family for Australia, sets an old man-trap directly in Fitzpiers's path. It is certainly one of the most sinister machines in fiction: "The sight of one of these gins, when set, produced a vivid impression that it was endowed with life. It exhibited the combined aspects of a shark, a crocodile, and a scorpion. Each tooth was in the form of a tapering spine, two and a quarter inches long, which, when the jaws were closed, stood in alternation from this side and from that" (W., p. 441).

It functions superbly both as a ferocious symbol of affronted sexuality, and as an emblem of the secretive old rural life. It is difficult not to wish that Hardy had allowed Fitzpiers to get his deserts in the gin, and Giles his with Grace in a happily-ever-after marriage. That one has the leeway to indulge such fantasies seems to me a measure of the failure of a nevertheless very great work of art.

The pentagonal novels are distinguished by a rhythm of attrition. They are dominated by characters like Oak, Venn, Clym Yeobright, and Giles Winterborne, whose speciality is endurance – suffering and martyrdom. The passionate characters in these books do "tragic" things without attaining the tragic personality. Boldwood, Eustacia Vye, and Felice Charmond all attempt to break out of something – they aren't quite sure what. At any rate they make futile gestures Hardy deliberately sets in a context which diminishes them. It is hard to take Eustacia's and Wildeve's drowning wholly seriously in a world of Egdon Heath, so much more impressive a tragic personality. So their end is merely Romantic. Boldwood on the other hand behaves passionately and achieves melodrama: he is really treated like a "case". Felice and Fitzpiers confirm the generally anti-heroic bias of these novels. They are defeated simply by the complexities of human involvement – complexities they had underestimated, and which finally exhaust them. Bathsheba Everdene is the potentially tragic personality who behaves in a quasi-comic way, then learns contrition and patience. The heroes and heroines of these books, in fact, are anti-tragic precisely in virtue of their willingness to endure. Whether they succeed, like Oak or Venn, or fail, like Winterborne and Marty, they do it quietly and in consonance with the natural order.

All this must be taken strictly in terms of the psychological constituents; the consistency of the structuring of these three novels emerges from the following schemata:

Statuesque   Nervous

Far from the Madding Crowd:
Oak – Boldwood – Troy – Bathsheba – Fanny Robin

The Return of the Native:
Clym – Venn – Eustacia – Thomasin – Wildeve

The Woodlanders:
Marty South — Giles — Felice — Fitzpiers — Grace

PART THREE

The Tragedies

Introduction

The tragic novels — *The Mayor of Casterbridge, Tess of the d'Urbervilles,* and *Jude the Obscure* — are based upon a psychological triad. Their greater impact must, I think, in part be explained by the more intense concentration given to fewer characters and their relationships. But this is not even half the truth. These are novels of passion, in a particular sense of the word, that can be understood only by reference to Hardy's total psychological scheme. Henchard, Tess, and Jude are all statuesques, dominated by the "rich *rouge et noir*" of passion. They are also archetypal characters in whose lives and deaths certain eternally recurrent human experiences are rehearsed. In Hardy's scheme of things, sin is associated with the Old Testament, and these are three sinners, in a biblical sense. Opposite them, and involved with them, are their anti types of the spirit — sin-free, merciless, Grecian. The intricate complexities of the pentagonal novels have been cleared away. Now the nervous and the statuesque fight it out to the finish.

8. *The Mayor of Casterbridge* (1886)

Hardy's finest fiction had always combined psychological profundity with intimate precision of social observation. In the early novels, it is often a weakness that the "serious" characters have nothing to do but lounge around being bored. The richly comic dialect writing of *Under the Greenwood Tree* plays second fiddle to the romance of Fancy and Dick. Nevertheless, the book breathes locality and a way of life: novels like *The Hand of Ethelberta* sacrifice this tender realism all but completely to a conventional conception of fiction as the intrigues of disembodied gentlefolk. If *The Mayor of Casterbridge* is, as I believe it is, Hardy's greatest single novel, it is certainly in part because its psychological preoccupations are welded securely onto a strong economic substructure. The Satanic hero of the book, Michael Henchard, is from the outset set deep in his trade. When he first appears, in fact, the vital physical details are subordinated to the details of his calling: "He wore a short jacket of brown corduroy, newer than the remainder of his suit, which was a fustian waistcoat and white horn buttons, breeches of the same, tanned leggings, and a straw hat overlaid with black glazed canvas. At his back he carried by a looped strap a rush basket, from which protruded at one end the crutch of a hay-knife, a wimble for hay-bonds being also visible in the aperture" (M.C., p. 1). Hardy's early heroes express their characters in their choice of abstract unemotional professions. But Henchard, the hay-trusser turned corn-chandler, really belongs to the world of *praxis.* So, significantly, does Donald Farfrae: their struggle takes place in the world of commerce. This is nothing to do with greater realism or probability. It is a matter of what Hardy wanted to say in this book. But it seems probable that the massive scale, solidity of structure, and weight of *The Mayor* derive from this great practicality.

This quality of practical solidity manifests itself also in the nature of the town itself. Curiously, *The Mayor* is the only one of Hardy's novels which takes place more or less entirely within a town, and yet it seems more solid, more permanent, than the novels imbued with the eternality of Nature. The explanation is simple enough. Only in a town or city is man really secure against Nature amid tokens of his own permanence. The very life. the restless change and variety Hardy records so intimately in *The Woodlanders* and *The Return of the Native,* the sense of seasonal change and cyclical growth, make the human enterprise seem insecure and uncertain. The city on the other hand is man's image of permanence: it is a guard against just that dependence on Nature and the weather which plays so vital a part in Hardy's fiction. Casterbridge is not just a city; it is a rampart against the wildness outside, a wall the Romans built round themselves to keep out the British gods and demons: "It was a compact as a box of dominoes", Hardy observes (M.C., p. 31). "It had no suburbs in the ordinary sense. Country and town met at a mathematical line." In other words, the ideal town for Hardy's purposes, not only close to Nature, but dramatically juxtaposed with it, its angular severity making no attempt to blend with or melt into the countryside, but insisting upon its own identity. Now, something of this determined squareness and inflexibility dominates Henchard himself. It will not do to say that Henchard *is* the town, or that Casterbridge symbolizes its mayor: but some such relationship of reinforcement or analogy subsists between Hardy's hero and the human organization of which he is, for a short while, the leader. Henchard is, in short, a tragic hero in the fullest sense of the words, a leader of the tribe whose very prominence tempts him to defy the gods, or the gods to bring him low.

But the novel has two eponymous heroes, if we disregard the subtitle: Donald Farfrae also becomes mayor of

Casterbridge, and the action of the tragedy concerns the conflict of the two men. At first sight the psychological structure of the novel seems quite simply triangular. There is the familiar Hardyesque struggle between the pair of men for the woman. Henchard's daughter, Elizabeth-Jane, marginally deflects the emotional stream, but does not seriously participate in the deeper contest involving her father, Farfrae, and her stepmother, Lucetta Templeman. Hardy was probably right to thin out the characters involved in the central psychical situation. *The Mayor of Casterbridge* is free of the twists and turns that so often mar the early novels. As a result, the decline and fall of Michael Henchard proceed with a gravity of movement and a severity of purpose that justify the comparison with Aeschylus and Sophocles, made by so many of Hardy's admirers. Apart from a little irritation at the comings and goings of Newson (Is he dead? Is he really Elizabeth-Jane's father? etc.), the reader is never distracted from the onward and downward course of this action by the accidents and quirks of fate that sometimes make Hardy seem less than wholly serious about the fate of his characters.

But the real significance of the thinning out of the characters goes beyond this. For the first time in Hardy's fiction, the narrative engineers a direct frontal confrontation between the two types, the two psychic principles that really underlie his whole *oeuvre*. In the real issue at the centre of the book, Lucetta Templeman plays only an instrumental role. She is the prize the two bulls battle for. Of course, she too is involved in the psychic tensions that always implicate Hardy's characters in each other's destinies. She finds herself torn between Farfrae and Henchard, and the conflict within her derives from the facts of her own constitution. Nevertheless, essentially, the deepest interest in the novel does not really concern Lucetta at all: it is the struggle between Henchard and Farfrae that drives the story along, not the emotional involvements of Lucetta. In this, too, it follows the pattern of great tragedy: for the greatest tragedies in European literature have not basically concerned themselves with love at all, but with a more primitive collision between man and the universe. Romance and tragedy are basically different genres.

There is no absolute difference between the fate of Michael Henchard and that of Tess, or Giles Winterborne, or Jude Fawley. But none of these other characters comes up against reality in the form of his own spiritual, archetypal opposite quite so starkly as Michael Henchard does. Henchard's collision with Farfrae alone has the quality of a fundamental tragic conflict not with that boring critical abstraction, Destiny, but with life itself. And this certainly has to do with the fact that Henchard only gets involved with Lucetta incidentally: the relationship is irrelevant to his conflict with Farfrae (or, as we could fairly say, with his own temperament). In all the other novels, the "tragedy" of the central characters derives directly — if not quite solely — from a decisive emotional crisis. All of which means that *The Mayor of Casterbridge* in an important sense is not about inter-sexual relationships at all, and that it owes its peculiar strength and impact somehow to this fact.

Hardy subtitles the book, "A Story of a Man of Character", a phrase which, in the context of his evolving psychological methods, acquires a more precise meaning than it would seem it could. Henchard's "character" emerges as a particular psychological force, precise in its definition. This fact alone reminds us yet again of the typological *donnés* behind Hardy's work. Yet in no other case is there greater need to insist upon the unique individuality of his characters. "Character" in the context is going to emerge gradually as a precisely configured force, yet there is only *one* Henchard.

The character in the specific sense reveals itself in Hardy's initial description. "The man was of fine figure, swarthy, and stern in aspect, and he showed in profile a facial angle so slightly inclined as to be almost perpendicular" (M.C., p. 1). What is Hardy doing here with the detail of the almost vertical facial angle? Something of Henchard's moral uprightness — not always very lovable — expresses itself in it.

Yet what other novelist is in the habit of noticing any variation at all in facial angle? Who else would even have been aware that there *was* such a thing as a facial angle? Hardy habitually works with such subtle physical details, psycho-physiological traits that are not yet mannerisms in the Dickensian sense. Gait is a more familiar expression of character: Henchard's walk is "measured, springless", "the walk of the skilled countryman as distinct from the desultory shamble of the general labourer" (M.C., p. 1). While Henchard's walk is characteristic of his social group, the way he actually sets his foot down tells us something of his own personality: "In the turn and plant of each foot there was, further, a dogged and cynical indifference personal to himself, showing its presence even in the regularly interchanging fustian folds, now in the left leg, now in the right, as he paced along" (M.C., pp. 1–2).

"Swarthy"; "stern in aspect"; "a dogged and cynical indifference": in such phrases Hardy establishes the character of the Man of Character. No reciprocity exists between him and his wife, Hardy tells us, yet his choice of woman does not altogether surprise the reader familiar with Hardy's methods: she turns out to have "mobility" of face. "When she looked down sideways to the girl she became pretty, and even handsome, particularly that in the action her features caught slantwise the rays of the strongly coloured sun, which made transparencies of her eyelids and nostrils, and set fire on her lips". She had finally, "the hard, half-apathetic expression of one who deems anything possible at the hands of Time and Chance, except, perhaps, fair play. The first phase was the work of Nature, the second probably of civilisation" (M.C., p. 2). The latter sentence prepares us for what we get, the most powerfully deterministic of Hardy's novels, and the one whose events most inexorably derive from the biochemistry of its characters.

Hardy takes a risk with narrative in *The Mayor* which could only be justified by the most spectacular success. He begins the novel with a scene that takes place two decades before the incidents that make up the main body of the story. It is not easy to persuade the reader to follow such a leap in time: the air of fictional contrivance ordinarily overwhelms the illusion of reality art depends on. Hardy pulls it off by concentrating energy into such a momentous act that we sail effortlessly over the time-space lapse and land expectantly on the other side. Henchard's sale of his wife in the opening chapter of the novel is an act with few equals for sinisterness in the history of fiction. It is of a piece both with Henchard's character, such as we have been allowed to glimpse it, and with the evil rustic atmosphere that pervades the book even when its action moves indoors. In the furmity tent scene, after the silent arrival of the trio at the Fair, Hardy entrenches Henchard into his character still more deeply, so deeply, indeed, that he can never get out again. When his fall finally comes, it is with a force that has been generated both by this initial crisis and by the energy and power of Henchard's own disposition.

The aura of low evil that attaches to the furmity tent never quite leaves Henchard. The strength of will that enables him to abide by the vow of abstinence he takes after waking up to find his wife and child gone, far from impressing us as morally "good", only testifies to that dangerous force of character that precipitated the unholy act. The vow of abstinence derives, fatally, from the most essential qualities of his being, just as the rum-laced furmity had only brought out all that was most formidable in him:

> At the end of the first basin the man had risen to serenity: at the second he was jovial; at the third, argumentative; at the fourth, the qualities signified by the shape of his face, the occasional clench of his mouth, and the fiery spark of his dark eye, began to tell in his conduct: he was overbearing — even brilliantly quarrelsome. (M.C., p. 7)

When he speaks it is with "a contemplative bitterness that was well-nigh resentful". Every detail here counts: the event that slowly shapes itself bears the stamp of Henchard's character. If one speaks of "determinism" in connection with this or any other of Hardy's novels, incontestably it is a psychological determinism one must refer to, not to some vague Destiny or Fate. One cannot read much of Hardy's poetry without being struck by his insistence upon juxtaposing the involvements of people with the impassivity of external Nature. After Henchard's wife has gone with Newson, Hardy does this more pointedly perhaps than anywhere else:

> The difference between the peacefulness of inferior nature and the wilful hostilities of mankind was very apparent at this place. In contrast with the harshness of the act just ended within the tent was the sight of several horses crossing their necks and rubbing each other lovingly as they waited in patience to be harnessed for the homeward journey. (M.C., p. 13)

And a little later, with something of the mood of *Two on a Tower,* he writes of the sunset:

> To watch it was like looking at some grand feat of stagery from a darkened auditorium. In presence of this scene, after the other, there was a natural instinct to abjure man as the blot on an otherwise kindly universe; till it was remembered that all terrestrial conditions were intermittent, and that mankind might some night be innocently sleeping when these quiet objects were raging loud. (M.C., p. 14)

The full advantage Hardy gains from the time-leap at the end of the second chapter is revealed only later, when he reintroduces Henchard with an impact augmented by twenty years' absence. The mental effect of the time-lapse, even if we encompass it at one reading, is to invest the hay-trusser-turned-mayor, with an extraordinary force. We experience the progress of his climb to power and eminence in a moment, through the eyes of his wife and daughter. Thus, the Character which we have witnessed in its more surly aspect now appears at its most august. Significantly, the two women discover Henchard again first through the same evil old hag of the furmity tent. The wife-selling incident in fact launched the mayor on his rise to prestige: without it Henchard would almost certainly not have taken the oath not to drink, and as certainly would not have gathered himself together sufficiently to be capable of any strenuous effort in life. Now, Susan and Elizabeth-Jane use it to stimulate the old hag's memory. Later, it will emerge as one of the decisive factors contributing to Henchard's fall. Again, the shape of Hardy's fable recalls the Attic tragedians: like Oedipus Henchard is dogged and finally brought low by an evil, violent act long thought forgotten. It is also interesting, incidentally, that the old hag remembers Henchard first by the details of his trade-gear — the cord-jacket and tool-basket. Prepared in this way, we wait for Henchard's reappearance at last as curiously as Susan Newson and Elizabeth-Jane. Interestingly, this second portrait goes far beyond the first in detail:

> Facing the window, in the chair of dignity, sat a man of about forty years of age; of heavy frame, large features, and commanding voice; his general build being rather coarse than compact. He had a rich complexion, which verged on swarthiness, a flashing black eye and dark, bushy brows and hair. When he indulged in an occasional loud laugh at some remark among the guests, his large mouth parted so far back as to show to the rays of the chandelier the two and thirty sound white teeth that he obviously still could boast of.
>
> That laugh was not encouraging to strangers; and hence it may have been well that it was rarely heard. Many theories may have been built upon it. It fell in well with conjectures of a temperament which would have no pity for weakness, but would be ready to yield ungrudging admiration to greatness and strength. Its producer's personal goodness, if he had any, would be of a very fitful cast — an occasional almost oppressive generosity rather than a mild and constant kindness. (M.C., pp. 37–38)

Hardy's achievement here is to build up rather than to exhaust energy in his subject. It stands at the opposite pole from the naturalist mode of portraiture, where an accurate enough delineation all but robs the character of any power to act, much less to interest us. Just as, earlier, Hardy had concentrated our attention on Henchard's thick-cord and fustian, so here he makes his evening dress set forth the peculiar strength of the man. Henchard's personal decoration, the "expanse of frilled shirt showing on his broad breast; jewelled studs, and a heavy gold chain" (M.C., p. 38), serve to measure the solidity of Henchard's character and standing.

The entire episode is impregnated with a suspicion of thunder: the two women walk into the middle of the controversy aroused by Henchard's bad wheat. The idea of bad bread is somehow deeply disturbing: it is associated obscurely with the evil and menace that pervade the whole novel. Henchard the mayor is also the biggest local corn-dealer. In some way, then, he is responsible for polluting the very staff of life. Moreover, he never escapes the evil underside of the civilized mind. Again and again, he is caught up with the gross or sinister aspects of the old rusticity. In general, the old country ways are associated with evil in *The Mayor of Casterbridge:* Mother Cuxsom, the furmity-woman, Mixen Lane, the prophet Fall, the skimmington ride – such characters and customs have little of the rich charm they had held in *Under the Greenwood Tree.* A strange kind of evil knowing is part of the atmosphere in Casterbridge – in contrast to the Roman squareness of the city itself. One senses behind this the old struggles that made England what it was: the British against the English, the English against the Romans, the Saxons against the Normans. Henchard's name and perhaps his character (he reminds one vaguely of Scott's Bryan, and is defined at one moment by a French phrase) are Norman. For all the refinements of their later courts, the Normans were skin-deep pirates. Henchard never frees himself from the ancient superstitions.

Hardy chose well when he made Henchard a corn-factor.

The whole business of milling and bread-making is encrusted with legends of poltergeists. As always, the evil, like the source of much of what is genuinely good in Hardy, permeates the speech of the rustics. We have already had "furmity", and "skimmington" — oddly horrible words to my ear. In a dialogue among the townsfolk immediately before the extended portrait of Henchard as mayor, one of them says to Susan: "But you must be a real stranger here not to know what's made the poor volks' plim like blowed blathers this week?" (M.C., p. 35). The verb "plim", of course, does the work with the witty pungency that characterizes all Hardy's dialect writing. One is tempted to regret that he ever abandoned it. Yet he never regarded it as at all appropriate to "serious" characters, apart from the diluted speech of Tess and Marty South. He knew that his readers — even himself — could not have focussed the serious issues if encouraged to patronize: there is much that is first-rate in dialect literature, but nothing really major.

Hereafter, the treatment of Henchard does not extend our knowledge of him: it merely follows with effortless accuracy the movements of his mind, or, since we do not in Hardy often think of that abstraction, of his very being: character is conveyed, as in *Wuthering Heights,* as much through gesture and physical action as through interior monologue or parallelistic commentary. From now on, behavioural details confirm the character laid out in the opening chapters. "Henchard's face darkened", "Henchard's face had become still more stern at these interruptions"; best of all, perhaps, when Farfrae's note reaches him, "The nettled, clouded aspect which had held possession of his face since the subject of his corn-dealings had been broached, changed itself into one of arrested attention. He read the note slowly, and fell into thought, not moody, but fitfully intense, as that of a man who has been captured by an idea" (M.C., p. 45).

The problem which had given rise to these changes in Henchard's mien, and to the solution of which Farfrae's note was a fated but casual contribution, itself contains the germ of the tragic narrative to come. Like the plague in *Oedipus Rex,* the popular dissatisfaction over the bad bread effectively charges the atmosphere with tension and dissonance. Like Oedipus, again, Henchard himself sets in motion the machinery that leads directly to his own destruction: by calling in Farfrae, Henchard initiates the process of his own downfall and disgrace. The scandal of the wife-sale is still in our minds, of course, so that the violent headstrong pride of "the Man of Character" serves to qualify our sense of the worldly success he has purchased with his resolve and determination. In fact, all of these aspects of Henchard help pack the man with the genuinely tragic potential. The material circumstances, too, are essential to the tragic myth: it is an important part of tragedy that the hero be seen in the full stature of worldly and material success. The kingly state of Greek and Shakespearean heroes is, in part of least, the pre-mercantile equivalent of supreme success and power. Hardy is one of the few artists of the capitalist era who have succeeded in translating the semi-mystical aura of the classical tragic hero into satisfactory commercial terms. Yet he manages also to make the action of his tragic myth derive wholly from the facts of Henchard's psychological constitution. And the nemesis that visits him is no agent of Fate, but his own psychological anti-type. His nemesis, of course, as always in tragedy, is strictly himself. But this is a truism, knowing rather than informative. The form the nemesis inhabits to bring Henchard face to face with himself is Donald Farfrae; and the meeting of the two is, as I have observed, the most direct confrontation in Hardy's fiction of two fundamentally antithetical types. (Later, it will be possible to make the comparison with Melville's *Billy Budd.*) If we follow Hardy's extraordinarily close narrative, we see how organically he persuades his action to shape itself.

Immediately before the decisive act of calling upon Farfrae in his hotel, Henchard is seen scornfully sober amidst the after-dinner drunkenness: "Only Henchard did not conform to these flexuous changes; he remained stately and vertical, silently thinking." This amounts to a direct contrast of the two sides of Hardy's type-transversal: on one side the "flexuous", on the other — for the moment in the ascendant — the "stately and vertical". Now in the context of Hardy's entire fiction to date, and of the preceding treatment of Henchard, we cannot read these phrases casually or lightly. Henchard's stateliness and his verticality cohere with all the other aspects of his character: we have seen his defiance, his hectic intensity under the pressure of alcohol, and his subsequent severity towards himself. We must bear in mind the glimpses Hardy gave us of the way he walked, and of the facial angle, "so slightly inclined as to be almost vertical". All this is contrasted with the "flexuousness" of the drinkers around the mayor in this scene. "Flexuous", of course, is a radical term in Hardy's psychological vocabulary. Its occurrence here seems at first sight odd, if not casual. Certainly, it usually indicates a positive quality — a capacity to bend, to move, to let life ride — something conspicuously absent in characters like Boldwood, Knight, and now, Henchard. Here, it is "silly". The detail adds to what has already begun to emerge as a dangerously decided character. It remains for Hardy to introduce him to the agent of his destruction.

Farfrae appears first through the eyes of Henchard's daughter, Elizabeth-Jane. The conception of Elizabeth-Jane herself owes something to Charlotte Brontë's governess-teachers. Like Jane Eyre and Lucy Snow, she inhabits the penumbral regions of society and the emotions, neither pretty nor brilliant enough to attract Farfrae very strongly, or at least to prevent herself being readily eclipsed by Lucetta Templeman. The treatment of the character in some respects surpasses Charlotte Brontë's. Elizabeth-Jane spices the Brontëesque brusqueness — the laconicism which is so attractive in Charlotte Brontë's Yorkshire heroines — with a touch of real malice, an almost witchlike lucidity of intuition which in the end owes much of its penetration to the bitterness of her experience. To the end of the book, when she has lost Farfrae to Lucetta, she remains a "dumb deep-feeling great-eyed creature". In this early scene, Hardy exploits these dumb feelings to colour his second male character, Donald Farfrae. He also succeeds in presenting that most elusive of simplicities — love at first sight. It is another of his secret watchings, though entirely without the element of voyeurism that runs through many of these incidents in Hardy's earlier fiction. Without any special emphasis, Hardy permits us to watch Elizabeth-Jane fall in love with the young Scot. She has already noticed him, in the street outside the inn when Henchard is at dinner. Now, helping out at a lesser inn, she finds herself serving him with his dinner:

> When she entered, nobody was present but the young man himself — the same whom she had seen lingering without the windows of the Kings Arms Hotel. He was now reading idly a copy of the local paper, and was hardly conscious of her entry, so that she looked at him quite coolly, and saw how his forehead shone where the light caught it, and how nicely his hair was cut, and the sort of velvet-pile or down that was on his skin at the back of his neck, and how his cheek was so truly curved as to form part of a globe, and how clearly drawn were the lids and lashes which hid his bent eyes. (M.C., pp. 52–53)

It is amazing that so much critical attention is focussed on Hardy's theory of Nature, on his pessimism, or his evolutionary meliorism, when the overriding impression the novels give is of a man to whom people were more attractive and interesting than anything else, for whom love was a reality, not a literary abstraction, and relationships the most important thing in human life. To account for the force of *The Mayor of Casterbridge,* we have to look not to the conception of the natural world, nor to any deterministic power, but to the nature of the psychological and emotional complexes at work in it, the flux and re-flux of attraction and revulsion. The saddest thing in Hardy's novels is not death, or that we are ruled by an external force at large in the universe, but simply that we are often doomed to love one another.

Thus, in the present instance, we witness the touching inception of a doomed love. We don't have to be told, we need only follow the motions of the girl's eyes: Hardy changes the angle of narration, so that instead of watching a girl carrying a tray to an unknown man, we see through her eyes. It is impossible to say quite when we slide into her shoes, though the vocabulary after a while makes it clear that we have: experienced novelists after all are not in the habit of using words like "nice". So, she falls in love with him and there is nothing that she — or he for that matter — can do about it. And that, Hardy says, is what Fate is all about. The point is even more important when Henchard himself comes to love the Scot. The tragedy in a sense is under way from the moment that Henchard and Farfrae meet: Farfrae is Henchard's opposite as wholly as Billy Budd is Claggart's.

In a way, the meeting of Henchard and Farfrae is the centre-point of Hardy's entire fictional output: the psychological investigations of the previous fifteen years have clarified and hardened to such an extent that he can offer a profound and universal confrontation which seems to involve not so much individuals as universal principles. Yet of course the achievement of such a universality presupposes the completely successful realization of the relationship in ordinary human terms. In such terms, the relationship between Henchard and Farfrae is crypto-homosexual. It is hard to find a suitable parallel elsewhere in English writing. The friendship of Japheir and Pierre in Otway's *Venice Preserved* — an obvious candidate — degenerates into slightly vulgar military camaraderie. The relationship between Steerforth and David in *David Copperfield* is more innocent and schoolboyish; so is David Balfour's hero-worship of Allen Breck in *Kidnapped,* though the love is returned there all right. In *Billy Budd,* the love is too intense, and becomes homicidal. The love of Henchard for Farfrae is more mature than any of these, and more deeply rooted. Yet it is one-sided: it is Henchard's love *for* the Scot that launches the

unbalanced relationship. Farfrae never fully reciprocates the
Mayor's affection, and this one-sidedness is central to the
meaning of the whole novel. The types represented in the two
men are differentiated at all levels.

It is possible, I have observed, that Hardy's work will
eventually enable us to speculate on the nature of a
specifically "tragic" personality. The great nineteenth-century
heroes, I also observed, have a common ancestor — Milton's
Satan. In the nineteenth century, the tragic and the Satanic
become more or less completely identified. Hardy's Henchard
is the most searching account yet given of the Satanic
personality.

The sombre, swarthy aspect of Henchard (with its
correlatives in Milton, Byron, Melville, and Emily Brontë) has
already been sufficiently stressed above, I think. What of his
anti-type? What, by contrast, can Farfrae's personality tell us
about Henchard? In the first place we have the glimpses
vouchsafed us through the eyes of Elizabeth-Jane. Farfrae is
further described as "a young man of remarkably pleasant
aspect", as being "ruddy and of a fair countenance",
"bright-eyed and slight in build". His first action in the novel
is to smile "impulsively". Because of the consistent
psychological system governing the whole Hardy canon, these
sparse details of Farfrae's appearance — "slight in build",
"bright-eyed", "ruddy" — create not merely a live human
being but also a psychic opposite to Henchard.

Farfrae catalyzes all that is warm and generous in
Henchard. Elizabeth-Jane (taking over the Nelly Deane role of
the recorder) notes the mayor's "tigerish affection" for the
Scot; when Henchard presses Farfrae to dine with him it is
with "impetuous cordiality". The "quiet eye" of Henchard's
daughter registers the growth of an intense and powerful
relationship: "She saw that Donald and Mr. Henchard were
inseparables. When walking together Henchard would lay his
arm familiarly on his manager's shoulder, as if Farfrae were a
younger brother, bearing so heavily that his slight figure bent
under the weight" (M.C., pp. 107–8).

The polarity is defined still more precisely a few sentences later. "The poor opinion, and but ill-concealed, that he entertained of the slim Farfrae's physical girth, strength, and dash, was more than counterbalanced by the immense respect he had for his brains" (M.C., p. 108).

I doubt if many readers of the novel really like Farfrae, in spite of the fact that we are meant to; everybody in Casterbridge does, and two women fall in love with him. The reasons are interesting. They relate, negatively, to Henchard's Satanism. Like Ahab and Heathcliff, Henchard coerces and bullies everybody around him and breaks every law of liberal decency. Yet when he dies, we weep. Farfrae, in contrast, does not really respond to Henchard's affection. He remains aloof, outside any ultimate emotional engagement, and this applies even to his courtship of Elizabeth-Jane and Lucetta. His courtship of Lucetta in fact is hardly more impassioned than his initial, purely reasoned, suit of Elizabeth-Jane. This is to oversimplify: there is the scene in Lucetta's room when his eyes fill with tears at the pathetic scene enacted below them on the pavement between the two young lovers; and he has his nostalgic Scottish songs about "haem". But on the whole we accept Lucetta's view of him as "free from Southern extremes. We common people are either all one way or the other — warm or cold, passionate or frigid. You have both temperatures going on in you at the same time" (M.C., p. 191).

A well-conceived piece of work, in fact — to reduce him to his literary essentials — avoiding the pitfalls of the critical romanticism that so often makes him merely cold. His is an emotional but equable disposition, genuinely moved on occasion; he is far from being the business-machine he is sometimes taken to be. (If he were this, indeed, the book could hardly have the immense power it has.) Yet, finally, we find Henchard's all-or-nothing will more sympathetic — more heroic simply. It is his crash we wait for. Henchard suffers: Farfrae is not the stuff tragedy is made of.

Farfrae attracts Lucetta immediately and more genuinely

than Henchard ever had. She makes it clear in fact that that embarrassing liaison grew out of loneliness rather than attraction. The types are beautifully counterpoised: Lucetta — as her name (*lux* plus gallic feminity) suggests — belongs with Hardy's Southern temperaments: "a dark-haired, large-eyed, pretty woman, of unmistakably French extraction on one side or the other" (M.C., p. 179). She moves with "innate grace" and is defined by Hardy's favourite "flexuous", an adjective whose connotations vary, but mainly centre on sensuousness or abandon. And it is her view of Farfrae that best fixes him. She sees not an intelligent Scottish businessman but a young man with "hypoborean crispness, stringency, and charm, as of a well-braced musical instrument" (M.C., p. 189). "Hypoborean" is the key-word, suggesting a definite and conscious antithesis with the "Tartarean gloom" of Henchard. Again the parallel with *Billy Budd* and *Moby Dick* is inescapable, though the confrontation in each case serves a quite different spiritual aim. Claggart, Ahab, and Henchard are all destroyed by what they most love and most fear — the pure, the absolute, or the successful. For what is perhaps most distinctive about Farfrae, as opposed, say, to Billy Budd, is that he represents that which will succeed, not through nastiness, or any drive in particular (though he has drive in plenty), but just because of what he is, exactly as Henchard fails — or destroys himself — because of what he is. It is more difficult to show how this is true of Farfrae, and this derives from the facts of the case: it is equally difficult to enlist the reader's sympathy for him, and for much the same reasons. What obtains in life does not necessarily obtain in our experience of life through literature. Few people would enjoy being pushed around and shouted at by Heathcliff, just as few sailors would willingly put up with Ahab's insane tyrannies. Yet it is not mere fantasy and self-deception that make us respond so deeply and warmly to these men in the pages of books. In the same way, the chances are that in life a man like Farfrae would be as popular as Hardy insists that he is, and that Henchard would be as strongly feared and hated as his bad temper makes him in Casterbridge. The truth is, I think, that Hardy had put his finger on a profound psychological truth in *The Mayor of Casterbridge*. And that is that men of a certain temperament, like Farfrae — "Hypoboreans", "once-born", in William James's terminology — accept the experience that comes their way, whether in the life of the emotions or of "business" (and what is "business", but a way of exercising the human organism in life?) and convert it naturally to the currency of their needs. Thus, Farfrae accepts Henchard's "friendship" (he would have been embarrassed probably at the word "love"), and the loss of it with about equal disturbance to his balance: in either case, he will think about it, adapt it to his life, and go on. If Henchard likes him then so much the better, if he turns against him, then, well, too bad — he must go somewhere else to work. Hence, his relatively easy change of mind when Henchard by sheer weight of personality persuades him to stay in Casterbridge. So with his emotional life, which is neither shallow nor superficial, but wholly experienced, accepted, and absorbed: he can adapt from Elizabeth-Jane to Lucetta without much more than a canny rethink. Nor is this just knowing which side his bread is buttered on — except in the profounder sense of being aware of what is the best course for his life to take. Hardy goes to great lengths to ensure that we do not think Farfrae either light or hard: he is several times shown to be emotional and easily reached by pathos — almost to the point of sentimentality.

However we choose to read *The Mayor of Casterbridge*, it cannot be as a morality in which the soulless New Man, Farfrae, prevails over the good old ways enshrined in Mike Henchard. Apart from anything else, the novel is pervaded, as I have already suggested, more strongly than any other of Hardy's works with the evil associated with "the old ways". Practically everything smacking of the old rusticity is steeped in evil ignorance, or the occult "knowledge" that civilization and enlightenment have become estranged from. To say it again, Henchard never escapes the old ways, and it is they that help bring him low. *The Mayor of Casterbridge* is both more modernistic and more timeless than the tempting Luddite reduction would suggest. Nothing in the book indicates that there is anything admirable in Henchard's rule-of-thumb way of doing business. On the contrary, it becomes symbolic of his dogged, hell-bent Character, as dangerous in its generosity as in its anger. The first sound of his laughter through the hotel window at the ceremonial dinner remains in our memory: "That laugh was not encouraging to strangers; and hence it may have been well that it was rarely heard." And so it proves: Henchard's excessive love for Farfrae, like his spasmodic bursts of magnanimity towards his workmen and fellow citizens, is as inconsiderate of its object as his wrath.

Every act that leads to Henchard's eventual downfall in fact proceeds from "Character": his estrangement from Farfrae starts when the Scot objects to his bullying of Abel Whittle. This fateful incident itself derives from his contemptuous refusal to honour the superior claims of Jopp to be his manager once Farfrae has arrived on the scene.

To place the significant incidents in the process in fact is to retail the structural skeleton of the work, with hardly a single omission. The unvarying ease of the movement, the plausibility of the mercantile intrigue, the part played by minor figures like Jopp, the unforced persuasiveness of the rising of Farfrae's and the setting of Henchard's star, the overwhelming sense of there being astral forces at work – all this makes for the final cathartic impact. The dialectic of Henchard's fall can be followed as a constant interaction of violence, impulsiveness, and inflexibility, so that the whole grows inevitably out of the man's psychological make-up. Perhaps the detail which brings the whole conception of Henchard closest to the classical psychology of Humours and temperaments is that of the "rich *rouge et noir* of his countenance". The redness – redness of passion and choler – is fatally associated with his headstrong lunge towards self-immolation. Like Claggart's, finally, Henchard's eyes hold the secret of his strange power: "His dark pupils which always seemed to have a red spark in them, though this could hardly be a physical fact — turned round under his dark brows until they rested upon her figure. 'Now, then, what is it, my young woman?' he asked blandly" (M.C., p. 79).

It is this profound and exact knowledge of Henchard's psychical constitution that makes for the inevitability and the bitterness of his death, a death that finally redeems the moody violence of his life, so that Hardy can take in his stride the dangerously self-conscious tragic image with which he attempts to define him: "A dark ruin, obscured by the shade from his own soul up-thrown."

The Miltonic overtones again emphasize the almost theological reading demanded by Hardy's diction: that Henchard and Farfrae are Manichean poles cannot be doubted. In everything opposed, in texture, colouring, consistency, build, timbre, the two men face one another across the void, Henchard turned towards the dark, Farfrae towards the sun.

9. *Tess of the d'Urbervilles* (1891)

Tess of the d'Urbervilles announces in its title a preoccupation with lineage that meant much to Hardy; birth, breeding, and descent distil an aura of grace that is translated naturally into Hardy's own habitual psychological terms. Yet no one who reads the book is really interested in the fact that Tess is of aristocratic descent, and the idea is beautifully satirized by Hardy himself, in the figure of "Sir John" Durbeyfield, Tess's father. Nothing, moreover, derives from the aspirations enkindled in the Durbeyfields by the vicar at the beginning of the book, except perhaps a little ease of plot-manipulation here and there. Yet Alec d'Urberville's nastiness plainly relates to his being an *arriviste,* a pretentious, vulgar upstart, while Angel Clare's confused liberalism continually reverts to the subject of birth and privilege, now deploring the decline of the ancient stock, now impressed by its achievements. It is strange how these ideas hover over Hardy's book, without ever settling anywhere, yet supplying a kind of unifying preoccupation.

Fundamentally, the "tragedy" of Tess has nothing whatever to do with birth, lineage, or anything else outside what Hardy is beginning to see more and more sombrely as the fatal facts of personality. We have seen how in the great novels leading up to *Tess,* the serious action has sprung from the way people are made. Henchard, Eustacia Vye, Winterborne — these characters are destroyed not by a malign external force, or by their refusal to submit to Nature (whatever that could mean), but through the chemistry of their own beings, and their interaction with others. Moreover, Hardy's own "pessimism" both created this vision and was created by it. What we can say to allay the paradox is that neither a doctrine of critical self-help ("You see, if *only* he hadn't done that, he would have been all right") nor a straight determinism defines Hardy's *Weltanschauung:*

> As flies to wanton boys are we to th' gods —
> They kill us for their sport.

Gloucester's couplet could serve — apparently — as an epigraph to works like *Tess.* Yet no one feels inclined to label Shakespeare a "pessimist" or a "fatalist". Like Shakespeare's, Hardy's greatness lies in a comprehensive duality of vision; he sees that tragedy is not to be avoided, but he does not therefore see life as a mechanical, predetermined pattern in which choice is illusory, and praise or blame inapposite.

It is no less misguided to analyze *Tess of the d'Urbervilles* in terms of the heroine's moral "weaknesses", as John Holloway by and large does, or to deplore her weak-willed sliding into the "typical rural fatalistic acceptance", with Roy Morrell. No one, surely, imagines that Hardy's great book has been made obsolete by certain subsequent improvements in social tolerance, or by greater moral and sexual emancipation, or even by dispelling rustic ignorance. If our only conclusion from reading *Tess of the d'Urbervilles* is that Tess should have had the courage or the strength to disregard the law and convention, then we must think it shallow and moralistic, something left behind with L'il Em'ly and the early D. W. Griffith. If it is the great book I and many other of its readers think it is, it must be concerned with deeper matter than Victorian narrow-mindedness, and tell a more interesting story than good-girl-gone-wrong. For one thing, we cannot be at all sure that our sexual mores represent a real improvement of those of the Victorians. For another, major art is never to be explained in such simple-minded terms.

This point emerges as clearly from *Tess* as from *The Mayor; Tess* is a great book because we feel at the centre the presence of a human being worthy of suffering. I have already referred to what is almost a distinct species of humanity in Hardy — those who constitutionally, and, as it were, inevitably, suffer, gather suffering, and translate it by a kind of metabolic process into themselves. This account must be modified slightly, in view of what Hardy achieves in characters like Grace Melbury and Sue Bridehead. But the modification need not take the form of a retraction of what has been said about Henchard and Tess, but on the contrary, of a further clarification and refinement of basic terms that confirm them anew. What is beginning to emerge is a fundamental distinction between those who suffer, like Henchard, by gathering weight to themselves, and those who, like Grace Melbury — and later Sue Bridehead — exasperate themselves into nervous exhaustion.

Any account of Tess Durbeyfield that contents itself with either totting up her strengths and weaknesses, or lamenting her passivity before the law, is to be ruled out of court immediately, therefore. Tess fits into and grows out of the complex evolution that has been governing the course of Hardy's novels all along. Her character, her identity, *is* the book; *it* is what Hardy has to say. Perhaps we can best clarify the point by asserting that Tess's "weakness" — the quality in her that makes her yield to Alec d'Urberville — is precisely what makes her herself, and what confers upon the book a greatness it could hardly otherwise have had. It is in her "sensuality" that we shall find the meaning of Tess, not in her lapsed nobility. The "blood" notion serves mainly as satire, as when Joan, Tess's mother, assures Sir John:

> "What's her trump-card? Her d'Urberville blood, you mean?"
> "No, stupid; her face — as t'was mine." (T.D., p. 63)

Joan's riposte in fact is a wry commentary on the whole book. For *Tess* is steeped in the evil old ways. It begins, indeed, with two episodes rooted in the past — her father's new conception of himself as Sir John Durbeyfield, heir to the ancient line of d'Urberville, and the Marlott walking-party, a survival of the old May-dance. We have noted the aura of evil hanging over the old rusticity in *The Mayor of Casterbridge*. Again and again, the talk of the rustics turns upon legend and witchcraft.

Some such tint of evil — in the sense of a semi-occult, semi-forbidden knowledge — is associated with Tess herself. It is not accidental that our first glimpse of her is as a votive sister of the local "cerealia" — a virgin on the threshold of experience; nor that her home hugs close the ancient optimism of the peasantry — a faith in the irrational that offsets the patent inauspiciousness of the present. Tess clearly inherits much from her mother, as the mother herself confesses. From her Tess takes the sensuality, the connection with the occult, and the good looks — the three things being closely related. Joan herself is a magnificent creation — a mixture of ignorance and insight, of vigorous maternalism and coarse sensuality.

Invariably, when using the folk-idiom, Hardy writes with a racy naturalness that sometimes makes an embarrassing contrast with the stilted poise of his official style. His comic dialogues dramatize brilliantly, and are instinct with an old wisdom-cum-obtuseness which draws upon a store of stories and wizardries. Often, as I have observed of *The Mayor*, this is linked with the obscene, the opposite of the warm good-heartedness one might have predicted from literary peasants. Yet although this is so in *Tess*, it is also true that there is something ambiguous in the awareness it reveals in Hardy of realms of experience that somehow undercut the preoccupations of his serious writing. To put it crudely, why does Hardy so often seem to be so horror-struck at the facts of sexual life? Was it simply the Victorian "double-think" — that what was all right among the servants was horrible for decent people? Perhaps. But there is a deeper reason, I think, and this reason "explains" Tess. In short, just as *The Mayor of Casterbridge* dramatizes the Satanic rebellion, so *Tess* is the fable of the Fall, the loss of innocence. And this is the universal theme that cannot be made obsolete, no matter how sexual mores evolve.

The point is of some importance, especially bearing in mind the sort of irritation D. H. Lawrence felt at the book. Tess is so alive, physically: why does Hardy want to whip out of her what should yield her her greatest experience in life? The subject is a little more complex than that suggests, admittedly; and to discover in what way, we must turn as usual to the relationships. Tess possesses a richness and a redness that unequivocally denote a species of the passion that dominated Michael Henchard. Henchard's passion drove him to self-destruction: he was possessed of a hectic carelessness that made his generosity as dangerous as his anger. Tess's blood, too, is Norman, and her passion is the passion not of pride but sensuality: "Tess Durbeyfield at this time of her life was a mere vessel of emotion untinctured by experience. The pouted-up deep red mouth, to which this syllable was native, had hardly as yet settled into its definite shape, and her lower lip had a way of thrusting the middle of her top one upward, when they closed together after a word" (T.D., pp. 14–15). It is the word "untinctured", with its Keatsian glow, that best suggests the richness of her being. Throughout the book, she is defined in terms of redness: Hardy observes in this first chapter of the novel how her "mobile peony mouth and large innocent eyes added eloquence to colour and shape. She wore a red ribbon in her hair" (T.D., p. 13).

Mingled with the sensuality is another quality, of course, a suffusing beauty of person we can only call Soul. But this too is subtly associated with the capacity for the occult and even the transcendent we have noted in her mother. Joan's "soul" reeks of small-village black magic, but it is real enough in its own way. Hardy both satirizes and acknowledges the quality in the scenes at Rolliver's: "A sort of halo, an occidental glow, came over life then. Troubles and other realities took on themselves a metaphysical impalpability, sinking into mere mental phenomena for serene contemplation, and no longer stood as pressing concretions which chafed body and soul" (T.D., p. 24). There is something else, too, that Hardy wants us to grasp about Joan's capacity for abandonment: "She felt a little as she had used to feel when she sat by her now wedded husband in the same spot during his wooing, shutting her eyes to his defects of character and regarding him only in his ideal presentation as lover" (T.D., p. 24). I have noted elsewhere Hardy's ability to transmit the quality of possession, either by music or dancing or alcohol. In *Under the Greenwood Tree* this quasi-mystical possession was associated with the demonic and with a source of vitality and non-rational awareness to which the new generations of daylight reformers are innately hostile. We must be careful here to avoid the reformist fallacy, that somehow we should throw off the inhibitions and repressions of the new shallowness, and get down (or back) to raw basic living. Hardy gives us little support for this view of things. As *The Mayor of Casterbridge* showed, he really found the old knowledge both disquieting and distasteful. Hardy understood the demonic as few of his English contemporaries did; nor did he panic at his conclusions, as James did in *The Turn of the Screw,* for instance. There is both loss and gain in evolution: in developing from Henchard to Farfrae, mankind loses some of its attractiveness, but it also loses its fears and ghosts. Moreover, of course, there is always the possibility of sheer self-deception in the notion of a past Golden Age, rich in sensual wisdom and demonic wit. But such illusions themselves tell us much about our idea of evil. What is important is not to brand evil and outlaw it, but to break it down into its components. This, I believe, is Hardy's aim in the Wessex novels. Tess Durbeyfield, one of the great "innocent" characters in fiction, is in fact deeply involved with much that has its roots in what we usually call evil.

Joan Durbeyfield's *Compleat Fortune Teller* is interesting in this light:

> A curious fetichistic fear of this grimy volume on the part of her mother, prevented her ever allowing it to stay in the house all night . . . Between the mother, with her fast-perishing lumber of superstitions, folk-lore, dialect and orally-transmitted ballads, and the daughter with her trained National teachings and Standard knowledge under

an infinitely Revised Code, there was a gap of two
hundred years as ordinarily understood. (T.D., pp.
24–25)

It is tempting to conclude from this passage that Hardy means
to indicate in Joan's folklore if not a wisdom at least a
capacity for handling, absorbing, and not being hurt by "the
facts of life". The tart ironies on the "Standard knowledge"
and the "infinitely Revised Code" suggest that the conclusion
would be consistent with Hardy's plan, though it would by no
means exhaust it. It would also go far to explain the raciness
of the dialect passages in Hardy: jacketted by
bourgeois-establishment censoriousness, Hardy's prose becomes
stilted and awkward. Yet the notion is put to flight
energetically when Tess goes to fetch her parents at Rolliver's,
when, "even to her mother's gaze, the girl's young features
looked sadly out of place amid the alcoholic vapours which
floated there, as no unsuitable medium for wrinkled
middle-age" (T.D., p. 31). Whatever Hardy felt about the old
peasant life – a strange mixture of common sense and
superstition – he was certainly in no danger of idealizing it.
There is a wide gulf between the alcoholic vapours and the
transfigured sexuality of Joan's world, and the genuinely
transcendental capacities of her daughter. These are first
revealed in the stories about the stars Tess spins to her
brother, Abraham: "They sometimes seem to be like the
apples on our stubbard-tree. Most of them splendid and sound
– a few blighted" (T.D., p. 35). I personally am far from
convinced by Tess's stoical asseveration that our star is one of
the blighted ones, or the narrative engineering which almost
immediately after results in the death of the horse (a
tremendous blow to the family). Such things reveal an
artistically dubious Hardy.

But these are mere hints and guesses. Nothing very definite
is known about Tess until we see her confronted by Alec
d'Urberville. Now the writing before Alec's appearance has
been thick with fatalism, with vague gestures towards
Providence, of which the "blighted star" passage is fairly

representative. Tess's determination to regard herself as a murderess of the family horse partakes of this doom-consciousness. When Alec d'Urberville lounges into the novel, smoking a cigar, a much more definite step is taken:

> He had an almost swarthy complexion, with full lips, badly moulded, though red and smooth, above which was a well-groomed black moustache with curled points, though his age could not be more than three or four-and-twenty. Despite the touches of barbarism in his countours, there was a singular force in the gentleman's face, and in his bold rolling eye. (T.D., p. 40)

The social allegory, which at one level at least *Tess of the d'Urbervilles* articulates, is worth outlining: the barbarian from the dark North (in its infernal significance) buys a noble name, and seduces the genuine inheritrix of the line he has bought. Shortly before the fateful meeting of the two, Hardy lays out the terrain:

> the soft azure landscape of The Chase — a truly venerable tract of forest-land, one of the few remaining woodlands in England of undoubted primaeval date, wherein Druidical mistletoe was still found on aged oaks, and where enormous yew-trees, not planted by the hand of man, grew as they had grown when they were pollarded for bows. All this sylvan antiquity, however, though visible from The Slopes, was outside the immediate boundaries of the estate. (T.D., p. 44)

The social allegory fits well in this scheme: the antiquity of The Chase lies outside the *nouveau riche* estate. And it is in The Chase that Tess is seduced, so that the name itself acquires a wry double meaning. As we shall see, The Chase has an entirely different atmosphere and function from the sylvan world of Hintock in *The Woodlanders*.

There is not much to be defended in Hardy's treatment of Alec d'Urberville (the only character in the book, perhaps, to get out of hand in the second half of the story). But there is no doubt of the effectiveness of his role in the fable. Few mature novelists would have risked "Well, my beauty", as an opening line for a character with a "bold rolling eye". Alec d'Urberville certainly toured up and down the Mississippi during the golden age of Hollywood, and still probably does his stint in *Woman's Own* serials. I do not feel particularly inclined to praise Hardy for taking the chance; it is one of a few too many, which undermine Alec long before his gory end. Yet the initial grasp of the type is strong and sure. Certainly, the characterization is confident – not least in the detail of "badly moulded" lips.

But it is principally in terms of Tess that Alec d'Urberville succeeds. Note, for example, the skill with which the scene that follows is handled; it is a kind of love-dance, before the eventual seduction. With what delicacy Hardy suggests Tess's utterly involuntary response, her real but inadequate protestations, when he wants to put the first strawberry in her lips: " 'Nonsense!' he insisted; and in a slight distress, she parted her lips and took it in. They had spent some time wandering desultorily thus, Tess eating in a half-pleased, half-reluctant state whatever d'Urberville offered her" (T.D., p. 48). Hardy's generalized commentary on the scene is of the utmost importance: "In the ill-judged execution of the well-judged plan of things the call seldom produces the comer, the man to love rarely coincides with the hour for loving" (T.D., p. 50). And further, placing the episode right at the centre of his entire scheme, he speculates: "We may wonder whether at the acme and summit of the human progress these anachronisms will become corrected by a finer intuition, a closer interaction of the social machinery than that which now jolts us round and along; but such completeness is not to be prophesied, or even conceived as possible" (T.D., p. 50). It seems to me important here that Hardy should speak of a "finer intuition" – implying the objective existence of objective emotional data. One intuits – as one knows and sees – only what is actually out there in the world. Hardy does not refer to loving, or even feeling, but to intuiting – i.e. recognizing an appropriate emotional correlative for oneself.

His language, beyond all doubt, here implies that if the plan of things were good (he clearly has in mind an evolutionary model of something imperfect struggling to realize its own best possibility, and to eliminate its own grossness), then we would not make these fatal blunders of judgment about the people with whom we become involved. These blunders Hardy sees as radical to human unhappiness. This view clearly rests upon the basic psychological scheme I have been trying to outline in the earlier novels. The idea that each man or woman has a certain psycho-physical cast or mould (even if we call the entity Soul) itself implies that the choice of another human being to love springs from the disposition of this cast or mould. It means that there are laws of attraction and revulsion and that these laws govern much of human behaviour. Much of the value of Hardy's fiction lies in his profound understanding of these laws. His conception of Fate or Destiny undoubtedly expresses this attitude towards human psychology.

This makes some important points clear. In the first place, Hardy definitely implies that it was Tess's "bad luck" to be subjected to Alec d'Urberville's pressure at a time when the man she could have loved was not around. In fact, he states it as unequivocally as he well might. "In the ill-judged execution of the well-judged plan of things, the call seldom produces the comer, the man to love rarely coincides with the hour for loving" (T.D., p. 50). This degree of "fatalism" can never be wholly washed from the linen. There is no question of its all being in some way Tess's "fault", as though she ought to have been a bastion of resistance.

For why should it worry Tess particularly, being wooed by Alec? The answer is simple, and springs from the entire psychological ordination of Hardy's novels: because she recognized in him some affinity with herself, because she responded to him in some measure, because her fundamental sensualism corresponds to his. In other words, because they were, in an important respect, of the same type.

People do not always, or even usually, find their own type

attractive. For one thing, people have spiritual needs, drives, affinities of enormous variety, that are often not satisfied by simple type-correspondence. For another, there is the familiar "attraction of opposites" — a cliché of little value now, but of which one can perceive the origination in fact. Often, there is a rightness about type-affinities. Giles and Marty, in *The Woodlanders,* for example, simply "went together". But Giles did not love Marty. By and large, his attraction towards Grace was more usual. The otherness of the other, perhaps, is the first prerequisite in sexual attraction. It is there in the crypto-homosexual love of Henchard for Farfrae. Again and again in Hardy, it is the tendency of relationship to cross the type-transversal: the "lymphatic" Eustacia Vye loves the light-in-build Damon Wildeve, for instance. Now Tess loves Angel Clare.

There is never the slightest shade of doubt that this is *the* relationship in the novel. From Tess's point of view, there is no one else. Why then, does Hardy subject her to d'Urberville, before she can establish real contact with him? Certainly not to consummate a "hard-luck" story, but in order to make this one point about her — she was a body as well as a soul. Although she never wavers in her love for Clare, and although Hardy seems to have regarded the strength of her attachment as sufficient to cement the relationship, in this one important respect, she has more in common with Alec d'Urberville. If we do not appreciate the reality of the pressure d'Urberville exerts on her, neither simply exploiting her frustration nor her social dependence, but insisting his sexuality on her until she yields and responds, we must fail, it seems to me, to do justice to the novel. If we do not see the seduction in this way, in these terms, then the novel is reduced to the level of melodrama. And our response shows that it is not this.

Hardy's handling of the episode surely makes this clear. It is, of course, the most decisive in the book, by far outweighing any of the minor diversions and accidents which threaten at times to inflect the course of the fable. There are three main phases in the seduction: the dance in

Chaseborough; the walk home through the moonlight with the workfolk, culminating in the fight from which Tess is rescued by Alec's arrival; and the seduction itself in the heart of The Chase. Hardy loads the scenes leading up to the incident with a heavy summer eroticism, in the midst of which Tess's isolation becomes more apparent to herself. Her distinction of bearing — her "soul" — is emphasized here, giving the Fall its maximum significance. She accompanies the workfolk to the weekly outing with an aloof fastidiousness, more than justified by the dance that brings it to its climax. The dance, as so often in Hardy, is vaguely evil and uncontrolled, and it is conceived overtly in terms of pagan mythology: the dancers are associated with the Bacchic underside to the human psyche: "Of the rushing couples, there could barely be discerned more than the highlights — the indistinctness shaping them to satyrs clasping nymphs — a multitude of Pans whirling a multitude of syrinxes; Lois attempting to elude Priapus, and always falling" (1912 edition, p. 78).[1] The process of possession transfigures them, translates them to a higher realm, one in which they are generalized, losing individuality. They become demiurges, only in the light of the lamp resolving themselves into the "homely personalities of her next-door neighbours". "Could Trantridge," Hardy then asks, "in two or three hours, have metamorphosed itself thus madly!" As usual, Hardy does not distinguish the "evil" possession of dancing from its transfiguring lift. Perhaps this is close to the heart of his sense of what evil is. Yet we must be careful not to idealize the thing: Hardy did not care much for this underside of the psyche. He preferred people sober, though he saw in the lower depths the source of a great deal of vitality. The weekly dance — with its highs — takes its place naturally in the workfolk's lives.

The dancing scares Tess slightly, for the scene is thick with a half-exciting, half-evil atmosphere, in which the possession and the sexuality ellide:

> Changing partners simply meant that a satisfactory
> choice had not as yet been arrived at by one or other of

the pair, and by this time every couple had been suitably matched. It was then that the ecstasy and dream began, in which emotion was a matter of the universe, and matter but an adventitious intrusion, likely to hinder you from spinning you from where you wanted to spin. (1912 edition, p. 79)

At this point, just where the prose threatens to take off into erotic rhapsody, Hardy brings things literally down to earth with a comic collision of the dancers. The sequence of events is wryly humorous: the dream ends on the floor, as it should. Hardy stages the whole episode — with d'Urberville's fortuitous appearance as a cigar-tip glowing in the dark — in order to set Tess in relation to the sexual intoxication she keeps aloof from. She refuses his offer of a ride home — the next of the Devil's bribes — though she admits herself flattered. Under the moonlight of the walk home, the transfiguration and possession of the workfolk are again conceived comically: an aura of release and sexual abandon adheres to the women, especially to the two sisters, nicknamed the Queens of Spades and Diamonds, both of whom have been d'Urberville's mistress, and are therefore rivals of the new favourite, Tess. Hardy's gift for rendering the peasant earthiness stands him in especially good stead here. Some of the sexuality of the Queens rubs off onto Tess, so that d'Urberville's reappearance at this point seems a little more than timely. Alec's rescue of Tess from the brawling sisters might have provided that external pressure of circumstances with which Hardy was often tempted to solve his technical problems. He almost suggests this at times here: "At any other moment of her life, she would have refused such proffered aid and company, as she had refused them several times before" (T.D., p. 84). But the scene ends with a strange serenity that militates against a simple-minded reading in terms of circumstances, or, at least, which compels us to interpret the pressure of circumstances in terms of the Devil's scheming: "The erratic motions seemed an inherent part of the irradiation, and the fumes of their breathing a component of the night's mist; and the spirit of the scene, and of the moonlight and of Nature, seemed harmoniously to mingle with the spirit of wine" (T.D., p. 83). Tone and rhythm here transmit an inner bliss that transcends the earlier mockery: the redeeming power of wine, of sensuality, of life, asserts itself through the grace of release. The workfolk are horrible, coarse and gross, but they wear haloes in the moonlight, and but for the brawl instigated by the Queens Tess would have been translated with them.

Hardy never at any point mitigates the coarseness of Alec d'Urberville, and at the moment of seduction, insists upon his total unworthiness of Tess's fineness of texture. (She is "sensitive as gossamer".) Yet it is not possible to accept Tess's seduction as other than the ancient myth — the loss of sexual innocence, the Fall — and this entails our acknowledging her own acquiescence in the event. Otherwise, there is really no loss of innocence at all, and the entire story is reduced to the level of Victorian pathos. Hardy's scene-setting guarantees the gravity of the act: "Darkness and silence ruled everywhere around. Above them rose the primaeval yews and oaks of The Chase, in which were poised gentle roosting birds in their last nap; and about them stole the hopping rabbits and hares" (T.D., p. 90). The writing has the deep calm of a Düreresque idyll, a paradisal solemnity that is at the same time desolatingly sad. Hardy does everything possible to allay the indignation of the Victorian reading public by making Tess as vulnerable as possible. ("But might some say, 'where was Tess's guardian Angel? Where was the providence of her simple faith?' " [T.D., p. 90].) By the inserted clause "might some say" Hardy dissociates himself from the sentimental clamour of this kind of pietism. Certainly, he sees the pathos of the situation as heightened immeasurably by the coarseness of d'Urberville, but it is a heightening of the pathos endemic to the myth — to the sexual initiation, no matter how, or by whom, performed. "It was to be. There lay the pity of it", Hardy observes. But the pity of it is reduced if it is not taken as universal, something that has no intrinsic relation to circumstances or Victorianism. Only compare the Gothic nightmare with which Dickens, as representative Victorian moralist, would have charged the "rape", with Hardy's paradisal, idyllic solemnity, and the point is placed beyond doubt.

Reference back to Tess's acquaintance with Alec, and to Hardy's treatment of her before, strengthens the point. One remembers Hardy's persistent reference to Tess's lips throughout Phase the First, her learning to whistle, with Alec looking on, savouring the pouting of her "full mouth". Then, we have this crucial interchange between them before the seduction:

> "I haven't offended you often by love-making?"
> "You have sometimes."
> "How many times?"
> "You know as well as I — too many times."
> "Every time I have tried?"
> She was silent. (T.D., pp. 84–85)

This admissive silence is followed by a fragment of nocturne:

> She was silent, and the horse ambled along for a considerable distance, 'till a faint luminous fog, which had hung in the hollows all the evening, became more general and enveloped them. It seemed to hold the moonlight in suspension, rendering it more pervasive than in clear air. (T.D., p. 85)

Beyond any doubt, the care Hardy has expended upon this scene raises the loss of Tess's virginity to a plateau of significance which by far transcends the level of pathetic melodrama. The Chase becomes a sacred grove, the seduction a religious rite, Alec d'Urberville — just for a while — the priest of initiation. A little over thirty years before Hardy wrote *Tess of the d'Urbervilles* George Eliot had allowed a similarly exalted tone to creep into a sternly moralistic account of the downfall of a foolish girl: *Adam Bede* leaves us in no doubt that Hetty Sorrel (black-eyed, petite, selfish, and passionate) is to be pitied and despised, and offers the worthy Dinah Morris for our admiration. Yet nothing in

George Eliot's treatment of Dinah Morris approaches the beauty and serenity of the scenes leading up to Hetty's seduction by Arthur Donnithorne. The general similarity of the two novels is unmistakable: in both, the incident is watched over by the ancient oaks of a Chase, in both the young squire has his way with the helpless working-girl; in both, too, the consequences are dire. But by far and away the most striking parallel is in the idyllic quality that suffuses the narration as the seduction is approached: Hetty's seduction, too, is like a religious ceremony. The Fir-tree Grove in which it takes place is seraphically transfigured; it becomes a "delicious labyrinthine wood", "a wood of beeches and limes, with here and there a light, silver-stemmed birch — just the sort of wood most haunted by the nymphs: you see their white sunlit limbs gleaming athwart the boughs, or peeping from behind the smooth-sweeping outline of a tall lime; you hear their soft liquid laughter — but if you look with a too sacreligious eye, they vanish behind the silvery beeches, they make you believe that their voice was only a running brooklet." This is the afternoon in the wood, "a still afternoon" when "destiny disguises her cold awful face behind a radiant veil". The evening is chill but equally rapt: "She hates the leveret that runs across her path: she hates everything that is not what she longs for." When he kisses her at last, he might be "a shepherd in Arcadia for aught he knows, he may be the first youth kissing the first maiden, he may be Eros himself, sipping the lips of Psyche — it is all one." Just a kiss. Yet, "There was no speaking for minutes after." Victorian convention demanded that the unspeakable begetting take place offstage; yet this surely is Hetty's loss of innocence. What else can explain the intensity of the writing, the use of the present tense, the powerful sense of regret "afterwards"?

> He walked right on into the Chase, glad to get out of the Grove, which surely was haunted by his evil genius. Those beeches and smooth limes — there was something enervating in the very sight of them; but the strong

> knotted old oaks had no bending langour in them — the
> sight of them would give a man some energy. Arthur lost
> himself among the narrow openings in the fern, winding
> about without seeking any issue, till the twilight
> deepened almost to night under the great boughs, and
> the hare looked black as it darted across his path.

Whatever we may think of George Eliot's puritanism, there is
no questioning the religious quality of the writing in these
pages — the exalted sensuality that makes the sexual union a
revered as well as feared end of human aspiration.

Something has happened, in both novels, that transcends
the level of sexual melodrama and social grief. The air of
solemnity before and after the event makes it impossible for
us to see it as anything less than mythopoeic.

If Michael Henchard is Hardy's Satan, Tess is his Eve.
Curiously enough, though it is consistent with her creator's
strange way of seeing things, she experiences Paradise only
after her Fall. The real significance of her lapse only strikes
her after she has fallen in love with Angel Clare at Talbothays
Dairy in the third Phase of the novel. In the second Phase,
Hardy is at pains to articulate a theory of consciousness
which is strikingly prophetic of Husserl's. After the birth of
her child, Tess interprets the aspect Nature happens to be
wearing at the given moment entirely in the light of her own
misery:

> On these lonely hills and dales her quiescent glide was of
> a piece with the element she moved in. Her flexuous and
> stealthy figure became an integral part of the scene. At
> times her whimsical fancy would intensify natural
> processes around her till they seemed a part of her own
> story. Rather they became a part of it; for the world is
> only a psychological phenomenon, and what they
> seemed, they were. (T.D., p. 107)

The last clauses of this passage put Hardy in line with
Schopenhauerian pessimism, but also with the philosophy of
intentionality being worked out by Brentano in Hardy's own
time, and by Edmond Husserl much later. Hardy's acute

understanding of the relationship between consciousness and "reality" is centrally important in the analysis of Tess after her fall. But — "what they seemed, they were": "reality" cannot be clapped inside the inverted commas at all. It is the Absolute Reality of the metaphysician that needs this sort of protection. Reality, Hardy asserts, is never without interpretation. Thus, Tess experiences the bitterness of her lapse in every moment:

> The midnight airs and gusts, moaning amongst the tightly wrapped buds and bark of the winter-twigs, were formulae of bitter reproach. A wet day was the expression of irremediable grief at her weakness in the mind of some vague ethical being whom she could not class definitely as the god of her childhood, and could not comprehend as any other. (T.D., p. 107)

The particularization of this idea — Tess's awareness of the social law she has broken — is therefore subsumed under the general law of consciousness, that reality is a creation of the perceiving ego.

The harvest-scene advances the time cinematically, that is by scene-presentation rather than sequential narrative. The prose conveys a powerful and moving rhythm of cyclical growth and transcendent evolution, restoring to Tess the ancient quality suggested in the "cerealia" of the opening chapters of the novel. She appears explicitly as an Old Testament matriarch, "the most flexuous and finely-drawn figure of them all". What the section principally imparts, indeed, is not the moralistic misery threatened in the title "Maiden No More", but just that surpassing majesty of the basic myth, at all times present in *Tess*, the universal myth of the loss of innocence. The harvesting ritual itself underscores the timelessness of the myth. It is more and more difficult to confine the tragedy to the social conventions of Victorian England. The Law, in fact, has taken on a decalogical significance. The law Tess feels herself to have transgressed is the law of God; thus, a law against herself. At every point, the vacillations of quality within the text make it clear that

this is the real purpose of the fable. Where the prose moves
deep and strong, we feel Hardy to be in touch with the
springs of the myth:

> In the afternoon and evening the proceedings of the
> morning were continued, Tess staying on till dusk with
> the body of harvesters. Then they all rode home in one
> of the largest wagons, in the company of a broad
> tarnished moon that had risen from the ground to the
> eastwards, its face resembling the outworn gold-leaf halo
> of some worm-eaten Tuscan saint. (T.D., p. 116)

Writing of this order — warm, rich, unstrained — alternates
with the shrill moralizing over the death of her child: "In the
blue of the morning that fragile soldier and servant breathed
his last, and when the other children awoke they cried
bitterly, and begged Sissy to have another pretty baby" (T.D.,
pp. 120–21). No one. ever wrote worse, more against his own
grain, or with less real interest in his subject, than Hardy
about children. Essentially, as *Jude the Obscure* later
emphasizes, Hardy's world is non-procreative; children are an
embarrassment, an irrelevancy — worse — a sign of the curse
over mankind. This blindness of Hardy's — compare Dickens's
marvellous sympathy with and intuitive understanding of
children — testifies more shockingly than any other aspect of
his art to his radical distaste for the physical side of human
existence.

   This shrill strain we can only regret, along with the episode
of the christening of the dead child, and the hanging of Little
Father Time in *Jude*. But there is a third strain, a vein of
abstract disquisition that does not break the fictional illusion,
yet is fascinating as philosophy. He returns to the
quasi-Husserlian view of consciousness I have referred to
above: "She was not an existence, an experience, a passion, a
structure of sensations, to anybody but herself. To all
humankind besides Tess was only a passing thought" (T.D., p.
115). So that her sufferings on the head of her neighbours'
censure of herself, are largely illusory — illusory but
inevitable. This is a hook there is no getting off, because that

is how consciousness is made. Our moral sense — our sense of guilt itself — is grounded in this quality of perception; our consciousness of reality is compact of everybody else's consciousness. Husserl calls it intersubjectivity: "Whatever holds good for me personally, also holds good as I know, for all other men whom I find present in my world-about-me."[2] The world — reality — despite all differences of angle and individuality is "an objective spatio-temporal fact-world" — "the world about us that there is for us all, and to which we ourselves nonetheless belong."[3]

Thus, when Hardy speculates about Tess's reactions to her situation on a desert island, where there would be no neighbours to censure her, we must not take it as a brief for supposing that he regarded her whole tragedy as merely brought about by the conventions: "Alone in a desert island would she have been .wretched at what had happened to her? . . . Not greatly . . . she would have taken it calmly, and found pleasures therein. Most of the misery had been generated by her conventional aspect, and not by her innate sensations" (T.D., pp. 115—16). The speculation certainly offers still more evidence of Hardy's profundity of thought; only George Eliot, in the English novel, thinks so clearly and penetratingly on an abstract plane. Nevertheless, the desert-island speculation has probably misled more readers of the book than anything else in it. What he says is, in one sense, perfectly true. On a desert island, she would have been outside the pale of the law, even God's law, perhaps. Would Milton have written *Paradise Lost* on a desert island? No. He would have found himself outside what Husserl calls the fact-world of intersubjectivity. His conscious world would have been different — as would Tess's moral sense. But Hardy's phrase — "she would have found pleasure therein" — implies another element in the situation than mere social censure; it implies that something was to be salvaged from something *un*pleasant, and this unpleasantness is the loss of innocence, her disturbing initiation with Alec. Her sexual fall constitutes an offence against herself, God, and the law, which cannot be reasoned away by talking about conventional morality. It is not fear of censure that dogs Tess, but her own sexual knowledge, her own sense of having fallen; and the force of this depends very largely upon her sense of having yielded out of her own sensualism.

The magnificent strength of the third Phase of the book begins to make us aware of the subtlety of Hardy's plan. For the Talbothays section surpasses anything Hardy ever achieved by way of natural sweetness of rhythm and fertility of invention. If Satan is a ruthless corn-factor, Eve is a dairymaid. No novelist without Hardy's background, one fancies, could have risked this parable.

Hardy's broad conception breathes beneficence, calm, and strength. It is regrettable I think that he should have committed himself at a crucial moment to one of his slightly grandiose cinemascopic panoramas, which, marvellously appropriate as it might have been to the world of Clym Yeobright and Eustacia Vye, here results in an almost pretentious stoicism, totally out of key with its context: "Not quite sure of her direction Tess stood still upon the hemmed expanse of verdant flatness, like a fly on a billiard-table of indefinite length, and of no more consequence to the surroundings than that fly" (T.D., p. 136). This is the sort of thing critics are apt to think of when the question of Hardy's philosophy is raised. Wrongly; for in the context, the sentence jars both technically and in conception, reducing the gentle yet powerful parable to the level of a facile humanism. Nothing else, either before or after, encourages or enables us to think of either Tess, or the rest of humanity, as fly-like. The obtrusiveness of thought matches the jerky change of focus it necessitates. The spectacular billiard-table certainly entails an eagle's-eye view, yet one is forced immediately after to zoom in, with nauseous abruptness, to focus the heron that flaps up at Tess's presence.

It is especially irritating that Hardy should have allowed this to happen at a stage when Tess is about to move in on the marvellous quiet rhythm of the Talbothays life. She has, as I have hinted, consistently been defined in Old Testament terms. A few paragraphs earlier, she has in fact with impressive casualness actually been identified with Eve:

> She has tried several ballads, but found them inadequate; till, recollecting the psalter that her eyes had so often wandered over of a Sunday morning before she had eaten of the tree of knowledge, she chanted: "O ye Sun and Moon . . . O ye Stars . . . Ye Green Things upon the Earth . . . ye Fowls of the Air . . . Beasts and Cattle . . . Children of Men . . . bless ye the Lord . . . Praise Him and magnify Him forever!" (T.D., p. 134)

Tess now finds peace — salvation of a kind — in work. The idea hardly recommends itself to this century. Yet Hardy's rhythm and tone-colour persuade us into acceptance of labour — digging and delving — as a valid mode of adjustment to suffering.

Quotation could be unintermittent, I think: the rhythm of milking, the cycle of the seasons, the slow movement of the cows, the luxuriance of the terrain, the strange isolated community life of the Dairy, the abundance of milk itself — everything contributes to an image of life and civilization that can, without pretentiousness or vagueness, be described as archetypal. Again, it does not seem quite right to call the mechanism symbolic. To introduce Tess, obsessed with her impurity and her sexual initiation, into a world dominated by the white purity of milk, cannot be absolved from a pathos bordering on the emblematic. One would do better to indicate Hardy's astuteness in choosing and interweaving the elements of the fable, so that each part gathers meaning from its relations to the rest, than indulge in such symbol-mongering, however. Thus, we can point to his deliberate counterpoising of the two Vales — the Vale of the Little Dairies (Blackmoor Vale, Tess's own), and the Vale of the Great Dairies, the Vale of the Froom:

> It lacked the intensely blue atmosphere of the rival vale,

and its heavy soils and scents; the new air was clear, bracing, ethereal.

The river itself, which nourished the grass and cows of these renowned dairies, flowed not like the streams in Blackmoor. Those were slow, silent, often turbid; flowing over beds of mud into which the incautious wader might sink . . . and vanish unawares. The Var waters were clear as the pure River of Life shown to the Evangelist, rapid as the shadow of a cloud, with pebbly shallows that prattled to the sky all day long. There the water-flower was the lily; the crow-foot here. (T.D., p. 133)

The new air, the River of Life — such details help to create the image of a parabolic landscape. In the significant passage immediately following this, Hardy describes Tess's alternations of mood:

Her face had latterly changed with changing states of mind, continually fluctuating between beauty and ordinariness, according as the thoughts were gay or grave. One day she was pink and flawless; another pale and tragical. When she was pink she was feeling less than when pale; her more perfect beauty accorded with her less elevated mood; her more intense mood with her less perfect beauty. (T.D., p. 134)

Hardy has isolated here the rhythm of alternating elation and depression modern psychologists call cyclothymic. Characteristically, he gives it a moral-aesthetic value: Tess's beauty has a moral force. It may well be that Hardy has uncovered an important psycho-physical correlation, incidentally: the cyclothymic pattern seems significantly dependent upon Tess's whole physical-spiritual constitution, as does her tendency to assume the worst on the smallest evidence. Such correlations are to be expected of Hardy's accuracy and consistency of observation.

Tess comes to know the full innocence of her nature only when she falls in love with Angel Clare. The purgatory of her guilty self-consciousness is over, and she embarks upon the experience of Paradise. Along with Damon Wildeve and

Donald Farfrae, Angel is usually disliked by Hardy's readers. Like Wildeve, he has a certain gallantry and a quality of fastidious, remote self-esteem which proves irresistible to the "dark villains": "Beneath the local livery was something educated, reserved, subtle, sad, differing." It is the gift of charm and the weakness for flirtation (he knows he can have his pick of the Talbothays milkmaids) that set him apart from the dour thinkers he in some ways resembles. Tess notes that "his mobile face had grown more thoughtful", and Hardy's full-length portrait confirms the point:

> Angel Clare rises out of the past not altogether as a distinct figure, but as an appreciative voice, a long regard of fixed, abstracted eyes, and a mobility of mouth somewhat too small and delicately lined for a man's, though with an unexpectedly firm close of the lower lips now and then; enough to do away with any influence of indecision. Nevertheless, something nebulous, preoccupied, vague, in his bearing and regard, marked him as one who probably had no very definite aim or concern about his immediate future. (T.D., p. 147)

Tess's reabsorption into a life of innocent labour and purpose coincides with Angel's initiation into a new rhythm — the rhythm of "the seasons in their moods, morning and evening, night and noon, winds in their different tempers, trees, waters and mists, shades and silences, and the voices of inanimate things" (T.D., p. 153).

So their two streams melt into one. It is significant that the first sign of the melting — Angel having initially remained completely oblivious of Tess — is his noticing her "fluty" voice and the thought she utters in the milkmaids' tea-time conversation: " 'I don't know about ghosts,' she was saying; 'but I do know that our souls can be made to go outside our bodies when we are alive' " (T.D., p. 154). One remembers the innocent passage earlier in the book when Tess talked about the stars to her brother. She is now describing a phenomenon, to which she herself is subject, and which is known to those who interest themselves in witchcraft and the occult: " 'A very easy way to feel 'em go,' continued Tess, 'is to lie on the grass at night and look straight up at some bright star; and, by fixing your mind upon it, you will soon find that you are hundreds and hundreds o' miles away from your body, which you don't seem to want at all' " (T.D., p. 155). John Holloway's commentary is interesting:

> Hardy brings this "fancy" up against the kindly dairyman's down to earth amazement, and Tess goes significantly on to say, "you will soon find that you are hundreds o' miles away from your body which you don't seem to want at all," reminding us for a moment of the price she will ultimately pay for her dream-world spirituality.[4]

In other words, Tess has been betraying an airy-fairy unreality which suffering will cause her to regret. But this reading is not supported by the context, nor by the drift of the whole novel. In the first place, Hardy does not deflate Tess's "fancy" with the dairyman's "down to earth amazement". On the contrary, Crick's eyes are "charged with serious enquiry", and he says to his wife: "To think o' the miles I've vamped o' starlight nights these last thirty years, courting, or trading, or for doctor, or for nurse, and yet never had the least notion o' that till now, or feel my soul rise so much as an inch above my shirt-collar" (T.D., p. 155). The passage contains nothing to suggest that Tess is being deflated by Hardy, or satirized for her dreaminess. This experience of Tess's, in fact, is not dreaminess or unreality at all; it is associated with her sexuality — via the baser aspects of the occult — and with her spirituality. Both qualities are united in the traditional figure of the witch. We recall that Eustacia Vye was thought a witch: one of the Heath folk made a waxen effigy of her, and she eventually suffered the traditional witch's fate of drowning. Tess has Eustacia's heavy-limbed sensuality, though in a sublimated form. This ethereality — one of the qualities no reader can have missed in Tess — is precisely what distinguishes her from Alec d'Urberville, with whom she nevertheless shares a physicality entirely absent from Angel

Clare. This is the central crux of the novel.

The experience of floating, of being detached from the body, is a common phenomenon of occult, mystical, and psychedelic literature. It is associated with the use of aphrodisiacs, hallucinogens, and also with certain purely physical experiments practised by ascetics and yogis in search of "enlightenment". It is also, incidentally, known to parachutists, who call it "free-fall". Country mystics and witches knew thousands of secret ways of producing the effect. Tess Durbeyfield is constitutionally prone to psychic phenomena of the same kind: she might, under the wrong stress, break down into hallucinatory schizophrenia; she might, in the wrong circumstances, have become a witch herself. Her spirituality is deeply associated with her capacity for powerful sensuous experience: what made her yield to Alec d'Urberville and what enables her to experience these strange spiritual flights are really the same thing. A similar aura of occult sexuality adhered, we have seen, to her mother, Joan.

Of all men, the fastidious, intellectual, refined Angel Clare is the least able to understand Tess, or to help her. He is her anti-type. Yet the attraction between them is powerful, over-mastering, all-consuming: or at least, it is for Tess. Just this imbalance in the relationship — he is capable of wriggling off the hook — brings about the novel's tragic *dénouement*. What begins to emerge is the patent fact that Angel Clare, in spite or because of his sensibility and fastidiousness, is incapable of total self-commitment to the relationship. It is not a question of censuring Angel Clare, but of acknowledging the type of man he is. It is a common notion probably that anyone can fall in love, and that we all fall in love in the same sort of way. But Hardy suggests that this is probably not true. I have referred above to Donald Farfrae's ultimate immunity to the kind of suffering endured by Michael Henchard, an immunity that really kept him aloof from the love that the mayor felt for him. Some people, Hardy intimates, are born to suffer and to love; others let both suffering and love pass through them, like electricity through a wire. On the cessation of the charge, these latter sooner or later return to their previous state. These happy spirits — Hypoboreans, Hardy calls them — seem destined to draw the love, the passion, of the dark, sombre sufferers. What Henchard endured through his love of Farfrae, Tess suffers through her love of Angel Clare. Neither Clare nor Farfrae really reciprocates: they cannot, and this is part of their attractiveness — in life at least. In literature, as I have noted already, they are unpopular. The tragic type — Henchard, Tess, Boldwood, Jude Fawley — teach us something the Hypoboreans cannot, and we reward them with our love.

It is the episode of Clare's harp-playing that succeeds better than any other in the book in capturing Tess's combination of spirituality and sensuality. The description of the overgrown garden Tess pushes through to hear the harp better almost repels by its gross abundance. Typically, Hardy does nothing to mitigate the sickly over-lushness of nature run to seed; Tess wades through its superabundance with cuckoo-spittle on her skirts, crackling snails underfoot, yet she emerges

> conscious of neither time nor space. The exaltation which she had described as being producible at will by gazing at a star, came now without any determination of hers; he undulated upon the thin notes of the second-hand harp, and their harmonies passed like breezes through her, bringing tears into her eyes. (T.D., p. 158)

At the end of the episode, after the conversation between them, Hardy observes that "Tess's passing corporeal blight had been her mental harvest" (T.D., p. 160).

So there *is* a harvest. Later, as Clare begins, in his own intellectual way, to fall in love with her, it is her spirituality he loves:

> Whilst all the landscape was in neutral shade his companion's face, which was the focus of his eyes, rising above the mist stratum, seemed to have a sort of

phosphorescence upon it. She looked ghostly, as if she
were merely a soul at large . . . It was then, as has been
said, that she impressed him most deeply. She was no
longer the milkmaid, but a visionary essence of woman –
the whole sex condensed into one typical form. He
called her Artemis, Demeter, and other fanciful names
half-teasingly, which she did not like because she did not
understand them. (T.D., pp. 167–68).

She has for him a "dignified largeness both of disposition and
physique, an almost regnant power" (p. 167). These are
important phrases; "dignified largeness", "almost regnant
power". Together with certain others – "her calm
abandonment", her "chastened calm" – they serve to create,
gradually, organically, an ideal model of the type of woman
Clare might be expected to find deeply attractive. And in
these beautiful pages, with their idyllic dawns, when it seemed
to them as if "they were Adam and Eve", we witness the
growth of a love which stands as one of the great archetypes
in European literature. The breadth of movement in this third
Phase of *Tess of the d'Urbervilles* is unique in Hardy's writing,
as indeed is the quality of the love. With time, it must pass.

Characteristically, Tess aids its passing: the order of
honesty she exhibits in revealing to Clare her liaison with Alec
d'Urberville seems indistinguishable from a fatal inability to
accept her own happiness. Anyway, the revelation brings out
what has all the time been latent in Clare, his chronic
inability to forgive, or to absorb into himself the facts of
recalcitrant experience. The somewhat aloof fastidiousness
which had so attracted Tess to him now reveals its nastier
aspect: he can watch her weep:

She broke into sobs, and turned her back to him. It
would almost have won round any man but Angel Clare.
Within the remote depths of his constitution, so gentle
and affectionate as he was in general, there lay hidden a
hard logical deposit, like a vein of metal in soft loam,
which turned the edge of everything that attempted to
traverse it . . . his affection was less fire than radiance,

> and, with regard to the other sex, when he ceased to
> believe, he ceased to follow: contrasting in this with
> impressionable natures, who remain sensuously infatuated
> with what they intellectually despise. (T.D., p. 312)

It is the final phrase, perhaps, which most damagingly reveals
Clare's viciousness, when once his intellectual fastidiousness,
his "hard logical deposit" of self-righteousness, has been
reached: "He waited till her sobbing had ceased." Clare's
sarcasms, however, conceal also a "back current of sympathy
through which a woman of the world might have conquered
him. But Tess did not think of this; she took everything as
her deserts, and hardly opened her mouth" (T.D., p. 313). In
other words, Tess hangs on to her doom, she accepts her
defeat, as she accepts her experience. In the same way as
Clare just could not sin (and if in a later more enlightened age
he did sin, it would not be sinning *to him,* and therefore not
at all), so he does not gather "the harvest of the experience",
as Hardy has already called it. Thus, Clare's "hard logical
deposit" makes him immune, both to experience in the
cumulative sense, and to sin, to repentance, and therefore to
forgiveness. Here, Hardy is working with the greatest
generality: Clare suffers differently from Tess. He wears away:
"His thought had been unsuspended; he was becoming ill with
thinking, eaten out with thinking, withered by thinking,
scourged out of all his former pulsating flexuous domesticity"
(T.D., p. 314). One thinks of Clym Yeobright censuring
Eustacia: "You are ambitious, Eustacia — no, not exactly
ambitious — luxurious."

Clym and Angel are different intellectual types, but they
are at one in their puritan inability to countenance any form
of possession or sensualism as well as in their ravagement by
thought. It will be observed that Hardy confers upon Angel
his favourite "flexuous"; in collocation with "pulsating", it
leaves no doubt of Hardy's basic approval of him, nor yet of
his kinship with Wildeve. Hardy's work in this field, I think,
suggests a reappraisal of some of our basic moral notions — of
forgiveness, for example, of suffering, of sympathy. We are

not concerned so much with psychology, with the type-classifications of Kretschmer and Sheldon, as with our means of ethical decision. It seems necessary, in important respects, to rearrange our entire moral vocabulary: what becomes of our basic ethical concepts — forgiveness, for example — if we admit that they are simply irrelevant to certain psychical types?

It is, of course, a weakness in the writing that one follows with comparative restlessness some of the intricacies of the action hereafter: Clare's comings and goings, for instance, Tess's visit to the Clares (potentially so good, but betrayed by an excess of close concentration of such details as Tess's boots stuck in the hedge, and her overhearing what Angel's brothers are saying), the absurdity of Alec d'Urberville's conversion and deconversion. The outer structure just does not support the meaning. The inner movement continues powerfully and relentlessly, nevertheless, so that d'Urberville's reappearance has a certain formal rightness. The novel reveals a quasi-Bartokian arch-structure, with the Talbothays and marriage sequences forming the top of the curve. Both formally and intentionally, Alec's reappearance assumes great significance: is not Hardy condemning Tess to him by the formal logic of the novel?

The bleak Flintcomb Ash episode is Tess's inferno, with the strange birds from behind the North Pole arriving "silently on the upland Flintcomb Ash; gaunt spectral creatures with tragical eyes — eyes which had witnessed scenes of cataclysmical horror in inaccessible polar regions of a magnitude such as no human being had ever conceived, in curdling temperatures that no man could endure" (T.D., p. 372). This is awesome writing, straight from the consciousness that could conceive the northern Hell of the Sagas. Forgetting the missed chances, the letter read too late, and so on, with which Hardy wearies us hereabouts, we cannot fail to observe a strange note that has entered the fable: "[Alec d'Urberville] was not her husband, she had said. Yet a consciousness that in a brute sense this man alone was her husband seemed to weigh on her more and more" (T.D., p. 464). We remember Hardy's earlier digressions on Tess's redness, on her hyper-physical yawn, like a cat — also that Alec is "the red ray in the spectrum of her life".

This is something I shall now explore in *Jude the Obscure* — not pessimism exactly, or ineffectuality, but a despair of ever writhing free of the wrong commitment, with the possibility in the background that the wrong commitment is, in some way, the right one.

10. *Jude the Obscure* (1896)

Four years separate *Tess of the d'Urbervilles* from Hardy's last serious novel, *Jude the Obscure*. He had by this time been writing fiction steadily for a quarter of a century. He had produced a dozen large-scale novels, three collections of stories, and a volume of poems. These are the rough statistics. In terms of creative energy, he had expended, I believe, a greater force of imagination than any English novelist but Dickens. This judgment is based not on prolificity or industry, but simply on the massed articulation of poetic detail, fused into a large spiritual, psychological, and philosophical account of human experience, the bases of conduct, the nature of moral law, and its relations to the natural order.

Just what all this entails can be understood perhaps from a rapid reflection on the quality of the nature-writing in the Wessex novels: I have been quoting spendthriftly enough, yet I could have trebled the amount of quotation without sacrifice of quality. This means a staggering outlay of imaginative capital of Hardy's part, which is to say, of intense concentration, maximum attention of the entire being — the kind of thing a poet, if he is any good at all, might ask of himself a dozen times a year. Now Hardy's writing at these points — I am thinking fairly straight-forwardly now of "descriptive" passages — demonstrates the most tremendous grip on phenomena: the vision is at once generally comprehensive and localized in the most minute particularity. So that the inverted commas round the adjective above will have to stand: this is not *descriptive* writing, but inhabitance, an act of communion, a mediumistic devotion to the world of objects and animals that is not a gift to simple naivety but the reward of sustained awareness and attack.

The detailed accuracy of his writing bespeaks a profound

animism: one is inclined to associate religious Nature poetry
with a generality, a sweep that carries it into the sublime at
the expense of local fineness, as often happens in Victor Hugo
and even Wordsworth. Hardy rarely strives after the
"sublime". He prefers to work close to the facts, the actuality
of Nature. Frequently enough, however, he employs animistic
metaphor or simile. John Holloway observes: "The doctrine —
it is an old one — is simply that the earth itself is a great
living creature."[1] I see no reason for quarrelling with
Holloway's main contention: his lists of Hardy metaphors
proves his deep sympathy with the texts. But I think he
over-rationalizes the process: I don't think there was a
doctrine, neither was there any sustained ideational pattern. I
do not believe Hardy saw a "system" at work in Nature. His
metaphor and symbol achieve with the natural world what
Dickens achieves with the city. Both writers concentrate
constantly and energetically upon the phenomena most
familiar to them — Dickens upon offices, houses, factories,
streets, ships; Hardy upon trees, heaths, water, and weather.
Both force things to yield animistic identities: both are poets
rather than just novelists. Both, finally, paid the price for the
ceaseless demands they made upon themselves. When Dickens
turned forty he was already tired in mind: although his
greatest work lay ahead, it was in a more controlled, relaxed
vein, without the intense empathy of his most characteristic
work. Similarly, by the time he came to write *Jude the
Obscure,* Hardy seems to me to have exhausted his stock of
natural imagery: *Jude* contains none of the nature-writing
which is one of the great pleasures (to put it mildly) of his
previous fiction. The trend is continued in his last novel, *The
Well-Beloved,* where the shots of the Isle of Slingers are
mainly graceful kodachrome studies, entirely without the
animistic power of the real Hardy. It hardly therefore seems
surprising that after this he stopped writing fiction: the
poetry that followed is full of beautiful observation but it is
governed by an increasingly conceptual, philosophical concern,
which to a large extent seems to have taken the strain off the

empathic imagination. The intense, totally committed absorption in phenomena we have witnessed in the great novels had gone forever.

Yet *Jude* ranks with *The Mayor* and *Tess* as the finest of Hardy's novels. It pushes Hardy's preoccupations to their last possible resort: Nature has gone, now people just fight it out. If we bear in mind what has all the time been Hardy's psychological drive, what conclusions he has been approaching, what types he has been distinguishing, we must see *Jude* as the logical end, the *ne plus ultra* of his canon. Thus, John Holloway's puzzlement is justified, bearing in mind what his basic position has been: "There is in this book no background at all of nature or of a harmonious common life in accord with it. Hardy portrays a whole world of *déracinés* – a neurotic woman intellectual who paints eccelesiastical figures, an artisan who aspires to learning, a barmaid, an eccentric schoolmaster – who hurry from town to town in trains, or live isolated in inns and extemporized lodgings."[2] In fact, as I shall try to show, Jude Fawley, Sue Bridehead, Arabella, and to a lesser extent Phillotson, continue what has all along been the fundamental psychological struggle in Hardy.

The relationship of the book to *Tess* and *The Mayor* is profound. All three are triadic novels, though in each the pivot is different. In structure, *Jude* is an inverted *Tess:* if I may parallel the characters of the two books, Sue is a kind of feminine Angel Clare; Arabella plays a part which is comparable (in a severely limited sense) with that played by Alec d'Urberville. Arabella seduces Jude, partly by coercion, partly by tapping his sensuality, as Alec taps Tess's. Like Tess, Jude is ashamed of his sensuality. Lastly, Alec and Arabella play little more than an instrumental part in the proceedings: they exist, in one sense, to prove Tess and Jude sinners. Tess and Jude return to Alec and Arabella as if inexorably, and this is part of the meaning of both books. Thus, the psychology of *Tess* runs parallel to that of *Jude:* the basic dichotomy, now long since clear, is almost consciously debated in *Jude*. In each of these three great novels, the central triangle of forces consists of the same psychological quantities: Henchard-Tess-Jude; Farfrae-Angel-Sue; Lucetta-Alec-Arabella. With whatever qualifications are necessary[3] (and we must remember that the characters are not only different but involved in different myths) we must scrutinize this constant structure to understand what Hardy is doing in these late novels.

If Henchard is Hardy's Satan, and Tess his Eve, Jude is his Adam, even though throughout the novel he appeals to the example of the Book of Job. Jude's story is the closest Hardy ever got to a personal myth, although his own participation is — as always — indirect. The arc of Jude's career — the youthful promise and industry, the intellectual aspiration bursting through the working-class identity, the bitter experience of marriage, the fascination with architecture — makes *Jude the Obscure* something like a personal testament. It is, as Holloway remarks, a bitter book.[4] We cannot afford to regard this bitterness as either incidental to the actual theme of the novel or in any way preconceived: it derives directly from the books which precede it, but also, I think, grew out of the novel's own ingredients.

In texture and structural proportions, *Jude* is curiously ambiguous. Its overall arc achieves a genuine movement of life and time, so that what starts in youth ends in bitter disabusement with enough unforced naturalness to make its *dēnouement* among the most moving things in Hardy. Moreover, its basic myth, like that of *Tess*, is representative enough to give it relevance outside the field of its own psychological insights. These insights, finally, develop the implications of the foregoing books with a thoroughness and lucidity that compensate for the absence of the natural dimension: it replaces the natural rhythm with a neurasthenic dialectic all its own.

In spite of all this, the novel in certain respects turns heavily back to those bad old ways of Hardy's: there is too much fussy incident, too many comings and goings, concerning too many different towns (Christminster, Aldbrickam, Alfredston, Marygreen), by means of too many trains and carts. Too often the real force of the psychological convulsions and contortions is lost, dissipated in the attention one has to pay to time-tables and dates. The strong, even movement of *The Mayor,* where every incident has enough time to digest itself, where time and action are perfectly married, has been replaced by a concentration on a string of events, several of which seem incidental to the book's inner momentum. But in the end perhaps this conduces to the effect, well noted by Holloway, of "a frustrated aggregate of querulous and disorientated individuals".[5] The strength of the novel's basic myth — it is Hardy's *Great Expectations* — first reveals itself in the mirage-like glimpses the boy Jude keeps getting of the distant city of Christminster. How much finer Jude's vision of the seat of learning is than the Victorian dream of money and success. Yet it works as powerfully as the purely social aspirations of his older contemporaries. Towards Christminster, the air itself changes — "a bluer, moister atmosphere, evidently, than what he breathed up here" (J.O., p. 17). And when he asks a workman whether the city can be seen from where they are,

> "You can't often see it, in weather like this," he said. "The time I've noticed it is when the sun is going down in a blaze of flame, and it looks like — I don't know what."
> "The heavenly Jerusalem," suggested the serious urchin. (J.O., p. 18)

The first real glimpse he has of the city has a Bunyanesque purity and fervour:

> In the course of ten or fifteen minutes the thinning mist dissolved altogether from the eastern horizon, as it had already done elsewhere, and about a quarter of an hour before the time of sunset the westward clouds parted, the sun's position being partially uncovered, and the beams streaming out in visible lines between two bars of slaty cloud . . . Some way within the limits of the stretch of landscape, points of light like the topaz gleamed. The

air increased in transparency with the lapse of minutes,
till the topaz points showed themselves to be vanes,
windows, wet roof slates, and other shining spots upon
the spires, domes, freestone work, and varied outlines
that were faintly revealed. It was Christminster
unquestionably; either directly seen, or miraged in the
peculiar atmosphere. (J.O., pp. 19–20)

The last sentence gives the lie, of course: this has been an
image not of the retina, but of the spirit. The minute
particularity of the details — vanes, slates, freestone work —
would be outrageous if this were supposed to be registering
what was there. Even if Jude could have seen the city below
in broad daylight, he could hardly have picked out such
details as those Hardy notes. So it is a vision that crystallizes
before us, an Atlantean incandescence, generated out of the
will. Later Jude watches for the city at night and sees,
miraculously, "a halo or glow-fog over-arching the place against
the black heavens behind it, making the light and the city seem
distant but a mile or so" (J.O., p. 21).

It is these visions Jude Fawley interests us for, rather than
for the excessively mature stoicism of the philosophy he
articulates to himself: "As you got older, and felt yourself to
be at the centre of your time, and not at a point in its
circumference, as you had felt when you were little, you were
seized with a sort of shuddering" (J.O., p. 15). The
preposterousness of putting such sentiments in the head of a
small boy indicates the falsity, I think, of the stance: this is
the vein of crypto-existentialist negativism Hardy must have
felt by now to be expected of him. Even real moments, such
as the farmer's punishing Jude for letting the birds eat his
grain, are vitiated by an excessively philosophized rationale in
terms of an inclement universe. Hardy had a vein of genuinely
philosophical thought, which furthers the articulation of his
meanings, and is valid in its own right. But this
doom-conscious stoicism is not it. The opening sections of
Jude are valuable primarily for the very real sense they
convey of a spiritual setting forth, a feeling of life opening

up, intensely exciting in their realized allegorical mode.

The disturbance of Jude's quiet stream of scholarship by Arabella Donn, or rather by the awakening of his own sensuality, apparently presents us with the "theme" of the novel. After all, Hardy makes it fairly apparent that the agitation she causes Jude effectively shatters his peace of mind, and weakens his concentration to the point of non-existence. Moreover, Hardy himself described the book as "a deadly war waged between flesh and spirit" (Preface to the first edition, 1896). And of course this is what the book *is* about. But not in quite such simple terms. For the fact is that a close reading of the story does not support the belief that the "tragedy of unfulfilled aims" is brought about by either Jude's or Arabella's sensuality. The truth is that Jude manages as well as anyone could have in his circumstances: his Greek, Hebrew, Latin, and Church History are as good as they ought to have been. The Master's letter, the most crushing single blow Jude receives, would have come if Jude had never met Arabella, or got drunk, or in any other way yielded to the brute in himself. So whatever may be the nature of the involvements in the book, Jude's "tragedy" cannot be described quite so straightforwardly as a battle between flesh and spirit. It *is* about unfulfilled aims – *Jude* is perhaps the greatest modern dramatization of that supremely modern disease, frustration – and it *is* about the guilt aroused in a certain intellectual type by sexual experience – the Old Testament background is more than usually relevant. But one must dismiss any simple presentation of the work as being concerned with these themes in quite the way Hardy himself suggests in his handling of Arabella's seduction of Jude.

Arabella herself immediately falls into place. Which means that Hardy knows the type thoroughly, and presents her surely. Hardy's major characters now wholly and easily inhabit their type-moulds, without in the slightest losing individual reality. This has largely been true since *The Return of the Native:* what is impressive now is the certainty of the handling, the certainty of a man who has got to the springs of personality. People are not bundles of qualities, nor can they be mixed like cocktails. But they are dominated by their basic psycho-physical constitution. Arabella is a type we recognize from our earlier reading of Hardy, as well as from life: "a fine dark-eyed girl, not exactly handsome, but capable of passing as such at a little distance, despite some coarseness of skin and fibre. She had a round and prominent bosom, full lips, perfect teeth, and the rich complexion of a Cochin hen's egg. She was a complete and substantial female human – no more, no less" (J.O., p. 42). Tess without a soul? Not quite. But compare this portrait of Arabella with the marvellous biblical glimpses of Tess at the haymaking: "the oval face of a handsome young woman with deep dark eyes and long heavy clinging tresses". Her figure is "flexuous and finely-drawn", and her "complexion may be guessed at from a stray twine or two of dark brown hair". Tess, too, despite her "soul" is, as the saying goes, all woman. Of her face, Hardy says that there was "nothing ethereal about it; all was real vitality, real warmth, real incarnation". Arabella Donn is a "substantial female human – no more, no less". The qualifying phrase makes the difference, of course. Arabella has, in fact, Alec d'Urberville's coarse consistency: Alec is swarthy, "with full lips, badly moulded". If this detail serves to fix d'Urberville, it is the "Cochin hen's egg" which establishes Arabella's richness, a richness that is slightly offensive. (It is a brilliant example of Hardy's skill with sheer sound and association: like the word "jonquil" in another image "Cochin", with its rich "ch" sound and exotic associations, delicately captures a very important quality in Arabella.) And of course Arabella does offend, so far as a good and amusing comic creation can. Everything, from the dollop of pig's flesh she throws at Jude to attract his attention, to the dimples she archly sucks into her cheeks, contributes to the effect of vulgar vitality. But this vitality is not, *pace* Lawrence, approved of: it culminates in the ghastly farce of the pig-killing after their marriage, and the uncanny incident when Arabella walks up and down outside their house in a species of fit:

Here, she began to saunter up and down, perversely
pulling her hair into a worse disorder than he had
caused, and unfastening several buttons of her
gown ... pedestrians turned to stare at the extraordinary
spectacle she now presented, bonnetless, her dishevelled
hair now blowing in the wind, her bodice apart, her
sleeves rolled above the elbows for the work, and her
hands reeking with melted fat. One of the passers said in
mock earnest: "Good Lord deliver us!" (J.O., p. 81)

The harridan side of animal sexuality in women – with, at
the end, just a hint of witchcraft – could hardly have been
more pungently presented, even by Chaucer. Her departure
now out of the novel – via emigration to Australia, that
panacea of the Victorian plot-monger – is of course a
convenience, but a convenience that is justified.

For we now want to find out more about Jude himself.
Hardy gains by focussing the character properly only after we
have seen him in action. The impact of the reacquaintance
derives its weight from a species of subtle reinforcement:

Jude would now have been described as a young man
with a forcible, meditative, and earnest rather than
handsome cast of countenance. He was of a dark
complexion, with dark harmonizing eyes, and he wore a
closely trimmed black beard of more advanced growth
than is usual at his age; this, with his great mass of black
curly hair, was some trouble to him in combing out and
washing out the stone-dust that settled on it in the
pursuit of his trade. (J.O., p. 91)

Hardy now wields the terms he has made his own and taught
us to understand with perfect confidence: we know precisely
not only the type, but the unique inscape of Jude Fawley
himself, because of the subtle inflection Hardy can now give
to words like "forcible, meditative, and earnest". The
masterstroke – in emerging naturally from the foregoing
type-mould and in establishing one man and one man only –
is "harmonizing eyes". Only Jude has "harmonizing" eyes.
Yet the quality is of a piece with those he shares with

Henchard, 'Clym Yeobright, and Giles Winterborne. The forcibleness of Henchard and the dourness of Giles Winterborne are centre-nodes of different characters. This ability to frame such organic unities, crossing his lines all the while, yet keeping them separate, clear, is surely Hardy's greatest gift as a psychologist.

What makes Jude a hero, where Winterborne for instance is not, is the combination of the force and the sensuality, the sensuality Arabella was able to trick out of him. Jude's susceptibility — to Arabella and to beer — is of crucial importance in our understanding of him. To write them off as moral "weaknesses" is to ethicalize the art out of the book. For Jude's drive towards self-realization stems from the peculiar mélange of qualities (whether a balance or an imbalance is again an ethical red herring) — concentration and restlessness, aspiration and recklessness, idealism and sensuality — that constitutes his identity. "He was a species of Dick Whittington," Hardy observes of his arrival in Christminster, "whose spirit was touched to finer issues than a mere material gain" (J.O., p. 93). This, baldly stated, is the myth of Jude Fawley. If we accept Hardy's word for it, that it is a tragedy of unfulfilled aims, it must be assumed that this tragedy, these aims, are, like Pip's in *Great Expectations,* part of the human condition, not to be lamented as errors or mistakes that could have been avoided with more thought or self-control.

Very substantially, the rest of the book concerns Jude's struggle with his cousin, Sue Bridehead. And this again is the deep, immitigable clash of two principles, two emotional systems, two laws, that of the flesh, perhaps, and that of the spirit. It is in articulating this clash that Hardy forces his basic insights to yield their most significant conclusions. For at this stage, the conflict between types, the complex interaction of which the whole canon of his fiction has been labouring to define, now crystallizes in its final form. Hardy arrives at the existence in personality of two principles which, transformed and modulated by a process of constant individuation, make up the complex of humanity.

Sue Bridehead flickers several times across Jude's vision before she settles long enough to be focussed: first, she is a face in a photograph, "a pretty girlish face, in a broad hat, with radiating folds under the brim like the rays of a halo" (J.O., p. 92). Then we learn in passing that she is some kind of artist. Finally, Jude comes across her in the street: "She looked right into his face with liquid, untranslatable eyes, that combined, or seemed to him to combine, keenness with tenderness, and mystery with both, their expression, as well as that of her lips, taking its life from some words just spoken to a companion" (J.O., p. 106). One thinks immediately of Thomasin Yeobright, with that "ingenuous, transparent life" in her eyes. The two characters diverge sharply — there is nothing ingenuous in Sue Bridehead — yet the affinity is deep. The definition of Sue that now follows turns attention, almost methodically, from "the windows of the soul" to that other source of information, the "general mould and build":

> He remembered now that she was not a large figure, that she was light and slight, of the type dubbed elegant. That was about all he had seen. There was nothing statuesque in her; all was nervous motion. She was mobile, living, yet a painter might not have called her handsome or beautiful. (J.O., p. 107)

Whether in antagonism or collaboration, in mutual discord or one-sided love, the nervous and the statuesque define each other as they define themselves — by an awareness of the other in themselves, and themselves in the other. When Hardy speaks of the "deadly war waged between flesh and spirit" in *Jude the Obscure* he is usually taken to be referring to Jude Fawley and his sexual lapses. But what of Sue Bridehead? Isn't it in her that the deadliest phase of the war is to take place? Isn't she to be the terrain chosen by the flesh to conduct its final campaign against the spirit? And isn't Jude's greatest sin to be the desecration of her purity? When Jude takes Arabella to wife, the distance he falls is far less than when Sue accepts Jude's penis into herself. And when finally they "settle down", and she dutifully bears him his children and labours (so bravely) to make herself the mother of Adam's brood, the war has surely entered its last frenetic spasm. The lull is to be protracted. She seems "reconciled"; the twentieth-century reader starts to think she has "matured". But when Little Father Time hangs their children it seems like the outward proclamation of an inwardly acknowledged guilt. She has lived, we must believe, in a state of permanent deadlock — a tension indistinguishable from peace. But all the time, the spirit is looking for a recognition of its guilt, and Little Father Time finally provides the occasion. Hardy is, we must admit it, a Manichean. The flesh is the devil's, and Jude is the embodiment of its spasmodic impulses. All this Jude knows when he sees her. His reflection has a morbid penetrativeness — "How could one of his cross-grained, unfortunate, almost accursed stock, have contrived to reach this pitch of niceness?"

This is not the first time in the book that Hardy has hit this note with Jude. Apart from the outbursts of precocious existentialism that mar the opening chapters, Jude sets out expressly to "battle with his evil star". When he arrives in Christminster, he chooses his lodgings in a suburb called Beersheba. His physiognomy and mind, in fact, have a strongly Hebraic cast: in several places Hardy refers to the Book of Job, and one of the minor irritants between Jude and Sue is her ridicule of his religion. In the context, this appears as Hellenism mocking at Hebraism, to use Matthew Arnold's terms. (They must surely have been in Hardy's mind at the time he conceived this relationship.) It is also of course the nervous mocking the statuesque: Hardy's terms work at several levels.

Readers are apt to be as irritated by Sue as by Wildeve and Angel Clare. Yet Hardy's description suggests that either he has failed or his readers have. The vacillations of her behaviour would try the patience of the saint Jude slowly becomes over the course of the action. But if we do not understand that Phillotson and Jude between them exert on her a pressure to which she is entirely unequal, and that Jude demands as much of her by way of self-denial as she does of him, then I think the novel must be judged a failure. It is not; and the failure is due to a combination of slovenly reading habits, and the peculiar psychological phenomenon I have referred to above, that people like Sue, and Angel Clare (and Donald Farfrae) simply do not excite sympathy. So the novel engages us fascinatingly even when we fail it. In the postscript he wrote to the 1912 edition of *Jude* Hardy wrote of her as "the slight, pale 'bachelor' girl — the intellectualised, emancipated bundle of nerves that modern conditions were producing". It is interesting to see the mastertouch still there, even if exercised with a slightly journalistic summariness. But Hardy's presentation of Sue in the novel, especially at the beginning, has a great deal of softness and affection: she is, after all, a "pretty, liquid-eyed, light-footed young woman" (J.O., p. 111). And there is one vein in her that simply cannot be neglected if she is to be focussed clearly. It emerges in the curious episode when Sue, out walking in the country near Christminster, meets an itinerant pedlar selling cheap statuary, "reduced copies of ancient marbles", among them "a Venus of standard pattern, a Diana, and, of the other six, Apollo, Bacchus and Mars" (J.O., p. 112). She eventually chooses Venus and Apollo, and sets them up in her room. Her reaction to the pagan emblems of sexuality is a strange mixture of luxury and apprehension: "Being of nervous temperament she trembled at the enterprise." "They seemed so very large now they were in her possession, one on either side of a Crucifixion", and, unable to sleep, she contemplates them with a thrill of release. At the same time, Hardy informs us with naive omniscience, Jude was chanting New Testament Greek alone in his room.

This impulse of Sue's recalls Grace Melbury's "Daphne-esque mood": almost invariably in Hardy, Greek myth is associated with lawless sensuality, with the whimsical, as opposed to the sober self-discipline and guilt-consciousness of the Old Testament. The Greek gods and demiurges signify the wayward, intoxicant aspect of sex, where the Hebraic sin-consciousness rigorously contains a more powerful physicality. Jude's intellectual conscience exacts full repentance for his few (and legal) acts of sensuality with Arabella: "What a wicked, worthless fellow he had been to give vent, as he had done, to an animal passion for a woman, and allow it to lead to such disastrous consequences; then to think of putting an end to himself; then to go recklessly and get drunk" (J.O., p. 110). Jude's conscience, in fact, is on a par with Henchard's temper, and Tess's remorse: it wrecks him.

Sue's almost autoerotic vein of cerebral enjoyment of release can hardly be reached by Jude's morbid sensuality. Once we understand this, the oscillations that follow begin to make some sense: and Sue becomes a little more sympathetic.

The reappearance of Jude's old schoolmaster, Phillotson, complicates yet clarifies the situation. The three characters are brought together under one lamp when Jude takes Sue along to meet Phillotson:

> The rays fell on the nervous little face and vivacious dark eyes and hair of Sue, on the earnest features of her cousin, and on the schoolmaster's own maturer face and figure, showing him to be a spare and thoughtful personage of five-and-forty, with a thin-lipped, somewhat refined mouth, a slightly stooping habit, and a black frock-coat, which from continuous frictions shone a little at the shoulder-blades, the middle of the back and the elbows. (J.O., pp. 123–24)

At this stage of the novel, before the neurasthenic alternations of mood have set in between Jude and Sue, Sue herself has a particular radiance. "She was so vibrant," Jude reflects, "everything she did seemed to have its source in feeling. An exciting thought would make her walk ahead so fast that he could hardly keep up with her: and her sensitiveness on some points was such that it might have been misread as vanity" (J.O., p. 124). Later when she is working with Phillotson, at Jude's suggestion, Phillotson in his turn is struck: "A new emanation, which had nothing to do with her skill as a teacher, seemed to surround her" (J.O., pp. 127–28).

These pages are very important not just in the characterization of Sue but in the final reading of the book as a whole: the "tragedy" also concerns the putting out of this radiance of Sue's, not by experience alone, but by the importunateness of Jude and Phillotson. Phillotson's designs on her, indeed, now begin to take on a sinister uncleanness. There is something unclean and clammy about him altogether — something redolent of close, stuffy rooms, laboured but unintellectual study, a negation of the life of the body. Hence, his musings and broodings take on an unpleasantly calculating air that cancels out the kindliness he actually treats her with. The situation is as exasperating to the reader — Hardy ensures that we identify with Jude — as to Jude himself. Yet the courtship and marriage develop out of the strange complex of nervousness and abandon that makes Sue such a bad bet for Jude. Basically, Phillotson's repellent unphysicalness is more acceptable to her than Jude's sensuality.

Unfortunately, Hardy felt himself committed to the thicket of fortuitous events, snags, and spurious obstacles that he felt must go for the "interest" of the quarterly readership. Hardy really needed here the intellectual poise and technical sophistication of the post-Flaubert novel in France to set forth his extremely modern subject matter. Thus one has, I think, to disregard the theme of cousinage, and Jude's and Sue's sense of the doom hanging over their stock; even the marriage to Arabella — though important in establishing Jude's sensuality — must be seen as a red herring. The real obstacle to the marriage of Sue and Jude is their profound spiritual incompatibility: *au fond,* Sue cannot tolerate Jude's animalism, and so allows Phillotson to court her. Hardy had put his finger here on some very new and disturbing themes. None of Hardy's contemporaries, in England or France, was as delicately sure as he of the real causes of sexual attraction and revulsion; of the reasons why one has to suspend judgment in cases where judgment seems demanded; of the morass of instincts, impulses, aversions, and false articulations that is the terrain of human relationships. Scenes like the one where we witness Sue's shuddering inability to tolerate Phillotson's touch, and the even more horrible one when she permits his legal claims — these are revolutionary in literature, and Hardy's narrative technicalities merely obscure the profundity of his insights.

Few characters in fiction irritate the reader more than Sue Bridehead. Yet the reader who admires Hardy's handling of Phillotson's court to her — a sure and masterly piece of timing — should think twice about Sue's "intolerable" treatment of Jude and of the young graduate she had earlier driven to suicide by letting him live with her without letting him touch her. The ease and inevitability of Phillotson's suit stands in direct ratio to the harsh importunateness of Jude's. She feels safe with Phillotson, and it is as reasonable to blame Jude for continuing to press her as to blame her for denying him.

On a return to his home-village, Jude learns from his aunt more about his cousin's waywardness — about her visionary recitation of *The Raven* as a child, for instance: " 'She'd bring up the nasty carrion-bird that clear,' corroborated the sick woman reluctantly, 'as she stood there in her little sash and things, that you could see un a'most before your very eyes. You too, Jude, had the same trick as a child of seeming to see things in the air' " (J.O., p. 136). More interesting still is her tomboyishness — her skill in the boys' games, and her teasing refusal to play on when they begged her. This is a beautiful piece of retrospection, in fact, both strengthening the known contours of the character, and articulating variations we could not quite have predicted. The sequence of events hereabouts makes this one of the strongest sections in the novel, a jarring crescendo, with Jude's despair of getting Sue, his flagging concentration in his studies, the shattering rebuff from the head of the college he applies to, the reversion to drink, the Job quotation he smears on the walls of the college, and finally the bitter laughter that shows how the experience has changed him: "The stroke of scorn relieved his mind, and the next morning he laughed at his self-conceit. But the laugh was not a healthy one" (J.O., p. 146).

It is on such sequences as this, an elaborate yet forthright series of relevant events, that fiction should turn: we really feel the bitterness seeping into Jude. This is even true — on balance — of the cat's cradle of futile journeys, decisions gone-back-on, missed appointments, and dramatic returns; the form of *Jude the Obscure* labours to create the image of the growth of bitterness and exasperation. In spite of some disastrous episodes (the infamous Little Father Time sequence, for example) the actual progression — the short tenure of people's arrangements, the abrupt *voltes faces,* the reversions to type and the sporadic assertions of will — elaborates a uniquely bitter design.

The motto of this design is seen also in Sue's behaviour towards Jude: again and again she snubs him, only to repent hours later with passionate little notes. Or he bitterly mocks her, and she recoils in tears. And the overall design continues to modulate through its larger phases. Sue marries Phillotson and Arabella returns from Australia to reassert her claim on Jude. This larger plan redeems (though it doesn't justify) some of the weak local incidents. When Sue and Jude actually get to the registry office for instance, they allow themselves to be deterred by the sight of a soldier and a girl with a black eye going through a charade of the horrible institution of marriage, as though for their instruction. Such inventions are crazy: Hardy ought to have known better, especially as they express a serious meaning. They milestone the progress of exasperation that the novel is mainly concerned with, and also serve to strengthen the sense of impossibility about the relationship: something will not let Jude and Sue live in harmony together.

Similarly, Arabella's return functions rather like Alec

d'Urberville's reappearance in *Tess:* to remind Jude of his sensuality, the sensuality he is in the process of shackling. He succumbs to her immediately, the spurious legality of the act being oddly counterbalanced by Jude's unnecessary guilt about it.

It is this deeper design too, that one resists, *if* one resists the movement of the book. For neither the irritating surface of the plot nor the various red herrings Hardy drags across the trail can explain any more than they can mar the actual inevitability of the narrative. That Sue should flee in horror from Phillotson's touch, bear Jude's children, then return to misery with the schoolmaster again, can only be explained in terms of the deeper psychological drives I have been trying to describe. It is wrong, of course, that Phillotson's unclean advances should be preferred to Jude's sensuality, or that he should be preferred in any sense or on any terms to Jude. Sue acquires over the period of living with Jude a force of character that successfully replaces her earlier radiance: she becomes a woman, but at the price perhaps of her inner light. Her return to Phillotson only makes artistic sense as an indication of her basic inability to accept the role of sexual mother. Similarly, Jude's remarriage to Arabella cannot — on pain of absurdity — be understood other than as his reversion to his centre of gravity.

Yet this seems the moment to say that a great deal of Sue's behaviour can be understood in de Rougemont's terms, as indeed can the whole novel.[6] According to such a reading, Sue would represent the spirit of Romance. Jude insists on destroying the "passion" that springs up between them by forcing her into a deadening marital union. Sue is hostile to marriage and to sex, both being in turn equally hostile to passion in de Rougemont's view of things. When Arabella (the spirit of sex-and-marriage) returns from Australia, Sue is frightened into marriage with Jude out of fear of losing him to the "wife" who can offer him the sex that is obviously so important to him. But she has no doubt about the hatefulness of "so hopelessly vulgar an institution as legal marriage". It is a "sort of trap to catch a man". What Sue says to Jude just before they do agree to get married might have come from the pen of de Rougemont himself: "Don't you dread the attitude that insensibly arises out of legal obligation? Don't you think it is destructive to a passion whose essence is its gratuitousness?" This frightens Jude too, and they live on for a while in a sort of "dreamy paradise". The passion, in other words, is granted a reprieve.

. Accepting this view of Sue, the attack on marriage mounted by the whole book acquires a higher significance. It is not merely the protest of a wise man against an inflexible institution that makes more people unhappy than it makes happy, but a last-ditch action by the Romantic consciousness. Marriage is hateful, on this view, because it destroys passion. The enemy to passion is, as Sue says, "coercion". So, the pattern of the narrative acquires fresh significance: what forces Sue and Jude back into the arms of Phillotson and Arabella is the Romantic hatred of tediously consummated union.

Jude dies reciting the Book of Job, and it is Old Testament wrath and despair that dominate the novel. Jude and Sue tend apart, perhaps, at the dictates of some deep Romantic force. Yet the terms of the logic are grounded in their personalities. Thus, Hardy's appeals to the gods, to Jude's evil star, are to be taken neither literally nor rhetorically. Hardy's unfortunate rashes of stoicism — the often near-pretentious aphorisms about life being a silly game, or accursed from the start — have encouraged the popular conception of him as a "fatalist". But fatalism is a boring and unintelligent substitute for real thought. Yet again, the sense of inexorability we feel in great art in one sense *is* identifiable with the view that there is nothing to be done about anything. In the same measure as we see it in *Lear* and *Agamemnon,* we see in Hardy's books the great movement of inevitability: we see it in Jude's great public outburst against the pharisees of Christminster, and in the marvellous cinematic scene where Hardy cross-cuts between Jude lying on his death-bed reciting the Book of Job, and the crowd outside shouting enthusiastically at the speech of a politician. Finally, and overall, it is there in the arcs of the lives of Jude and Sue. When the widow Edlin suggests that Sue has found peace with Phillotson, Arabella sums up the strange fatality behind their frustrating experience:

> " 'She may swear on her knees to the Holy cross upon her necklace, till she's hoarse, but it won't be true!' said Arabella. 'She never found peace since she left his arm and never will till she's as he is now.' "

That people should end up in the wrong beds that are nevertheless somehow the right ones suggests some kind of curse on humanity. The idea seems both disagreeable and old fashioned, yet there is depressingly little in twentieth-century experience to suggest that this is not so.

PART FOUR

The Philosophy of Typology

11. "The Nervous and the Statuesque"

Hardy's evolution as a novelist can be followed in his increasing rationalization of personality and behaviour. The early novels have genuine and accurate insights set in characters whose other traits and actions are unrelated to them. Hence, the plots of these novels hold little real interest for us now. There are exceptions, such as when Elfride Swancourt lets her horse make for her an important decision in her emotional life; or the generally passive behaviour of reserved intellectuals like Stephen Smith and George Somerset in contrast to the aggressiveness of sexual predators like Manston. Since money is a seasoned motivation, Hardy often resorts to conventional devices like stolen plans, and even murdered wives, to rescue his story from stagnancy. On the whole, there is no organic relation between the narrative and the characters. This is a familiar truth about the early fiction of most novelists. It is the particular path Hardy's maturation took that concerns us. As he develops, we see that not only do people do the sort of thing that could be expected of them — a *sine qua non* of any good fiction — but that they behave in ways geared more specifically to the psychological content I have been trying to describe above.

It would be an unimpeachable but useless general truth to point out that Hardy's characters act consistently according to their type — and "type" would lose its significance. Of course, Pip in *Great Expectations* does Pip-like things; Casaubon in *Middlemarch* fails because of the kind of man he is, and so on. What is the difference, then, between Hardy's methods of characterization and those of non-typological novelists such as Dickens and George Eliot, who are equally faithful to the facts of psychology?

The answer is really quite simple. Even when George Eliot

and Hardy overlap in creating a character the psychologist would identify as being of a particular type, say, as melancholy, introverted, or asthenic (according to their jargon), they concern themselves with quite different things. The general consistency of their characterization derives from different perceptions about the characters is question. Dorothea Brooke and Tess Durbeyfield appear as quite similar types (probably what Sheldon would call viscerotonic); in both cases we believe their creators make them act consistently according to their personalities. And though their biographies are not entirely dissimilar (each suffers a kind of martyrdom at the hands of an intellectual prig), the "content" of the two novels is widely different, and reflects differing attitudes towards life and people. Perhaps the most important of these, in the given instance, is the fact that George Eliot does not acknowledge the existence of Dorothea's sexuality at all, while Hardy, on the other hand, comes several steps closer to D. H. Lawrence and the modern age in forcing a showdown between Tess's sexuality and Clare's lust for righteousness. After all, no twentieth-century novelist could have married Dorothea off to an old stick like Casaubon without wondering what they did at night, and making their conclusions "explain" her disabusement. Dorothea's spiritual disabusement, though, is just as real as Tess's sexual initiation, and the real difference between the two books goes deeper. For in the mature Hardy, the characters' actions, or failures to act, derive not only from their personalities according to the laws of normal fictional consistency: they follow directly the lines of their psychological cast or type, and are proffered by Hardy as explicable in terms of it. Some examples will suffice.

Tess Durbeyfield yields to the sensuality that is an important part of her type — much as she yearns towards spiritual communion with Angel Clare — while Clare himself is constitutionally unable to forgive her: thus, the tragedy derives from the conflict between their particular types — the soft, luxurious Tess and the unforgiving, slightly priest-like

Angel. Giles Winterborne cannot break out of his melancholic reticence to compete with the rival Fitzpiers on Midsummer Eve, and hence allows Grace to slip away from him; similarly, he cannot meet her half-way when she apologizes for cutting him during the fog-scene in the woodland, even though such a relenting might well have brought her to him. Thus, Winterborne's very strength of character — what emerges in his dealings with Marty South as quiet reserved kindliness and considerateness — causes his ultimate destruction. Michael Henchard maintains the rigidity of pride towards all comers, and a contemptuous generosity that indicates violence and moodiness; he is unable to bend and adapt when the circumstances he has hitherto coerced begin to take their own course. Donald Farfrae, on the other hand, meets Henchard's friendship and hostility with about equal ease, and hence rides the novel out, even when the dark powers of ignorance and possession are turned against his wife, Lucetta, in the Skimmington ride. Jude Fawley falls to the demon of his own sensuality and crucifies himself on guilt. Sue Bridehead cannot ultimately live with his sexuality, yet neither can she quite live without him. Farmer Boldwood is incapable of living equably when the wall of his self-created world has been breached by consciousness of a desirable woman who might desire him. Similarly, Knight must make Elfride Swancourt part of his own inner familiarity before he can achieve the peace of mind disturbed by awareness of her beauty. Clym Yeobright settles to a life of quiet ruminative philanthropy, symbolically blinded to the irrelevant beauty of the actual physical world: Eustacia Vye for violence and death, like the unknown sailor of Lermontov's lyric, "Hoping in storm to find peace".

In all these cases — many, many more could be set down with the same sort of commentary — what the characters *do* stems directly from the facts of their psychology: and the facts of their psychology are, I maintain, such as I have been describing throughout this work. In other words, Hardy describes personality increasingly in terms of a restricted number of psycho-physical moulds, and explains their behaviour *directly and causally in terms of them.* This is the important point. It is not a question of our effecting upon passive material a quasi-psychiatric analysis, regardless of the artist's professed explanations, in the way that a Marxist might tells us that Hamlet is really motivated by disgust with the political and economic bondage to which Denmark subjects its proletariat; or a Freudian that Ahab really misses his mother, or Heathcliff needs affection. In every case — my argument is — Hardy really does provide the explanations I have retailed above: in fact he is unusually explicit in such matters and leaves little to the reader's speculative faculty. (When he feels there is room for speculation, he immediately takes the reader into his confidence about it, as when he wonders whether Grace Melbury might have re-accepted Giles Winterborne had he come down from his high perch: such speculations are to be taken with absolute good faith in Hardy. He is that rare thing, the totally honest artist.)

Most of the examples given above come from the later novels for the reason stated at the beginning of this chapter, that Hardy's artistic maturation takes the form of a deepening clarity about his subject matter — the types of human personality, and their consequences expressed in action. At first, the relations between the psychological insights and the plot-line are sporadic and intermittent, which means simply that Hardy is still unsure of what he really does think about behaviour and personality. As he matures, the action of the novels turns increasingly upon the psychological divisions and dispositions of the characters: just as *Wuthering Heights* explicates the inner tension in Catherine Earnshaw between the aspects of herself drawn to Linton and those drawn to Heathcliff, so all the major novels of Hardy concern the actions and interactions of carefully delineated and distinguished human types.

The question arises finally, whether we can draw up a general table of conclusions rationalizing Hardy's continually distinguished, varied, and consistent insights, to yield the kind of diagrams we have been given by psychologists of all ages, from the Humours physicians of the middle ages, to Wundt, Jung, Kretschmer, and Sheldon. My title suggests my own opinion that we can, though only with hesitancy and care. Throughout this work I have been assuming a kind of rough congruity between predominantly psychological systems of type-distinction (such as those of the later descendants of Galen — mainly the German philosophers of the Enlightenment and after); and morphological theories such as those of Hippocrates, Kretschmer, and Sheldon, concerned strictly with the variety of human physique, to borrow one of Sheldon's titles. In fact, a lot of work would have to be done to establish with even moderate conclusiveness that Hippocrates' two types — leptosomatic and pyknic — really do correlate tidily with Galen's system of the Humours. However, the evidence suggests — to the present writer at least — that the correlation can be made, and that Galen's work was probably done very much in the shadow of Hippocrates' earlier formulations. (A gap of some six hundred years in fact separates the two men.) This is particularly relevant in the case of Thomas Hardy. For his attitude to "the mind" and to the types of personality is framed — as I believe I have shown amply enough — consistently in terms of body-build and physical constitution.

More consistently than any other novelist, Thomas Hardy made the physical facts of personality the basis of his treatment of character. His habitual approach to the task of presenting these facts — the sustained visual portrait — derives from this fundamental concern for establishing the basic constitution, which is to say the physical type. By now it will be plain that any suggestion that the "mind" or "soul" exists independently of the body must be dismissed out of hand. In Hardy's novels "Character is destiny", and destiny hangs very largely upon the mould into which a man or woman is set.

The task of subsuming the various insights Hardy offers into the workings of the mind under general headings must be done, I think, strictly in his own terms; it would be useless to show how his general conclusions can be correlated with the schemata of existing psychological systems. Where, then, would be the value of Hardy's work? There are of course clear indications both of Hardy's debt to the traditions of typological analysis in general, and to the work carried out by creative artists like the Brontës and Scott. These artists in their turn owe much to broad popular and learned streams of character analysis. I have suggested examples also to show how Hardy anticipates, if he does not actually inspire, the findings of modern researchers like Sheldon. Thus, again, the loose unity of the whole field is confirmed rather than weakened by the shades of difference that exist among its various contributions. Referring to the extraordinary longevity of some modern psychological notions, H. J. Eysenck writes: "Descriptively, agreement between these modern studies and the old doctrine of the temperaments is quite surprisingly good."[1] Eysenck's book includes a diagram correlating the old structure of the Humours with modern extrovert-introvert, stable-unstable axes, showing the extraordinary coincidence of the descriptive adjectives applied by modern psychiatrists with the implicit qualities of the equivalent mediaeval label. The Melancholic, for example, occupying the Unstable Introverted quadrant of the circle, is described as "Moody, Anxious, Rigid, Sober, Pessimistic, Reserved, Unsociable and Quiet". Now this list, though the result of much laborious interviewing, analysing, and so on, in fact adds precisely nothing to the mediaeval concept: nor to the analysis of melancholics by artists like Cervantes, Shakespeare, Jonson, and Molière. Eysenck's list – accurate enough – might come from an undergraduate essay describing the character, say, of Hamlet or Don Quixote.

We can see right away how such a list could apply to certain Hardy characters: Boldwood, Henchard, Giles Winterborne, Clym Yeobright are all introverts or melancholics, with Henchard and Boldwood coming right at the top of the list, towards the point of extreme instability. Similarly, Gabriel Oak is a stable introvert (Eysenck gives

"Passive, Thoughtful, Careful, Peaceful", etc.); Sue Bridehead is an unstable extrovert — "Touchy, active, optimistic, changeable, excitable . . . ", and so on. And so we could go through Hardy's characters, adding little to our knowledge of human nature by subsuming his findings under known categories. There could be value in this. It would demonstrate for instance the extreme care and accuracy with which Hardy worked — to use the psychologists' language, the congruence and homogeneity of his characterization. We might respect him even more. But, as I have pointed out several times already, much of the value of Hardy's extremely delicate and profound studies is lost if we try to translate them out of his own special terminology. He rarely uses the Humours vocabulary. (I doubt if there are more than half a dozen examples in the whole of his fiction.) Moreover, he is sparing and careful in the use of the significant words I have been trying to isolate as specifically his own. Generalization, then, must be carried out in his own terms — and very carefully.

Something like the pattern I think we shall find in Hardy has probably begun to emerge over the last few pages. Consistently, Hardy's characters fall either side of a transversal, the inevitable transversal of type-thinking: Clare and Tess, Sue and Jude, Farfrae and Henchard, Bathsheba and Boldwood, Wildeve and Eustacia, Cytherea and Manston, Fanny Robin and Troy, and so on. In *Jude the Obscure* he finally arrives at his own terms for this dichotomy: the nervous and the statuesque. Right away it must be said that it would be unreal not to indicate the rough parallel between this dichotomy of Hardy's and the introvert-extrovert distinction of modern psychology, and indeed, the classic melancholy-phlegmatic/choleric-sanguine distinction of Galen. The basic structure remains the same: and it would be a serious breach of credibility if it did not. We would find it hard to pay serious attention to two students of the human mind who failed to agree at such a fundamental level. Similarly, the basic categories of the Brontës follow the scarcely varying structure: the Brontë heroes, dark, scowling earth-worshippers, stocky and strong, can be seen as typical pyknics, the fair-haired angels as typical leptosomatics.[2]

A résumé of Hardy's achievement in the field must begin with his Brontë heritage, with the habitual contrasting of a light, fair, blue-eyed type with a dark, powerful, hirsute type. In Hardy, the first fair-haired angels are (simply) feminine, as opposed (simply) to the dark masculine villains. More, the angels are characterized by mobility, and emotional changeability. This is Hardy's first essay in the nervous type. Opposite them are the dark, moody, thoughtful predators: Knight, Manston, and Shiner all subject the nervous angels to pressure, whether of aggressive sexuality, or simply of masculine weight of character. Cytherea is afraid to be with Manston simply because he attracts her too much, and Fancy Day definitely quivers in response to Shiner's domineering presence. Between these two types falls a third: the handsome young thinkers who usually get the girl. (The exception is Stephen Smith in *A Pair of Blue Eyes*, who yields to Knight.) The type is still unindividuated at this stage. Their interest is really confined to the structure they confer on the whole psychological world, and to the insights they embody into a type later more deeply explored. Dick Dewy of course is no intellectual: he foreshadows another version of the type, having the reticence of the thinkers without their ruminativeness. Perhaps the most significant results of this first phase of Hardy's explorations are the "mobility" of the angels (an original contribution to the typological scheme), and the already subtle range of the "thinkers". There is already a marked difference between the moody instability of characters like Manston and Knight (dangerously disturbable), and the phlegm of Shiner.

The second phase — which consists principally of *Far from the Madding Crowd* and *The Return of the Native* — initiates the differentiation of character and personality. In *Far from the Madding Crowd*, Bathsheba Everdene has the mobility of Fancy Day (as witness the horseback routine where she is compared to a "bowed sapling"), but she is also described as "heavy-limbed" — a significant departure. Thus, she shares the "versatility" of the later Ethelberta and the earlier angels (an important aspect of the type); she toys captiously with Oak, and teases Boldwood. But two facts about her put her beyond the angels: the sexuality implied in the heavy-limbed-ness, which responds so powerfully to Troy, and the "character" which makes her bitterly regret the devil she has roused in Boldwood. This is not simply fear, although she does grow to fear him: it is mature regret, such as Sergeant Troy would have been incapable of. Dominated by impulse, like Bathsheba, yet, unlike her, knowing neither past nor future, regret nor expectation, Troy possesses no *character* at all, in spite of his forceful masculinity. One of Hardy's profoundest contributions to psychology in fact is his demonstration that a light, graceful man (such as Angel Clare or Damon Wildeve) can have more force of character than an ostentatiously virile philanderer like Troy, whose front collapses at the feeble push of a Fanny Robin. Troy's apparently fortunate sanguine receptivity in fact rests upon a chronically unstable basis: he is an emotional bankrupt. Boldwood's vulnerability on the other hand derives from neurotically *over*-developed character. If personality is defined as that which serves the individual best in the present moment, Boldwood has suppressed his personality out of existence: he is all rigid inflexibility, dominated entirely by routine and the familiar. Like Knight, in fact, he is incapable of adaptation to stimuli, and must watch warily before he allows anything past his guard. Both are "square" in the true meaning of that modern idiom, perpendicularly entrenched in preconceived behaviour-routines. The word "flexible", therefore, so radical to Hardy's psychological vocabulary, receives enhanced definition by contrast with the rigidity of men like Boldwood. Gabriel Oak is entirely without impulse (the dominant concept of the book), yet, governed by "quiet energy", forges sturdily through whatever experience brings to him. He and Boldwood represent stable and unstable extremes of the same type. Fanny Robin, on the other hand, is the earliest example

Hardy offers of the extremely unstable nervous type of which Sue Bridehead is the logical end-product: a filament overcharged with current which must break under the intensity. Thus, Oak and Fanny Robin — tree and bird — may be seen as the polar extremes of the basic Hardy categories — the statuesque and the nervous. Between fall varying shades of impulsiveness and rigidity, the two notions which really, perhaps, underlie and explain the terminology.

In *The Return of the Native,* the extremes of the continuum are represented by Damon Wildeve and Clym Yeobright: reading from statuesque to nervous, we get

Clym Yeobright — Eustacia — Wildeve
Venn — Thomasin Yeobright

Eustacia Vye is a more developed version of the type initiated in Bathsheba Everdene: the significant adjectives with which Hardy defines her are *lymphatic, luxurious, ambitious, heavy-limbed, soft,* and *cloudy.* The angel of the piece — Thomasin Yeobright, all light and expectancy — gravitates towards the demon, Wildeve, but is saved from him by her guardian angel, Diggory Venn. Like her blue-eyed, Venn is associated with the earth and its rituals, but mobile, moving around the Heath with his caravan like a vigilante. As with Dick Dewy, and the later Giles Winterborne, though, Venn's reticence — skilfully contrasted with the volatile self-centredness of Wildeve — might be negative *or* positive. All three characters have their own Dionysiac side: Dick in the dance, where he can claim Fancy for his own, Venn in the sly, mobile unity with the Heath, and Winterborne in the practice of his two trades. They can all "get with" their natural surroundings, in spite of the guarded reserve of their social manner which places them with the statuesques, being entirely without nervous electricity.

An important new light is thrown on the angels by the arresting passage where Hardy describes the fantasy horrors projected onto the stormy night by Eustacia Vye's imagination. To Thomasin Yeobright, he observes, the rain would have been just rain, the wind just wind. To Eustacia, they were devils and tormenting spirits. The angelicism of Thomasin is associated here with a significant absence of imagination. We may imagine Venn's sober industriousness — it is he who carries on with the work of mending wrecked lives — likewise to derive from a rationalistic contemplation of the facts before him. This seems to relate him to the predominantly intellectual cast of the Brontës' Edgar Linton and St. John Rivers. Such characters — Venn, Rivers, Linton, Hawthorne's Dymmesdale — are capable of the utmost piety, consistency, and spirituality: yet even their spirituality, even their devotions, are detached, often to the point of coldness. By contrast, Heathcliff and Rochester are "of imagination all compact"; moody or phlegmatic, they are *involved*. Eustacia Vye needs more from life than is promised by Clym Yeobright's studious, speculative "bright deity". Her lymphatic, heavy-limbed luxuriousness, and her need to be loved, make demands more likely to be satisfied by Wildeve's "grace", demonic, volatile, irresponsible as it is. Where Troy's systematic living in the present, the planned carelessnes of his seductions, is brought down by its own ignorance of itself (eluding grief by adjourning it), Wildeve's self-centredness succeeds even in self-destruction. The pattern of attraction-revulsion is more highly evolved in this novel than in *Far from the Madding Crowd.* Yeobright and Eustacia are different kinds of statuesque, one preoccupied with its own "inner strenuousness", the other vividly projecting its own fantasy demands upon the external world. The implication of the plot is that Eustacia is the more likely to be fooled, which is to say, to run counter to the objective situation by misinterpreting it according to her needs. Hence, her mischoice of Yeobright. He, we note, is first to see through the relationship. Like Hardy himself, Clym has brooded long enough to know the score: "I ought to be of the same vein to make you happy, I suppose", he observes, thus putting his finger not only on the source of their own failure to satisfy each other, but on that "reciprocity of influence" which Hardy himself saw at the root of successful relationship.

Thus, Eustacia Vye, like Bathsheba Everdene before her, represents an intermediate type in Hardy's system, having the "flexuousness" of the nervous and the heavy-limbedness of the statuesques. Few characters in fact are extreme. The pure statuesque type is dominated by a certain stolidity, an immobility of the body, which can combine either with rigidity of mind to make a Henchard or Boldwood (the type is potentially homicidal), or with quiet energy to make a Gabriel Oak. In either version – stable or unstable – the result is Character. Eustacia's type on the other hand is heavy-limbed like the statuesques, and mobile and well-moving like the nervous. "Flexuous" – together with "lymphatic" the most important adjective used to describe her – usually connotes the more heavily physical aspect of the characteristically nervous "flexible". Its use suggests a habitual luxuriousness: such characters are highly charged, passionally orientated, sensitive to the higher grace of the ideal, yet fatally vulnerable to the demands of appetency. Alec d'Urberville, if we discount as we should his absurdly contrived conversion, remains untouched by any demands of conscience or the mind. He has the *"rouge et noir"* colouring of the Henchard temperament, though certainly not the character. Tess with her leanings towards possession and the spirit is equally distinct from an otherwise similar character, Arabella Donn in *Jude,* whom I have described as "Tess without a soul". It may well be that the "flexuous" type is characteristically "soulful".

Farfrae, Clare, Wildeve, and Sue Bridehead are quite clearly distinct characters, yet they fall within the same type-mould. They attract statuesques of varying hues, and are capable of frigidity, moral hauteur, or neurasthenic oscillations of mood. Farfrae with his ability to keep "both temperatures going on at the same time" is the stable end of the continuum of which Sue Bridehead is the unstable opposite. If I am right in my general contentions, then this question of mutual attraction, "the reciprocity of influence", is the very essence of the whole business of emotional engagement, and some attempt must be made to give a clear picture of Hardy's overall conception of it. The lines of the picture have already begun to emerge. It remains to follow the detail of his hardening conclusions. Who, in short, attracts whom? And for what reasons?

Most of the relationships summarized here so far have straddled the type-transversal. Yet really the subject matter is just too complicated to allow of any very clear generalizations: not everybody is *just* one type. People like Oak and Fanny Robin are extremes. Most people are complicated by admixtures of other qualities. Bathsheba and Eustacia belong with statuesques (another novelist might even have used the word to describe them). Yet they have the mobility of the light-winged angels. So that the increasing attention to the notion of nervousness as opposed to elasticity and mobility will have to be sustained: the simple morphological picture has been complicated by factors of instability, introversion, intensity. With the increasing complexity comes increased uncertainty of emotional choice. And from this uncertainty comes the tragedy in Hardy's fiction. Every Hardy novel except *The Mayor of Casterbridge* turns on the confusion created by people pursuing a projection of a sexual ideal somehow at variance with their own "real" needs. The inverted commas are important. Ultimately, Hardy implies in his last books, it is just impossible to establish what people's "real" needs are: we need what we think we need. Sometimes it seems that what really disturbed the Victorians was the suggestion in Hardy's novels that every woman needs more than one man to satisfy her varying needs. This is outstandingly true of Eustacia Vye: basically, her response to Clym Yeobright is more powerful than any emotional *frisson* Wildeve can provide her with. They are both statuesques. The author of the *Kama Sutra,* who ought to know, insists on the correct "matching" of lovers strictly according to size; sexual orthodoxy seems to demand it. But man is not just natural: there is the mind, the reason, the more complicated emotions. Some of these Clym can satisfy with his intellectuality, others not. Women like Eustacia, Hardy implies, think they are in love with the minds of men like Yeobright; in fact, it is probably a physical attraction, which, if unsustained by a more intense fascination, soon fades. Wildeve, a man "in whom no man would have seen anything to admire, and in whom no woman would have seen anything to dislike", possesses what Clym does not — sexual magic, or, charm. Thus, the morphological matching breaks down, even though the punishment of Eustacia and Wildeve in drowning may be construed as a kind of judgment.

In the middle novels, the direction of the emotional libido is from the women to the men. And in general Hardy was better at showing women falling in love with men (usually basically indifferent), than the contrary situation. In Hardy, as a rule, men who pursue their suit do so aggressively, uglily, if not actually violently: Boldwood, Phillotson, de Stancy, Manston, even Jude — all either insist their own private emotion upon an unwilling object, or become destructive. For the rest, it is a question of a passive endurance, like Gabriel Oak's, Giles Winterborne's, and Diggory Venn's. The only really Romantic suitor in Hardy is Troy, a professional philanderer.

But this is mere cataloguing. What matters is the underlying psychological explanation. For the real point is that there is a more or less consistent movement of emotional energy from the more highly to the less highly charged characters. Tess loves Clare more than he loves her; Henchard loves Farfrae, who remains more or less indifferent; similarly, Viviette Constantine loves Swithin St. Cleeve, Jude loves Sue, Ethelberta loves Julian, Eustacia loves Wildeve, Felice Charmond loves Fitzpiers — in all these cases the recipients fail to respond with anything like adequate warmth or intensity, if they respond at all. Now, with the single exception of Ethelberta (insufficiently defined), all the characters in the left-hand side of the above list fall into the statuesque category: the women are nearly all Hardy's favourite "lymphatic", "luxurious", "flexuous", "soft", "heavy-limbed" types, endowed with Romance temperament and dark hair: the men, Henchard and Jude, are the outstanding examples of Hardy's analysis of what the Humours psychology would describe in terms of black bile and melancholy, and what we have described in terms of introversion, repressed violence, an almost Hebraic aversion to happiness. Boldwood's passionate fixation on Bathsheba and Manston's on Cytherea, and Winterborne's hopeless love for Grace, partake of the same unstable unloading of excess libido. The recipients in the list, on the other hand, are all incapable of strong and lasting emotional response: Clare, Sue Bridehead, Farfrae, Wildeve, are all characteristic nervous or cerebral types, lightweight, once-born, their capacity to being affronted greater than their capacity to forgive, their changeability greater than their devotion.

The middle and early novels also contain another affective pattern, which fades out towards the end of Hardy's fiction: the helpless faith of an extremely pure, optimistic, rather abstracted type of girl (usually fair) for a selfish or changeable man: the best examples of this are Fanny Robin's love for Troy, Thomasin Yeobright's for Damon Wildeve, Grace Melbury's for Fitzpiers.

It seems then that Hardy distinguishes three main types of emotional discharge (whether it results in relationship or not depending upon the object of the discharge). First, the movement of affection from the more highly charged to the less highly charged (the statuesque to the nervous), as in Henchard's love for Farfrae and Jude's for Sue. Second, the "gravitation" of emotion from the smaller to the greater mass, or often simply from femininity to masculinity. The third category is what we could call the natural mating of like characters, of which the best examples are Alec d'Urberville's seduction of Tess, and Arabella Donn's of Jude. The use of the word seduction betrays what I think is true, that Hardy held this "natural" mating in some distaste. The point is of some significance.

To avoid the risk of over-schematicism according to alien terminologies, the following list based largely upon Hardy's own usage can be offered:

Nervous

Hypoborean (Farfrae)
flexible (Fancy Day)
flexuous (Angel Clare)
motion (Damon Wildeve)
grace (Wildeve)
versatile (Ethelberta)
fair (Thomasin Yeobright)
impulse (Troy)
luminous (Thomasin)
light build (Wildeve)
Daphne-esque (Grace Melbury)
elastic (Grace Melbury)
stringency (Farfrae)
crispness (Farfrae)
logical (Clare)

Statuesque

Tartarean (Henchard)
flat-footed (Boldwood)

dignity (Boldwood)
stillness (Boldwood)
impassive (Knight)
rouge et noir (Henchard)
inflexible (Knight)
stern (Henchard)
full-limbed (Eustacia)
perpendicular (Boldwood)
coarse (Arabella)
lymphatic (Eustacia)
luxurious (Eustacia)
heroic (Marty South)
placidity (Winterborne)
guardedness (Winterborne)
reserve (Winterborne)
restraint (Winterborne)

12. The Problem of Pessimism

Almost without exception, criticism of Hardy has concentrated on his "philosophy", his ideas, his *Weltanschauung*, to the more or less total exclusion of any real interest in his psychology. Often enough it is affirmed that the main character in the novels is Nature — Egdon Heath, or the Isle of Slingers, or the Vale of Blackmoor. And usually the reader is pleased enough with the conceit to question no further than his initial surprise the strange idea that a "fiction", a novel, could be built like this. John Holloway has given the best account I have come across of the living actuality of Nature in Hardy.[1] But Holloway's conception of Hardy seems to derive less from actual experience of the words on the page — from the aliveness and breathing subtlety of Hardy's writing — than from a feeling that Hardy's "pessimism" and predestinarianism are somehow related to and redeemed by his sense of Nature. The critic, in other words, goes from delight and awe in Hardy's nature-writing, to an awareness of the overall fatalism of the *Weltanschauung*, returns to the reverence for Nature, and makes a causal connexion between the two. And of course this is right up to a point. Hardy's experience of the processes and powers of Nature obviously influenced his predominantly predestinarian vision of human life. Or did it? Isn't this basically unscientific thinking? Shouldn't one rather see Thomas Hardy as part of his environment, his nature and emotions alike coloured by its mood? There isn't really any causal connexion. It makes no more sense to ascribe his "pessimism" to his environmental conditioning, than his conception of the overriding power of Nature to his natural or "innate" pessimism. Both views are equally barren and arbitary. Neither can be confirmed or confuted. Both, therefore, should be abandoned.

What gives rise to much of this speculation is the acute embarrassment occasioned by Hardy's fictional devices. Like the pessimism-environment debate, these much flogged charges should be raised only with apology and to be decisively jettisoned. Hardy's coincidences, misunderstandings, overheard conversations, and the like must be treated as at worst naive jobbing, at best, unsuccessful attempts to communicate a vision of life later expressed more powerfully and convincingly in another medium: Hardy's poems, for very interesting reasons, persuade us of his convictions with the kind of finality art must achieve. It is precisely the absence of finality and persuasiveness that vitiates Hardy's coincidences and unforeseen eventualities.

Any critical attempt, therefore, to explain and justify such incidents as Tess's happening to come across Alec d'Urberville preaching, or Mrs. Yeobright's failing to wake Clym up when she visits him, can immediately be dismissed as some order of special pleading. The plain fact is that the reader just doesn't accept them as he reads: something like an incredulous smile breaks over his face, and he attributes the circumstance to Hardy's naivety. The last thing he does is to. accept Hardy's vision of, to quote John Holloway, "a determined system of things which ultimately controls human affairs without regard for human wishes". Though this, patently, is what Hardy is trying to put over. One of the reasons why so much Hardy criticism remains academic (in the sense of being a pedantic and otiose restatement of what everyone feels anyway) is just that his intentions are so obvious that they need no comment.

In a material sense, it is true to say that art can tolerate any fault but failure. The novels of Dickens are packed with incidents which, taken separately, are outrageous if not farcical violations of decent probability. Yet such incidents as the convict's gesturing to Pip with a file, years after the Magwitch Christmas; or Mr. Wopsle's glimpsing Compeyson in the audience at one of his Shakespearean performances; even Martin Chuzzlewit's happening to be sitting on the night of his return from the U.S.A. in one of the few inn-windows in London to be passed by Pecksniff on his triumphal progress to the ceremonial opening of the school he has designed with Martin's ideas — these raise no difficulties, not because Dickens is a more skilled and persuasive artist than Hardy (though he is), but because they fit into the Dickens universe, which is an expressionistic universe, impregnated by the thought and feelings of the artist himself. It is, in other words, an "inner" universe, dictated ultimately by the projects of the subject. Now, Hardy's universe is supremely objective. For all the magnificence of the nature-writing, the world of Hardy's novels is severely external to the will of the creator. Its integrity depends supremely on the maintenance of, let us say, objectivity. We believe that Hardy is at all times keeping out of things, precisely because his evocations of the natural world are so accurate, so clinical that any suggestion of the pathetic fallacy is impossible. In other words, the nature-writing sets a standard of truth and objectivity that is outraged by the twists of fortune — even though these twists can and do happen in real life. It is no defence of Hardy's coincidences to say, "that's how he saw things" What we are concerned with is not truth or fact, but artistic integrity.

Nor is the point simply that Hardy's nature-writing is truthful, where, for example, Dickens's is somehow subjective or inaccurate: on the contrary, Dickens writes with magnificent exactitude. But the details of his recollected experience — presented with all the affection of a great master of nostalgia — are selected, ordered, and coloured with an eye to the immediate contextual problem. In Hardy, the whole point of the particular detail seems somehow to lie in its impartial precision. Somehow, in other words, the uncanny articulateness with which Hardy's world of Nature declares itself seems part of the whole enterprise of the novel. Perhaps it is just this audibility of the spirit of woods and heaths that makes the activities of Hardy's actual *dramatis personae* often seem unimportant. But this too is to over-simplify — and to anticipate. Why so often do the events the characters get involved in seem like mere foolery? What, in the second place, is the relation between the actions of the humans and the environment they find themselves in?

To answer the first question first, one has, I think, to concede the criticism so often levelled at Hardy. The actions of the humans seem trivial and arbitrary often not because Nature is the real hero (or heroine) of the novels, but simply because Hardy violates the laws of his own art. The primary law he offends against is one more brilliantly observed than anywhere perhaps in *Wuthering Heights*. Satisfactory structure in works of fiction derives not from the balance and contrast of events themselves, but from the balance and contrast of the relative *weight* of events. Thus, the real trouble with Hardy's coincidences is bathos, bathos that derives from the turning of huge significance on hugely insignificant events. In other words, there must be relative equilibrium of force between cause and effect in the action of a novel or drama. The cause must seem capable of producing the effect, or at least worthy of it. Only in very exceptional circumstances can an artist get away with weighing thistledown against lead. The most brilliant example in our literature occurs, probably, in Mallory's *Morte d'Arthur,* where the great armies do battle upon one of the knights drawing his sword to slay an adder. Significantly, we do not feel that the act tells us much about the way Mallory saw life. No specific import, in other words, attaches to the incident, although the whole episode is at once a beautiful comment on the futility of war and a genuinely philosophical irony. It is probably because Hardy works so hard to make his events and coincidences *tell* that the coincidences creak, or produce the resounding tinkle of bathos.

Two things, in fact, have to be sharply distinguished in Hardy: such imbalances in the cause-and-effect relation, and the use of coincidence, are different kinds of mistake. Both sorts of mistake do occur in the novels: of this I submit that no reader *qua* reader has ever entertained the slightest doubt, though later, *qua* critic, he may feel inclined to justify them as part of a total philosophy. If these devices *are,* indeed, attempts to convey a philosophical scheme, then they must be condemned along with Voltaire's *Candide,* Johnson's *Rasselas,* the contrived mechanisms of Graham Greene, the pretentious quasi-mystical charades of Hermann Hesse, and indeed all "illustrations" of ideas, which qualify neither as philosophy nor as art.

Often, one feels that the point Hardy is trying to illustrate could have been conveyed better with another choice of incident. For example, Clym's mother feels a comprehensible resentment against Clym and his bride. The situation is strong and well realized, so that the book survives the bathos of the incident in which Clym's midday catnap causes his mother to go away from his house, convinced of his callousness towards her. The passages describing Mrs. Yeobright's grief after her knocking at the door has been ignored are very moving: the particular situation acquires a universal significance in spite of the silliness of the actual incident. George Eliot and Arnold Bennett would have described her grief directly without bothering to contrive the fictional episode. In this light, such incidents reflect only Hardy's naivety, and it just seems a pity that he felt bound by a fatuous convention of romantic eventualities. That he did, of course, is his own fault, and nobody else's.

This incident from *The Return of the Native* illustrates the first type of the errors of judgment so often met with in Hardy's novels. The second type is the use of coincidences and improbabilities. It is this, probably, that most readers have in mind when they censure Hardy's plots. Thus, for example, Tess happens upon Alec d'Urberville preaching, is spotted by him, and again becomes involved with him. Everything is wrong about the episode, yet basically the story is strong here. It is unthinkable that Alec should become a preacher — this is a violation not of probability but of Hardy's own psychological plan. It is even more unthinkable that Tess should, as it were, re-corrupt him with an argument against the existence of God half-remembered from the conversation of Angel Clare. All the laborious ironies fall flat here. We simply have to wait until Alec re-emerges in his real colours — that is, until Hardy's psychological premises are allowed to assert themselves and dictate the conclusions.

So, here, as is usually the case, it is not the coincidence that is really either at fault or in question. We are not meant to think, if only Tess hadn't chanced upon Alec preaching she would have been all right, and we do not so think. And the same goes for the run of the coincidences and improbabilities in his books. In the main, they are not to be defended or excused as attempts to express a vision of the world, because they are by and large irrelevant to the course of the action. I have already given the example of Mrs. Yeobright's resentment against Clym, and the subsequent bitterness of her death. The incident of Tess's letter, on the other hand, does rather beautifully heighten the poignancy of her state of mind, wanting to confess, yet wanting to be happy. It is a matter of speculation whether the effect would have been achieved better by having Tess write a letter and tear it up, or merely think about writing one. Probably Hardy's way was the best here: all the time that the letter is out of her hands Tess is exposed — the letter is part of herself, and her awful vulnerability becomes extraordinarily moving. There is no question of Fate's taking a hand, or of things being out of Tess's hands: "The incident of the misplaced letter she had jumped at as if it prevented a confession but she knew in her conscience that it need not; there was still time" (T.D., p. 241). Coincidence, Fate, and the rest of the critical bores are not even shadowily invoked here.

And yet in a strange way they are. For although it is true that the course of Hardy's novels is not really deflected by these little incidents he so enjoyed engineering, they still tell us something about Hardy's conception of experience. The problem is subtler than is usually allowed. For in spite of the fact that the agonies endured by Hardy's characters are not arbitrarily inflicted by the gods or Fate or the President of the Immortals, but organically derive from their being *the kind of people they are,* still, Hardy intimates, there is immense sorrow in the fact that things are as they are. When, at the end of *Tess,* Hardy writes: "Justice was done, and the President of the Immortals, in Aeschylean phrase, had finished his sport with Tess" (T.D., p. 496), he does not intend any irony, as Roy Morrell maintains.[2] He does not mean that our destinies are in our own hands, and only our stupid self-deception causes us to bewail our lot and blame the gods. Nor is the point of *Tess* the weakness of the heroine, as both Morrell and John Holloway imply. Life *is* painful, existence *is* an agony to be endured — to deny that Hardy felt this is to misread him, perversely or wrongheadedly. Thus, Holloway speaks of "the price [Tess] will ultimately pay for her dream-world spirituality".[3] Morrell lays the blame for Tess's tragedy partly on Tess's own shoulders, partly on the man-made morality, from which she suffers, and which, Morrell thinks, Hardy regarded as "obsolescent, ready to be swept away".[4] Hence, it is "not possible to excuse Tess herself",[5] since she should have resisted and made a better job of things. Similarly, Morrell believes the *Titanic* poem "The Convergence of the Twain", can be absolved from any charge of pessimism or predestinarianism by going outside the poem to the context of the actual events. Here, Morrell's account in terms of irony seems even more strained. It is surely not enough merely to brand an artist's statements as ironical with no appeal to something in the words themselves: surely, for a statement which appears perfectly plain and unambiguous suddenly to be revealed as irony, the critic is obliged to justify the new reading by pointing out something in the text that had escaped previous readers and critics. Morrell's approach is original. Instead of finding something in Hardy's words, he quotes Joseph Conrad's. The lines in question seem to be at the heart of the poem:

> Till the Spinner of the Years
> Said "Now!" And each one hears,
> And consummation comes, and jars two hemispheres.

The "Spinner of the Years", says Morrell, though an

unfortunate usage perhaps, like the "President of the Immortals" in *Tess*, must be read ironically. Not only did Hardy not literally believe in the Deity, he did not even share the spirit which to all appearances lies behind the use of the phrase. For the point of the poem, he argues, is the ironical one that what humanity attributes to blind Fate, implacable Destiny and so on, really derives from human stupidity. Hence the Conrad quotation, which refers scathingly to "a sort of marine Ritz". We blame the gods, we speak of a finger pointing to the sky, accusing the Almighty – and all the while we should have seen to it that there were more lifeboats on board, and "that they should work efficiently" (to quote Morrell).

It would seem difficult to misread a poem or a writer more totally, and, I should have thought, more diminishingly. For Conrad's reaction is one thing – the old sea-dog was naturally furious and contemptuous of the brash floating palace and all it stood for. Now Hardy's reaction is both totally different and incomparably more profound. And it is the profundity Morrell scants. To support his reading he refers back to the satire (the poem is in the *Satires of Circumstance* collection) at the beginning of the poem:

> Over the mirrors meant
> To glass the opulent
> The sea-worm crawl – grotesque, slimed, dumb, indifferent.

And later, to the fish's dumb question, "what does this vaingloriousness down here?" Now, this certainly partakes of Conrad's scorn – "a sort of marine Ritz". But how different are their real responses to the event. Where Conrad speaks of "a most miserable, most fatuous disaster", Hardy refers, with sombre awe, to "an august event" (Morrell has "austere"). And, of course, none but a perverse reading would have needed this explicit phrase: the essence of the whole poem is the awe at the collision of the two great things – the biggest liner and the hugest iceberg – the most than man can achieve, and Nature's tremendous answer. No one who can read poetry at all can have failed to receive the thrill, the *frisson* of awe, as the ship is built in the dockyard, at the same time as:

In shadowy silent distance grew the Iceberg too.

The poem is, still, a satire, but of a profounder sort. In this, the "vaingloriousness", the vanity of opulence, plays a crucial part. The irony of the poem *is* that the magnificence now lies in mud. But the real meaning of the poem is in the grandeur of the collison — that we feel is not a "miserable, fatuous disaster", but an "august event".

Morrell's misreading exquisitely violates Hardy's intentions: "Does Hardy's 'determinism' make us more deterministic ourselves? Or does it make us more anxious that lifeboats should be numerous enough and that they should work efficiently?" he asks. In other words Hardy's irony, Morrell argues, works to make us more careful next time. Thus, the whole point of Hardy's poem is lost. For the real irony, the significance of the event to Hardy, was that *this* of all ships, should be singled out, and destroyed. Conrad's invective blurs the real issue. For, it is one thing to decry the lack of lifeboats, it is another to suggest, as Morrell does, that in some way, the disaster *could have been avoided.* Fewer people would have been drowned — but the irony remains that the greatest ship ever constructed was ripped open like a tin can, and the passengers scattered over the water like seeds on a dog's back. *This* is the irony, this is the reverberation of Hardy's great poem. For the engineers, when they claimed the ship could not be sunk, had taken the greatest precautions, precautions so thorough and technically advanced that they thought they could dispense with lifeboats. Thus, precisely what Morrell implies — that tragedy can be avoided — is the view which is being so superbly dramatized in the poem: man cannot avoid tragedy, no matter how secure he tries to make himself. The question of the lifeboats is therefore a red herring. *Some of the people* would have drowned anyway no matter how many lifeboats had been on board and the point would still have remained, emphasizing the essential precariousness of the human condition: *the liner would still have been sunk.* And this is the point of Hardy's poem. This is the goal of his satire. For him the lack of lifeboats was a snap of the fingers in God's face, a gesture of human insolence, that had to be punished. And in this we can see the Aeschylean core of Hardy's art: the poem, the drama, the novel, are all libations to the gods. Spectacularly, on a tremendous scale Hardy himself could never have dared, the wreck of the *Titanic* proved the essential sanity, the pitiless accuracy of his vision of life. At a distance of fifteen or twenty years, Hardy says to the critics who picked holes in his stories, "I told you so."

It will not do either to absolve Hardy from the predestinarian charge altogether, by making him an existential ironist, as Roy Morrell does. But although it is misguided to try to defend the coincidences and improbabilities of the novels as somehow "working" in a larger vision of things, the larger vision is certainly there – I doubt if anyone has ever doubted it. It is a religious, deeply ironic vision which can only be satisfied with the sacrifice of the human victims chosen by Hardy to illustrate his theme. In a sense, fiction proved inadequate: by a curious paradox, poetry, apparently so personal and subjective a medium, proved more congenial to Hardy's meanings. For the novel is by definition a fictional organism. It works, that is to say, by means of specially chosen scenes and crises, which have to be invented for specific purposes. Hardy never quite solved the problem of presenting a fatalistic, deeply religious conception of life in terms of invented action. To the end – though his novels show a steady improvement in probability and verisimilitude from *Desperate Remedies* to *The Well-Beloved* – his tales are apt to seem contrived at crucial points. He turned to poetry, I think, simply because poetry has a higher truth-content. In the stories and novels we nearly always feel that the characters haven't a chance, that Hardy means them to be dragged down in the end. This is the proper approach to the coincidences and improbabilities: they betray too blatantly

Hardy's *will* that his characters should fail to achieve lasting happiness. So the debate ultimately has nothing to do with probability, or "what actually happens" at all. The poems are gleaned from what actually happened and what Hardy had understood of his experiences, his regrets about his first marriage, his fear of age, his nostalgia for the past, for the missed opportunities. Hence, the air of willed contrivance yields to reality, though a reality, of course, coloured by the same sombre mind as conceived the fiction.

The greater of the novels do produce the genuine tragic catharsis. But only the greatest of them all, which is, I think, *The Mayor,* completely sheds the tricksy irritations of the other books — the rapid turns of fortune, the fortuitous meetings, overheard conversations, and so on — and sustains to the end a massiveness of movement that places it with the greatest achievements in the English language. Only in the fall of Michael Henchard, I think, does Hardy give completely satisfying expression to his vision, though Jude Fawley has an extraordinary bitterness, and Tess Durbeyfield a profoundly moving tenderness and vulnerability.

The full understanding of these characters and their chronicles can only be reached, I have argued, through an appreciation of the psychological scheme of which they are part. The progress of Hardy as a novelist mainly concerns the steady clarification of the psychological bases of his vision. Progressively, he refines and purifies the fundamental qualities of his psychology, until he achieves a subtle and powerful grasp of the human situation. His pessimism — if we can still use the notion at all — finds itself confirmed in the basic relationships between men and women and then, upon his looking still closer, in the actual physical make-up of humanity. Thus, the tragedy of human unhappiness springs not from the violation of Nature, as Holloway has it, or from our inability to throw off the Law, as Lawrence holds, but from the basic psychological laws that govern human behaviour. I have noted above that the type-vision in literature tends to occur in men of a basically fatalistic bias.

Although this is not proffered as a fixed rule, it occurs often enough to be remarkable. The novels of Thomas Hardy demonstrate the phenomenon more spectacularly than any other art of which I am aware.

Thus we must be wary of the notion of pessimism. We have to distinguish between two apparently similar things, both of which might receive the same label. The first is negative, a lack of hope, of interest in things; the second is a positive belief about the nature of the universe, of the purpose and direction of things. This second, teleological belief, is strictly metaphysical and religious: it is what Schopenhauer held — and Hardy. This is why we can maintain the contention that the typological vision generally accompanies a profound determinism that always threatens to become pessimism. This is why Emily Brontë and Thomas Hardy are so deeply akin. Both were sustained by a *positive* belief about reality. Emily Brontë believed, if not in any frameable set of propositions, at least in a mystical dynamic of life, a purpose working itself out like the cycle of Nature. This mystical belief is embodied magnificently in her marvellous novel, and in her finest poems:

> With wide-embracing love
> Thy spirit animates eternal years,
> Pervades and broods above,
> Changes, sustains, dissolves, creates, and rears.
>
> Though earth and man were gone,
> And suns and universes ceased to be,
> And Thou were left alone,
> Every existence would exist in Thee.
>
> There is not room for Death,
> Nor atom that his might could render void;
> Thou — Thou art being and Breath,
> And what Thou art may never be destroyed.

Whatever criteria we use, we know that the assertion behind and in that verse, in contrast to the vast majority of Victorian "optimism", is deep and real. We know that the mind that conceived it also "believed in" the assertion, as literally as it believed in the actuality of the objects in a room. It is this kind of belief, not any vague optimism, that sustained Hardy. Hardy likewise held a definite belief in the purpose and meaningfulness of Nature, of life, of the universe. The great mistake is to confuse this positive act of belief, which is quite a cool, waking thing in Hardy, having nothing to do with merely wanting things to be a certain way, with the absence of belief, the sheer negative lack of purpose that characterizes so much modern thought. The critical fallacies attacked above spring from some such source. The reasoning runs as follows: We feel a definite force for good in Hardy's novels, yet he apparently thought little of human life, and was pessimistic about our chances of happiness. Therefore, there must be something we have missed. Whence the positive explanations such critics as Roy Morrell and John Holloway have striven to demonstrate. Whence also the dismissals of disapproving critics: Why bother to read someone so patently against life? Now, it is pointless to look for any "explanation" of Hardy's views — for some unsuspected facet that makes them appreciable as the exact opposite of the "apparent" beliefs they convey. As I have said again and again, nobody without actually refusing to believe what Hardy states explicitly in clear and simple English, can fail to understand his "philosophy". So all the "explanations" — e.g. "Hardy is presenting satires on human self-deceptions, and is therefore not really a pessimist at all" — are absurd. Hardy is a classical pessimist in the sense that he believed that life was a largely pathetic sideshow in a wonder circus open all the year round. He believed that most men will be unhappy most of the time, the more so as they are sentient and intelligent. Consciousness is a disease, because happy ignorance cannot reflect on the necessarily pathetic part human life plays in the great design. He believed that most men misunderstand their relationship to their universe, generally in the direction of ridiculous self-glorification and an exaggeration of the part humanity plays. *But it is a great design.* This is the theme of the majority — if not actually all — of Hardy's poems. It is most explicit perhaps in the *Titanic* poem, and in the lyric he wrote during an episode even more likely to exaggerate man's sense of his own importance, the First World War:

I
Only a man harrowing clods
In a slow silent walk
With an old horse that stumbles and nods
Half asleep as they stalk.

II
Only thin smoke without flame
From the heaps of couch-grass;
Yet this will go onward the same
Though Dynasties pass.

III
Yonder a maid and her wight
Come whispering by;
War's annals will cloud into night
Ere their story die.

Hardy beautifully turns the tables both on man and on himself here. For the weight is taken off ·the War anxiety precisely by the tiny, slight human rituals that are more genuinely part of Nature. Nowhere perhaps in the novels did he so perfectly express his unchanging view, that human life is very fragile, very insignificant, and very beautiful.

Notes to Text

CHAPTER 1

1. Ernst Kretschmer, *Physique and Character.*
2. W. E. Sheldon, *The Varieties of Human Physique.*
3. Rostan in nineteenth-century France distinguished three types, *le type musculaire, le type digestif,* and *le type cérébrale.* After Rostan, many such systems were devised, such as that of Samuel Wells, who called the types motive, vital, and mental. Sheldon gives a useful survey of the subject in *Varieties of Human Physique;* a more thorough discussion is given by G. W. Allport in *Personality.*
4. "At home, even so near as Cossethay, was the vicar, who spoke the other, magic language, and had the other, finer bearing, both of which she could perceive, but could never attain to. The vicar moved in worlds beyond where her own menfolk existed. Did she not know her own menfolk: fresh, slow, full-built men, but easy, native to the earth, lacking outwardness and range of motion. Whereas the vicar, dark and dry and small beside her husband, had yet a quickness and a range of being that made Brangwyn, in his large geniality, seem dull and local" (*The Rainbow*). Lawrence's whole relation to the typological tradition is fascinating.
5. *The Human Pair.*
6. D. H. Lawrence, "Study of Thomas Hardy", p. 437.
7. *The Human Pair,* p. 103.
8. Ibid., p. 104.
9. *Thomas Hardy,* p. 151.
10. *The Human Pair,* p. 100.

CHAPTER 4

1. F. E. Hardy, *The Early Life of Thomas Hardy 1840–91.*

CHAPTER 5

1. "Hardy", in *The Victorian Sage.*
2. Hardy had noted the phenomenon — so fundamental to symbolism and to modern psychological techniques — in *Desperate Remedies.* When Cytherea Graye watches her father fall to his death, she also sees "without heeding . . . white sunlight shining in shaft-like lines from a rift in a slaty cloud". Hardy's comment is profound:

"Emotions will attach themselves to scenes that are simultaneous — however foreign in essence these scenes may be — as chemical waters will crystallise on twigs and wires. Ever after that time any mental agony brought less vividly to Cytherea's mind the scene from the Town Hall windows" — i.e. the death of her father — "than sunlight streaming in shaft-like lines" (D.R., p. 11).

    Baudelaire describes the formation of the poetic symbol in the same way. "In certain semi-supernatural conditions of the spirit, the whole depths of life are revealed within the scene — no matter how commonplace — which one has before one's eyes. This becomes its symbol" (*Fusées*).

3.   *Thomas Hardy: The Will and the Way.*
4.   John Schlesinger's film confirms, in fact, that the effect cannot be translated into cinematic terms at all, since it depends upon the brilliant use Hardy makes of metaphor: it is the blood-spot image that makes Hardy's passage so powerful.
5.   Cytherea Graye was praised for her strange ability to recover her footing when it seemed impossible (D.R., p. 2).

CHAPTER 6

1.   Cf. A. J. Guerard, *Thomas Hardy,* p. 141.
2.   Under the firelight, under the brush,
Her hair spread out in fiery points
Glowed into the words, then would be savagely still. (*The Waste Land*, lines 108—110)
3.   Cf. Robin Vote in Djuna Barnes's *Nightwood.*
4.   "Study of Thomas Hardy", p. 417.
5.   See W. E. Sheldon, *The Varieties of Human Physique.*

CHAPTER 7

1.   This is the sort of situation so well analyzed by Roy Morrell. See *Thomas Hardy: The Will and The Way.* chapter 10.
2.   See Fancy Day's letter to Maybold, quoted on p. 47 above.

CHAPTER 9

1.   This episode was added by Hardy to the 1912 edition.
2.   *Ideas,* p. 105.
3.   Ibid.
4.   *The Victorian Sage,* p. 285.

CHAPTER 10

1. *The Victorian Sage*, p. 258.
2. Ibid., p. 289.
3. One of which simply cannot wait: Lucetta is psychologically miles removed from Arabella and Alec. The similarity here is only the instrumentality of roles.
4. *The Victorian Sage*, p. 289.
5. Ibid., p. 289.
6. De Rougemont rather summarily includes it in a list of nineteenth-century novels guilty of degrading the obstacle in the Romance myth. See *Passion and Society*, p. 232.

CHAPTER 11

1. *Fact and Fiction in Psychology*, p. 58.
2. Charlotte Brontë notes that Rochester's build is "athletic", anticipating Sheldon.

CHAPTER 12

1. *The Victorian Sage*, p. 244 ff.
2. *Thomas Hardy: The Will and the Way*, p. 35 ff.
3. *The Victorian Sage*, p. 285.
4. *Thomas Hardy: The Will and the Way*, p. 39.
5. Ibid., p. 40.

Select Bibliography

THOMAS HARDY

Dates refer to first publication in book form. References in the text are to *Thomas Hardy's Works,* published by Osgood, McIlvaine and Co., London, 1895–1913, in twenty volumes.

Novels

The Poor Man and the Lady. Written in 1868, but never published.
Desperate Remedies. London, 1871.
Under the Greenwood Tree, or The Mellstock Quire. London, 1872.
A Pair of Blue Eyes. London, 1873.
Far from the Madding Crowd. London, 1874.
The Hand of Ethelberta: A Comedy in Chapters. London, 1876.
The Return of the Native. London, 1878.
The Trumpet-Major. London, 1880.
A Laodicean: A Story of To-day. New York and London, 1881.
Two on a Tower. London, 1882.
The Mayor of Casterbridge, the Life and Death of a Man of Character. London, 1886.
The Woodlanders. London and New York, 1887.
Tess of the d'Urbervilles: A Pure Woman Faithfully Presented. London, 1891.
Jude the Obscure. London, 1896.
The Well-Beloved: A Sketch of a Temperament (entitled The Pursuit of the Well-Beloved). London, 1897.

Stories

Wessex Tales. London and New York, 1888.
A Group of Noble Dames. London, 1891.
Life's Little Ironies. London, 1894.
A Changed Man and Other Tales. London, 1913.
The Short Stories of Thomas Hardy. London, 1928.

Verse

Wessex Poems and Other Verses. London, 1898.
Poems of the Past and Present. London, 1901.

Time's Laughingstocks and Other Verses. London, 1909.
Satires of Circumstance, Lyrics and Reveries. London, 1914.
Moments of Vision and Miscellaneous Verses. London, 1917.
Late Lyrics and Earlier with Many Other Verses. London, 1922.
Human Shows, Far Fantasies, Songs and Trifles. London, 1925.
Winter Words, in Various Moods and Metres. London, 1928.
Collected Poems. London, 1930.

Drama

The Dynasts. A Drama of the Napoleonic Wars.

Part First, London, 1903–1904.
Part Second, London, 1906.
Part Third, London, 1908.

The Famous Tragedy of the Queen of Cornwall at Tintagel in Lyonnesse. London, 1923.

BOOKS AND ESSAYS ON HARDY

ABERCROMBIE, LASCELLES. *Thomas Hardy: A Critical Study.* First published 1912. London, 1919.

BEACH, J. W. *The Technique of Thomas Hardy.* Chicago, 1922.

BLUNDEN, EDMUND. *Thomas Hardy.* London, 1941; New York (St. Martin's Press), 1941.

BOWRA, SIR M. *The Lyrical Poetry of Thomas Hardy.* Byron Foundation Lecture, Nottingham, 1946.

BROWN, DOUGLAS. *Thomas Hardy.* First published 1954. Rev. ed., London, 1961; New York, 1954.

CECIL, LORD DAVID. *Hardy the Novelist.* First published 1943. London, 1960.

CHAPMAN, F. "Hardy the Novelist." *Scrutiny* 3 (June 1934): 22–37.

CHILD, H. *Thomas Hardy.* London, 1916.

COLLINS, V. H. *Talks with Thomas Hardy at Max Gate 1920–22.* London, 1928.

DE ROUGEMONT, D. *Passion and Society.* London, 1940.

DAY-LEWIS, C. *Lyrical Poetry of Thomas Hardy.* New York, 1953.

D'EXIDEUIL, PIERRE. *The Human Pair.* London, 1930.

DIKE, D. A. "A Modern Oedipus: The Mayor of Casterbridge." *Essays in Criticism* 2 (1952): 169–79.

DUFFIN, H. C. *Thomas Hardy: A Study of the Wessex Novels.* First published 1916. London, 1921. Rev. ed., London, 1937.

ELLIOTT, A. P. *Fatalism in the Works of Thomas Hardy.* Philadelphia, 1935.

ELLIS, HAVELOCK. "Thomas Hardy's Novels." *Westminster Review,* n.s. 63 (1883): 334–64.

————."Concerning Jude the Obscure." *Savoy* 3 (1896): 35–49.

GARWOOD, HELEN. *Thomas Hardy: An Illustration of the Philosophy of Schopenhauer.* Philadelphia, 1911.

GOLDBERG, M. A. "Hardy's Double-Visioned Universe." *Essays in Criticism* 7 (1957): 374–82.

GOODHEART, EUGENE. "Thomas Hardy and the Lyrical Novel." *Nineteenth Century Fiction* 12 (1957): 215–25.

GUERARD, ALBERT J. *Thomas Hardy: The Novels and Stories.* Cambridge, Mass., 1949.

HARDY, EVELYN. *Thomas Hardy: A Critical Biography.* London and New York, 1954.

————.*Thomas Hardy's Notebooks.* London, 1955; New York, 1956.

HARDY, EVELYN, and GITTINGS, ROBERT, eds. *Some Recollections by Emma Hardy together with Some Relevant Poems by Thomas Hardy.* London, 1961.

HARDY, F. E. *The Early Life of Thomas Hardy, 1840–91.* London, 1928.

————.*The Later Years of Thomas Hardy, 1892–1928.* London, 1930.

HAWKINS, DESMOND. *Thomas Hardy.* London, 1950.

HOLLAND, NORMAN. "'Jude the Obscure': Hardy's Symbolic Indictment of Christianity." *Nineteenth Century Fiction* 9 (1954): 50–60.

HOLLOWAY, J. *The Victorian Sage.* London, 1953.

HOOPES, KATHLEEN R. "Illusion and Reality in 'Jude the Obscure'." *Nineteenth Century Fiction* 12 (1957): 154–57.

HOWE, IRVING. *Thomas Hardy.* London, 1968.

HYDE, W. J. "Hardy's View of Realism: A Key to the Rustic Characters." *Victorian Studies* 2 (1958): 45–59.

HYNES, SAMUEL. *The Pattern of Hardy's Poetry.* Oxford, 1961.

JOHNSON, LIONEL. *The Art of Thomas Hardy.* London, 1895.

KETTLE, ARNOLD. *An Introduction to the English Novel.* Vol. 2. London, 1953.

LAWRENCE, D. H. "Study of Thomas Hardy". In *Phoenix: The Posthumous Papers of D. H. Lawrence,* edited by Edward C. MacDonald. New York, 1960.

LEAVIS, F. R. *New Bearings in English Poetry.* First published 1932. London, 1954.

———— "Reality and Sincerity". *Scrutiny* 2 (1952): 90–98.

MACDONNELL, ANNIE. *Thomas Hardy.* London, 1894.

MACDOWALL, A. S. *Thomas Hardy: A Critical Study.* London, 1931.

MILLER, J. HILLIS. *Thomas Hardy: Distance and Desire.* Cambridge, Mass., 1970.

MILLGATE, MICHAEL. *Thomas Hardy.* London, 1971.

MIZENER, ARTHUR. " 'Jude the Obscure' as a Tragedy." *Southern Review* 6 (1940): 193–213.

MORRELL, ROY. *Thomas Hardy: The Will and the Way.* Kuala Lumpur, 1965.

MOYNAHAN, JULIAN. " 'The Mayor of Casterbridge' and the Old Testament's First Book of Samuel: A Study of Some Literary Relationships." *PMLA* 71 (1956): 118–30.

MUIR, EDWIN. "The Novels of Thomas Hardy." In *Essays on Literature and Society.* London, 1949.

NEVINSON, HENRY W. *Thomas Hardy.* London, 1941.

PATERSON, J. " 'The Mayor of Casterbridge' as Tragedy." *Victorian Studies* 3 (1959): 151–72.

PORTER, KATHERINE ANNE. "Notes on a Criticism of Thomas Hardy." *Southern Review* 6 (1940): 150–61.

PURDY, RICHARD L. *Thomas Hardy: A Bibliographical Study.* London, New York, Toronto, 1954.

SCOTT-JAMES, R. A. *Thomas Hardy.* First published 1951. London, 1957.

SHORT, CLARICE. "In Defence of Ethelberta". *Nineteenth Century Fiction* 13 (1958): 48–57.

SLACK, ROBERT C. "The Text of Hardy's 'Jude the Obscure' ". *Nineteenth Century Fiction* 11 (1957): 261–75.

SOUTHWORTH, J. G. *The Poetry of Thomas Hardy.* New York, 1947.

SPIVEY, TED R. "Thomas Hardy's Tragic Hero." *Nineteenth Century Fiction* 9 (1954): 179–91.

STEWART, J. I. M. "The Integrity of Hardy." *English Studies* 1 (1948): 1–27.

SYMONS, A. *A Study of Thomas Hardy.* London, 1927.

WILLIAMS, R. *The Wessex Novels.* London, 1924.

WING, GEORGE. *Hardy.* London, 1963.

YOUNG, G. M., ed. *Selected Poems of Thomas Hardy.* First published 1940. London, 1960.

MISCELLANEOUS

ALLPORT, G. W. *Personality.* New York, 1937.

AVICENNA. *A Treatise on the Canon of Medicine of Avicenna.* Translated by O. C. Gruner. London, 1930.

BRONTË, Charlotte. *Jane Eyre,* 1847. *Shirley,* 1849. *Villette,* 1853.

BRONTË, Emily. *Wuthering Heights.* London, 1847.

EYSENCK, H. J. *Fact and Fiction in Psychology.* London, 1965.

GALENUS. *De Temperamentis.* Cambridge, 1881.

HIPPOCRATES. *On Ancient Medicine: The Genuine Works of*

Hippocrates. Translated by F. Adams. London, 1849.

HUSSERL, E. *Ideas.* Translated by W. R. Boyce Gibson. London, 1931.

JUNG, C. G. *Psychological Types.* Translated by H. Godwin Baynes. London, 1923.

KRETSCHMER, Ernst. *Physique and Character.* Translated by J. H. Sprott. London, 1925.

LAWRENCE, D. H. *The Rainbow.* London, 1913.

MELVILLE, Herman. *Moby Dick.* New York, 1851.

SHELDON, W. E. *The Varieties of Human Physique.* New York and London, 1940.

Index